With Portfolio in Hand

VALIDATING THE NEW TEACHER PROFESSIONALISM

With Portfolio in Hand

VALIDATING THE NEW TEACHER PROFESSIONALISM

NONA LYONS

Editor

Teachers College, Columbia University
New York and London

Published by Teachers College Press, 1234 Amsterdam Avenue, New York, NY 10027

Chapter 14 is adapted from "The Vermont experiment in state-mandated portfolio program approval," *Journal of Teacher Education, 47,* 85–98. © 1996 by *Journal of Teacher Education.* Reprinted by permission of Corwin Press, Inc.

Library of Congress Cataloging-in-Publication Data
With portfolio in hand : validating the new teacher professionalism
  /Nona Lyons, editor.
   p.   cm.
   Includes bibliographical references and index.
   ISBN 0-8077-3717-8.—ISBN 0-8077-3716-X (pbk.)
   1. Portfolios in education—United States. 2. Teachers—Rating of—United States. I. Lyons, Nona.
   LB1029.P67W58   1998
   371.14′4—dc21   97-49365

ISBN 0-8077-3716-X (paper)
ISBN 0-8077-3717-8 (cloth)

Printed on acid-free paper
Manufactured in the United States of America

05   04   03   02   01   00   99   98   8 7 6 5 4 3 2 1

Contents

Preface

This book, *With Portfolio in Hand: Validating the New Teacher Professionalism,* highlights my belief that portfolios hold the possibility of becoming a new kind of credential of competent and effective teachers. This possibility is hinted at in one meaning of the word portfolio, "a case to carry documents of state, hence the office and functions of a minister of state" (Webster's Seventh New Collegiate Dictionary, 1963, p. 662). In this sense the portfolio can be a credential assuring a certain, well-qualified teacher–envoy to schools and their students.

But the word portfolio carries another meaning, "a portable case for keeping, usually without folding, loose sheets of papers, prints, etc." (p. 662). In this sense the portfolio can simply be a mundane collection of papers. These different meanings capture some of the tensions in today's portfolio experimentation in teaching and teacher education. The great danger is that portfolios can easily become elaborate paper collections, glitzy scrapbooks undifferentiated from the files most teachers now keep. Present portfolio experimentation is, however, shaping a new portfolio meaning: the dynamic process of teachers documenting the evidence of their work and growth, gathered and authored by them through careful reflection, shared with colleagues and students, and presented for public discussion and debate about their conceptions of good teaching. *With Portfolio in Hand* presents the evolution of this conception of a teaching portfolio: the warrant of a new kind of professional teacher.

The development of this book has, I believe, mirrored this emerging meaning of the portfolio. It was created over time through a collaborative process of reflective dialogue among colleagues. For that, I am indebted to several people, especially the participants of the Portfolio Conference ("Portfolios in Teaching and Teacher Education"), held since 1994 each January in Cambridge, Massachusetts. The book has its origins in a not quite casual suggestion made by Lee Shulman at the first conference gathering. As an organizer of the conference, with my colleague Grace Grant, I had invited Lee to present a historical perspective on portfolios, especially to discuss the role of the Stanford Teacher Assessment Project (TAP) in introducing the portfolio idea into teacher assessment. In his expansive and insightful way, in his cautions and encouragements about portfolio possibilities, Lee caught the imagination of several conferees. They began portfolio explorations of their own. Lee casually mentioned that it might be a good idea for people working with portfolios to share their work and in general to continue their dialogues. This recommendation had two results: the forming of a Special Interest Group of the American Educational Research Association (AERA), "Portfolios in Teaching and Reflective Teacher Education"; and, the annual Portfolio Conference.

This book reflects the continuing conversations about portfolios that grew out of these beginnings. I am indebted to Lee Shulman for his vision, encouragement, and enduring and contagious interest in the puzzles of teaching and learning. Grace Grant helped to think through the original idea for the book. Several colleagues—Vicki La Boskey, Helen Freidus, and especially my associates at the University of Southern Maine with whom I worked to place portfolios in a performance-based teacher education program—have sustained and nurtured my interests. Linda Darling Hammond's vision of competent and effective teachers for America's schools and their students has been a standard of excellence and hope.

Intellectually my work with portfolios, especially my long-standing interest in the development of reflection and reflective practice and the place of narrative in that, has deepened through deliberations over time with Maxine Greene, Carol Gilligan, Jean Clandinin, Blythe Clinchy, Mary Belenky, Miriam Clasby, Jane Attanucci, and Janie Ward. I value too my most recent colleagues—the "narrative group"—at the Wellesley College Center for Research on Women.

But above all, I prize my ongoing conversations and interviews with portfolio makers. They have continually stretched my thinking and understanding. I am especially grateful to the teacher interns of the University of Southern Maine's Extended Teacher Education Program whom I mentored in their portfolio developments and who in turn became mentors to me in understanding the portfolio process. I am grateful too, to students at the Harvard Graduate School of Education and Brown University—Pixita del Prado and Kelly Salazar—who in sharing their thinking first made me glimpse the power of a reflective portfolio process.

The College of Education and Human Development of the University of Southern Maine supported the Portfolio Conference over several critical years of these developments. Dominican College has also been generous in making the conversations happen.

Recently, I have had the great pleasure of introducing the portfolio idea into workplace education through the faculty of the Casco Bay Partnership for Workplace Education at the University of Southern Maine. Taking the portfolio into a new arena made it possible to see in sharper detail the power of the portfolio process. Hearing the first portfolio presentations of teacher interns at Dartmouth College this year reaffirmed the near-magic of creating a portfolio for portfolio makers and their mentors.

I am indebted to Jonas Soltis and Carol Collins of Teachers College Press. Jonas made significant and useful suggestions early on and Carol has been a guide all along the publishing way. Joan Moon at a critical moment did yeoman's work in her help in editing this book. Robert Lyons is ever a good and critical listener to the narratives of learners, their teachers, and to writers as well.

Introduction

Nona Lyons

UNIVERSITY OF SOUTHERN MAINE

Portfolios in teacher education are a recent phenomenon. Although they have a prized history with other professionals—artists, writers, and architects, for example—and had gained currency with elementary and secondary writing teachers for student use, portfolios were introduced into teacher education only in the 1980s. At that time a second wave of school reform carried with it an urgent imperative for a needed, new teacher professionalism.

That imperative had its origins in the massive dissatisfaction with American schools that emerged in the 1970s and continued into the 1980s. Documented by a series of reports beginning with the alarming *A Nation at Risk,* and buttressed by scores of keen observers of American schooling, dissatisfaction kept the American public alert and American education under indictment. Reform goals called for fundamentally new conceptions about the nature of knowledge and competence, immediate implementation of the teaching of higher-order thinking skills emphasizing problem solving, developing students' ability to exercise personal judgment, and a curriculum designed to accomplish these ends for all students, not just an elite few. In the late 1980s, school reformers saw at last that teachers, with their students, were at the heart of their enterprise and that any school reform needed to go hand in hand with the reform of teacher education: They began arguing the case for high and rigorous standards and the demonstration of actual performance by teachers as well as by students (Carnegie Forum on Education and the Economy, 1986; Darling-Hammond, 1986; Goodlad, 1990, 1994; Holmes Group, 1986; Lieberman, 1995; Shulman, 1987).

Schools, the argument ran, would never be reformed without accomplished teachers. That meant teachers who could demonstrate that they had the knowledge and skills to reach all of their students, had pledged their commitment to those students, and were part of a profession that assumed responsibility for the "definition, transmittal, and enforcement of professional standards of practice and ethics" (Darling-Hammond, 1988, p. 12). A new professionalism for teachers was born, child-centered, knowledge-based—and accountable. Albert Shanker (1985), President of the American Federation of Teachers, argued in answer to the question: What does it mean to have a profession, to be a professional? for at least four things.

> First, you cannot have a profession without standards. . . . Second, there is no profession without a knowledge base. . . . Third, there is no profession without a well established, formal set of collegial or peer relationships. And, Fourth, there is no profession unless the practitioners are seen as acting in the interest of their clients. (p. 15)

Shanker saw that teachers "must be viewed as professionals, as experts whose judgment can be counted on, as a group that acts on behalf of its clients and takes responsibility for the quality and performance of its own ranks" (p. 15). It would, Shanker believed, take a revolution equal to that caused by the successful emergence of teacher unionism to achieve such a goal.

But teachers and administrators knew too that twentieth-century school reforms—of the 1930s, the 1950s, and the 1970s—had foundered in trying to provide high-quality education. Historian Lawrence Cremin (1965), offering one example, points to a larger issue: "Progressive education demanded infinitely skilled teachers, and it failed because such teachers could not be recruited in sufficient numbers" (p. 350).

In the 1990s, then, on the eve of a new century, reformers recognized the critical need for good teachers, well-grounded in their subject matter, in child development, and in effective learning strategies that could challenge children to their highest achievement (Darling-Hammond, 1988; Lee, Smith, & Croninger, 1994; Meier, 1992; Resnick & Resnick, 1992). Above all, to be credentialed, teachers would need to demonstrate their knowledge and skill in actual teaching situations, not simply on paper and pencil tests. At once, teacher assessment became a high stakes activity. With that began the search for innovative, performance modes of teacher assessment and the discovery of the possibilities of portfolios. The portfolio idea, carrying with it the notion of a document, a set of credentials of the authority of one's office, was to become a vehicle for a new professionalism.

This volume offers a context for considering the history and the present place of the portfolio in teacher education and teacher assessment. The portfolio can be many things: from the sleek leather case of the artist to a modest manila folder; highly or loosely structured in the kind and number of its entries; representative of a person's best work or a sample of many works, including failures; or considered a collection of products and documents that constitute a body of work.[1] The editor and authors of this volume, however, working with teaching portfolios, hold as a model Lee Shulman's (1994) pioneering definition of the teaching portfolio.

> A teaching portfolio is the structured documentary history of a (carefully selected) set of coached or mentored accomplishments substantiated by samples of student work and fully realized only through reflective writing, deliberation, and serious conversation.

In high stakes decisions for certification or licensure, the portfolio usually is considered along with other evidence—classroom observations, assessments of cooperating teachers, and so forth. In a more sophisticated adaptation, the portfolio becomes embedded within a larger learning and assessment system, acting as its anchor and organizing focal point.

In examining the origins of the portfolio idea in teacher education, this book highlights the work of Lee Shulman and the creation of the National Board for Professional Teaching Standards (1989). It considers the rather rapid and accelerating use of portfolios in teacher assessment in several settings: locally by teacher education programs in the education of new teachers; nationally by the National Board for Professional Teaching Standards (NBPTS) for Board certification of experienced teachers; and, by a number of state departments of education aligned with the Interstate New Teacher Assessment and Support Consortium (INTASC), an alliance of states for the renewal of beginning teacher certification and licensure.

This book also looks at the possibilities and inherent tensions of portfolios: for redefining validity and reliability by considering new modes of judging portfolios; for fostering the idea of authoring one's own learning; and, most important, for making public what until now has remained nearly hidden from view, that is, debate and discussion about teaching practices, about what in fact constitutes good teaching. Ultimately, the portfolio as a process demanding at its best constant reflection on teaching and learning holds the promise—however fragile—of forcing a broader reflection on the ways teachers are educated and continue in their professional development. Although historically intertwined with the search for a new teacher professionalism, portfolios may never accomplish the daunting task of transforming teaching into a self-monitoring profession. Yet—as this book reveals—creating a teaching portfolio can be transformative.

A CONCEPTUAL FRAMEWORK FOR CONSIDERING PORTFOLIOS

The teacher portfolio may be considered from three perspectives: as a credential, as a set of assumptions about teaching and learning, and as making possible a powerful, personal reflective learning experience. While portfolios have all of these features, they at times can appear in contradiction to one another, creating the paradoxical aspects of portfolios and some of their extraordinary and creative tensions.

As a set of documents and evidence that validate one's teaching authority, the portfolio is a kind of credential representative of the emerging, new teacher professionalism. Here the portfolio can be seen as a mode of teacher assessment, the process by which a new or experienced teacher is evaluated against a set of standards and judged responsible for a class of students. But at a time of vigorous attacks on standards as mindless bureaucratization and a wrong-headed development that is increasing the top-down hierarchy of the federal or state role in education through such projects as Goals: 2000 (Clinchy, 1995; Howe, 1995; Meier, 1995) or state mandates, it is important to see the portfolio—as Lee Shulman asserts in Chapter 2—as revealing a set of assumptions about teaching and learning, ones shaped by a portfolio maker. Shulman asks: What vision of teaching underlies a given portfolio? Finally, to the novice teacher or to the experienced master, the portfolio process can be a compelling personal experience, offering an opportunity to reflect on one's learning and to articulate just who one is as a teacher. For some experienced as well as novice teachers, this can be "terrifying" and "exhilarating" all at once. From this perspective the portfolio is a highly individualized portrait of the self as a professional that sometimes may involve personal risks for a portfolio maker.

The real power of a portfolio process for teacher interns or master teachers may well be in the acts of constructing, presenting, and reflecting on the contents or the evidence of a portfolio. This inevitably involves sorting, gathering, and reflecting on the work of teaching—considering lessons taught, reviewing samples of the work of one's students, defining effective teaching moments or failures—and articulating why these are important to one's own philosophy and practice. Validation and understanding emerge through portfolio conversations with peers and mentors, the presentation of portfolio evidence, and the recognition of the new knowledge of practice generated through this process. This reflective, interpretive activity can result in the surety of the realization, "Yes, I am a teacher. I am ready to take responsibility for a class."

Here the portfolio serves its most significant purpose: as a scaffolding for reflective teacher learning. Instead of presenting a set of courses and credits earned for purposes of credentialing and certification, the teacher apprentice—or expert—stands at the center of his or her own learning, defining and defending the authority of a credential. It may be these two aspects—the portfolio as a mode of appraisal and assessment and as a means for validating one's personal development as a professional—that create the fundamental tension of portfolios. Several authors of this book attest to that. This tension is heightened by the fact that a portfolio can be used simultaneously for both purposes, it is highly personal, and it engages the individual in a reflective awareness of oneself as a professional. Paradoxically, the very personal aspect of the portfolio simultaneously serves another purpose: It makes public and concrete what teaching is all about, and holds up to consideration and scrutiny the question of what constitutes effective teaching for the individual and a profession.

It is important to recognize the dangers of the portfolio process—the possibilities for trivialization as well as mindless standardization. Yet, above all, the authors of this volume—all engaged in portfolio implementation—argue for the potential possibilities of a portfolio process and for continued experimentation with portfolios. While portfolios in teacher education are yet in their infancy, they hold great promise. This book sketches several of these possibilities.

AN OVERVIEW OF THE BOOK

Part I, "Prologue" of this book, recounts the discovery of the teaching portfolio. Nona Lyons places portfolios within the new teacher professionalism of the second wave of school reform. Lee Shulman, an originator of the teacher portfolio, tells the story of its discovery in a search for a new and more appropriate means to capture and assess the complexities of teaching. He relentlessly views the portfolio as a theoretical activity, that is, the portfolio construction process as guided inevitably by one's theory of teaching and learning.

Part II, "Emerging Portfolio Practices: A Sampler," presents rich and varied examples of current portfolio practices in teaching and teacher education. Dennie Wolf argues for the fundamental necessity of creating a portfolio culture in a school and its classrooms, if the portfolio is to be more than some throw-away fad. Steve Seidel considers how to look at student work using the collaborative assessment conferencing technique so that it is possible to understand what a portfolio maker—elementary or secondary student, apprentice or master teacher—might work on most ardently in constructing a portfolio. Examples of the current portfolio practices in several different teacher education programs are presented—by Helen Freidus of the Bank Street College of Education and by Carol Lynn Davis of the University of Southern Maine and Ellen Honan of the Yarmouth, Maine Public Schools. Nona Lyons examines the uses of interviews with students about the portfolio process as narrative structures that can scaffold teacher reflection.

Part III, "The Tensions: Portfolios for Professional Development or for Assessment," takes up the questions, tensions, and puzzles portfolios create: Are portfolios valid surrogates for teaching performance? What kind of surrogates are they? Several authors—Jon Synder and his teacher educator colleagues at the University of California at Santa Barbara and Lee Teitel and the experienced teachers of the Everett (Massachusetts) Public Schools—consider the critical question: Are portfolios most productively used for professional development or for performance assessment? Or can they be used for both? In "The Portfolio Question" Grace Grant and Tracy Huebner examine the lasting power of one form of organizing a portfolio through the use of an action research question called the portfolio question. What difference do these explorations make to the ongoing development of teachers? Finally, Larry Cuban tells the story of his unwitting development of a post-tenure portfolio at Stanford University, one he found himself constructing when he made the unheard of request for a post-tenure review of his teaching, research, and scholarship. Can the portfolio serve as a vehicle for post-tenure reviews?

In Part IV, "Judging and Validating Portfolio Evidence," other authors begin to extend the exploration of issues surrounding judging and validating portfolio evidence. Initiating this discussion are Walter Kimball of the University of Southern Maine and Susie Hanley of the Gorham, Maine Public Schools. They offer the case study of one teacher intern and follow the processes of gathering and judging portfolio evidence. For these authors the portfolio is not a stand-alone activity. Rather it is seen as part of a larger support and assessment system. Pamela Moss, research director for the portfolio assessment project of INTASC, broadens the discussion of examining and evaluating portfolio evidence as she looks at the thorny issues of validity and reliability in judging portfolios. What evidence and what kinds of reliability and validity are necessary for judging portfolios? Who decides? Moss advances the relatively new idea of using interpretive communities to judge portfolios in contrast to the traditional practice of individuals independently judging separate portfolio entries.

The next chapter addresses considerations for state credentialing when the portfolio is introduced as part of initial teacher certification. Richard Dollase, formerly of Middlebury College (Vermont), examines the question: What happens when states—Vermont, for example—mandate portfolios? In concluding this part, Gloria Ladson-Billings takes up the "missing portfolio entry" and considers the moral and ethical dimensions of today's teaching, raising the issue of where they fit in a portfolio process or in a teacher's portfolio.

Part V, "Epilogue," asks, in conclusion: What difference do portfolios make to the lives of teachers and their students? To a teacher's practices or students' learning? To a new vision of teacher professionalism? Here several examples outline with caution the possibilities of portfolios for continuing to shape a new teacher professionalism—however daunting, but critical, a challenge.

NOTE

1. Portfolio in the *Compact Edition of Oxford English Dictionary* is defined in three ways: (1) "a receptacle or case for keeping loose sheets of paper, prints, drawings, maps, music, or the like, usually in the form of a large book-cover, and sometimes having sheets of paper fixed in it, between which specimens are placed"; (2) "such a receptacle containing the official documents of a state department; hence figuratively, the office of a minister of state"; and (3) "-portfolio-stand, a piece of furniture for holding portfolios, drawings, music, etc." or "portfolioed—furnished with a portfolio" (p. 2245). (See also Bird, 1990.)

REFERENCES

Bird, T. (1990). The schoolteacher's portfolio: An essay on possibilities. In J. Millman & L. Darling-Hammond (Eds.), *The new handbook of teacher evalu-*

ation: *Assessing elementary and secondary school teachers* (2nd ed.; pp. 241–256). Newbury Park, CA: Sage.

Carnegie Forum on Education and the Economy. (1986). *A nation prepared: Teachers for the 21st century.* Washington, DC: Author.

Clinchy, E. (1995). Sustaining and expanding the educational conversation. *Phi Delta Kappan, 76*(5), 352–354.

Cremin, L. (1965). *The genius of American education.* New York: Vintage Books.

Darling-Hammond, L. (1986). A proposal for evaluation in the teaching profession. *Elementary School Journal, 86,* 531–551.

Darling-Hammond, L. (1988). Accountability and teacher professionalism. *American Educator, 12,*(4), 8–43.

Goodlad, J. (1990). *Teachers for our nation's schools.* San Francisco: Jossey-Bass.

Goodlad, J. (1994). *Educational renewal: Better teachers, better schools.* San Francisco: Jossey-Bass.

Holmes Group. (1986). *Tomorrow's teachers: A report of the Holmes Group.* East Lansing, MI: Author.

Howe, H. III. (1995). Uncle Sam is in the classroom. *Phi Delta Kappan, 76,* (5), 374–377.

Lee, V., Smith, J. B., & Croninger, R. G. (1994). *High school restructuring and student achievement: Issues in restructuring schools* (Issue Report No. 7). Madison: University of Wisconsin, Center on Organization and Restructuring of Schools.

Lieberman, A. (1995). *The work of restructuring schools.* New York: Teachers College Press.

Meier, D. (1992). Reinventing teaching. *Teachers College Record, 93*(4), 594–609.

Meier, D. (1995). How our schools could be. *Phi Delta Kappan, 76*(5), 369–373.

National Board for Professional Teaching Standards. (1989). *Toward high and rigorous standards for the teaching profession.* Washington, DC: Author.

Resnick, L. B., & Resnick, D. P. (1992). Assessing the thinking curriculum: New tools for educational reform. In B. R. Gifford & M. C. O'Connor (Eds.), *Changing assessments* (pp. 37–75). Boston: Kluwer.

Shanker, A. (1985). The making of a profession. *American Educator, 9*(3), 10–48.

Shulman, L. S. (1987). Those who understand: Knowledge growth in teaching. *Educational Researcher, 15*(2), 4–14.

Shulman, L. S. (1994, January). *Portfolios in historical perspective.* Presentation at the Portfolios in Teaching and Teacher Education Conference, Cambridge, MA.

PART I

Prologue

HISTORICAL AND CONCEPTUAL GROUNDINGS OF THE BOOK

Why teaching portfolios? Why just now? With what promise for the future? This Prologue offers some answers to these questions. It traces the arrival of the portfolio, already in use by other professions, as it makes its way into teacher education. Not simply the result of efforts to reform teacher testing, portfolios are presented here as an effort to capture the complex mindfulness of competent and effective teachers.

Recently, analyzing the promises and disappointments of school reforms, David Tyack and Larry Cuban in their book, *Tinkering Toward Utopia* (1995), suggest that goals and plans of school reformers ought to be considered more realistically as hypotheses about change rather than as blueprints for it: Schools are as likely to change a reform as to be changed by it. Consequently, adaptations of reform goals in this view would be expected and encouraged to fit local school conditions. How one school reform measure, the teacher portfolio, and some of its adaptations in teacher education are encouraging the new professionalism is the theme of this book.

REFERENCE

Tyack, D., & Cuban, L. (1995). *Tinkering toward Utopia: A century of public school reform.* Cambridge, MA: Harvard University Press.

CHAPTER 1

Portfolio Possibilities: Validating a New Teacher Professionalism

Nona Lyons

UNIVERSITY OF SOUTHERN MAINE

Twelve-year-old Amy sat with the small group of visitors in the music room of the Town Junior High School sharing a fat notebook of her writing and term projects, her portfolio. She opened the book, slid out a blue brochure, and handed it to a college student: "This is the brochure I made for the exhibition we just completed. I did mine on the Plains Indians. The brochure explains what is in the exhibit."

"What made you want to include this in your portfolio?" asked the college student.

"Well," said Amy, "When I began this project I wasn't really interested in this subject at all. I include it because I became interested in it."

"How did that happen?" continued the undergraduate.

"Well, I just started to wonder what the lives of the people were like. What did they do everyday? How did they live? I became interested."

Just then Amy's teacher joined the group. "Did you show them the science test," she asked, clearly encouraging Amy. "Did you finish it?" "Yes," Amy said, taking several sheets of paper from her notebook. The teacher explained: "Amy's group for the new science project decided that they would like to create their own unit test. And Amy volunteered to put it together." "I think I will put it in my portfolio," Amy announced, as the thought occurred to her. "Don't forget to complete your chart about the multiple intelligences," reminded the teacher. "Which intelligences do you think this test will touch upon?"

The visitors to the junior high school, college seniors from the local university, who were preparing portfolios of their own as part of an application to the university's teacher education program, were clearly nonplussed by their visit. "I can't believe it," one student commented. "I am a senior in college. I never heard of a portfolio until I started one of my own. These junior high school students have already finished one this year and this is not the first time they have done one!" The seventh graders had just presented portfolios to their parents as part of an end-of-semester reporting process. Town Junior High School was experimenting with portfolios as an alternative mode of assessment in its own and its district's efforts at school renewal and reform. The college students, who had just completed a study of Howard Gardner's theory of multiple intelligences, left the school rethinking not only what they would include in their own portfolios, but the kind of teachers they needed to become if they were to teach these junior high school students. Their professor, a teacher educator and instructor of their course, Developing a Teaching Portfolio, caught her breath. Amazed, she contemplated the easy way Amy had shared her processes of mind, her thinking, and, similarly, how easily her teacher engaged Amy in reflecting on that, on multiple intelligences and her ways of knowing. She pondered: What would happen when the junior high school students reached the university? What would a portfolio course look like then? The study of theory? In what direction was the portfolio, this one fragile effort at school reform, taking student learning? What did it portend for shaping the role of the teacher as a professional? Where might that be leading teacher education?

The realization of the critical role that teachers needed to play in any effective school restructuring characterized the school reform of the mid-1980s and the search for a new mode of teacher assessment. It upset an older view of the teacher and the teaching profession. This chapter considers this history as a context for the emergence of the teacher portfolio. It first looks at the portfolio as a manifestation of a new professionalism. It then examines the portfolio as revealing a set of assumptions about teaching and learning; finally, it presents the portfolio as a powerful reflective tool of professional and personal teacher growth and development.

THE PORTFOLIO AS A MANIFESTATION OF A NEW PROFESSIONALISM

Previously cast as an occupation, teaching for more than a century had viewed the teacher as the occupant of a role, subject to the rules of a bureaucracy. Teacher evaluation was something done to teachers. Then the vision of reformers in the 1980s transformed the role of the teacher. It placed the teacher "at the heart of what is known as 'educational excellence'" (Sykes, 1986, p. 365). Teaching would cast off its old bureaucratic image and, like other professions, create a new professional one. Linda Darling-Hammond (1986), contrasting the bureaucratic model of teaching with the emerging professional one, characterized a bureaucratic concept as follows: "In a pure bureaucratic conception, teachers do not plan or inspect their work: they merely perform it."

> In a more professional conception of teaching, teachers plan, conduct, and evaluate their work both individually and collectively. Teachers analyze the needs of their students, assess the resources available, take the school district's goals into account, and decide on their instructional strategies. . . . Evaluation of teaching is conducted largely to ensure that proper standards of practice are being employed. (p. 532)

If a new professionalism was to consider the evaluation or assessment of teaching against "standards of practice," it also had to create those standards and assessments and, in the process, upset an existing industry: teacher testing.

While the school reform movement had created a flurry of development in teacher assessment during the 1970s and 1980s, by the late 1980s teacher testing had been criticized effectively (Haertel, 1991; Shulman, Haertel, & Bird, 1988). Consisting largely of multiple choice questions and writing samples, and sometimes including descriptions of brief teaching scenarios for which one selected a correct answer, teaching tests were denounced for their failure to measure adequately or accurately actual teaching performance. Tests were criticized, too, for treating pedagogy as generic rather than subject matter specific. While the National Teachers Examination (NTE) of the Educational Testing Service (ETS) was the most vilified teacher test, most tests shared similar criticisms. One review (Haney, Madaus, & Kreitzer, 1987), concluded that: "it is . . . a sad delusion to think that current teacher tests hold promise for improving education in the United States" (p. 209).

Most disturbing to reformers was the image of teaching embodied in existing tests, the view of teaching as teacher centered, characterized by direct instruction, predominantly a lecture mode. Missing was teaching's complexity, the varied approaches and sophisticated responses of individual teachers to their students, those unique learners with histories and contexts of their own. The judgment, skill, and know-how, the professional competence of excellent and effective teachers needed to be part of any new assessment.

If teaching was to become a profession similar to others, it also would need to create the means to guarantee that members had met requirements for entry into the profession, had the knowledge and skills required to practice, and had the power to participate in the governance and decision making of schools. Above all, teachers would need to take part in the creation of the new assessments.

Standards and Assessments for a New Profession

In 1986 two important reports took up these issues, linking teacher assessment and professionalism. The Holmes Group suggested a structure for a new teaching profession, with different requirements and assessment procedures at each of three levels. There were to be subject matter examinations and observations of teachers' practice using portfolios and exhibitions as well as spot observations. The Carnegie Task Force on Teaching as a Profession (1986) suggested in their report, *A Nation Prepared: Teachers for the 21st Century,* that a national board for professional teaching standards be created in order to "establish standards for high levels of competence in the teaching profession, to assess the qualifications of those seeking board certification, and to grant certificates to those who meet the standards" (p. 62). The following year, the National Board for Professional Teaching Standards (NBPTS) was established, with teachers constituting the majority of its board and its membership. It became the lightening rod for professional teacher assessment.

At once the Board created assessment development laboratories for the purpose of constructing new teacher assessment instruments for the certification of teachers in several content areas. To guide its work, the NBPTS (1991) identified five propositions in its fundamental statement of policy, "What Teachers Should Know and Be Able to Do": (1) Teachers are committed to students and their learning; (2) teachers know the subjects they teach and how to teach those subjects to their students; (3) teachers are responsible for managing and monitoring student learning; (4) teachers think systematically about their practice and learn from experience; and (5) teachers are members of learning communities. Haertel (1991) emphasizes the significance of these propositions:

These propositions, as elaborated in the NBPTS document, go far beyond the domains of knowledge, skills, and dispositions that could be addressed under existing tests or any tests on the horizon. They emphasize the role of professional judgment and commitment; express the importance of teachers' lifelong learning; acknowledge the extensive, detailed, contextually bound knowledge that teachers must possess; and, set forth an ethical stance as well as a conception of professional capabilities. Aspects of pedagogical content knowledge are woven through several of the propositions. The importance of teachers' knowledge of student preconceptions and points at which they are likely to have difficulty, specific instructional strategies and materials, alternative instructional approaches and when to try them, and other aspects of subject-specific teaching knowledge are included. The Board's vision of the teacher is complex and demanding. It "acknowledges that even state-of-the-art assessments probably cannot fully capture teaching's complexities, and the standards it eventually will ask candidates to meet may not be as rich as the portrait of a Board-certified teacher sketched above" (NBPTS, 1989, p. 43). (p. 11)

In 1986, as the Board began to define its propositions for a new teacher professionalism, it also began its search for assessments that could capture the complexity it sought. At that time the Carnegie Corporation, sponsor of the Board, turned to Lee Shulman at Stanford University to undertake the challenge. Independent of the NBPTS, Shulman's newly developed Teacher Assessment Project (TAP) was to generate assessment approaches that would inform the Board's own work as it created a voluntary program for the national certification of teachers.

THE PORTFOLIO AS REVEALING A SET OF ASSUMPTIONS ABOUT TEACHING AND LEARNING

As Lee Shulman and his colleagues at the Stanford TAP began developing prototypes for teacher assessments, they challenged traditional views of both teaching and assessment (Shulman, Haertel, & Bird, 1988). In tracing the evolution of the project and its rationale, Shulman asserts that the process–product, input–output model of teaching that dominated assessment failed to capture the complex, messy, multiple dimensions of teaching and of teacher learning. Thus, in 1994, when Shulman addressed a conference of teacher educators gathered under the theme "Leadership in a Climate of Standards and Assessment," he reminded his listeners that the work undertaken by the Stanford TAP came from a profoundly different conception of the teaching act.

Eschewing the existing model, Shulman and his colleagues sought assessments that would be faithful to teaching's complexity and effective teachers' actual competencies. The point, Shulman stressed, is that discussions about standards and performance assessments that focus primarily on outcomes, their number or language, without clarifying the conception of teaching and learning they embody, clearly miss the mark.

In the then current teacher research, Shulman noted especially the absence of questions about teacher knowledge. Shulman's earlier research, the "Knowledge Growth in Teaching" project, had focused on teacher knowledge and the content of the lessons taught, the questions asked, the explanations offered. It raised a host of questions.

> Where do teacher explanations come from? How do teachers decide what to teach, how to represent it, how to question students regarding it, and how to deal with problems of misunderstanding? The cognitive psychology of learning has focused almost exclusively on such questions in recent years, but strictly from the perspective of learners. . . . Research on teaching had tended to ignore those issues with respect to teachers. What are the sources of teacher knowledge? . . . How is new knowledge acquired, old knowledge retrieved, and both combined to form a new knowledge base? What are the sources of analogies, metaphors, examples, demonstrations, rephrasing? . . . And what are the pedagogical prices paid when the teacher's subject matter competence is itself compromised by deficiencies of prior education or ability. (Shulman, 1987, pp. 12–13)

Shulman (1987) knew that the professional knew not only *how*—the capacity for skilled performance—but *what* and *why:* "The teacher is not only a master of procedure, but of content and rationale, capable of explaining why something is done to himself and to others . . . capable of reflection leading to self knowledge" (p. 43). The implications of this work pertained directly to the new teacher assessment: "We can begin to conceive differently of how professional examinations for teachers might be organized and constructed. . . . They must be defined and controlled by members of the profession, not by legislators or laypersons. They must reflect an understanding that both content and process are needed by teaching professionals. . . . They would be a good deal tougher than any examination currently in use for teachers" (Shulman, 1986, p. 43).

This was the task Shulman himself had to undertake with the TAP, to make teacher assessments that would be faithful to the teaching act. The story of the fortuitous road to the portfolio discovery—from the first efforts to replicate the life of classrooms, to the idea of a set of activities, demonstrations of teaching, that were carried out by teachers who came to an assessment center, to the idea of a "movable" assessment center brought to a classroom and captured in a portfolio—is told in Chapter 2.

THE PORTFOLIO PROCESS AS A POWERFUL, REFLECTIVE LEARNING EXPERIENCE

The story of the portfolio as a personal learning experience, powerful in the kind of reflective process it fosters, perhaps is best revealed in the stories of those who create their own portfolios. Take the following example.

The three teacher interns—Martha, Anna, and Sarah—who gathered on the warm spring morning had come to talk about their experiences in constructing a teaching portfolio. Looking back on their year's internship in learning to teach, the interns ought to have felt a sense of accomplishment, of pride in their achievement. They had been judged by their mentors as ready to take responsibility for classes of their own. But as they reflected on the year, and on the experience of creating a portfolio used in judgment of their readiness to teach, the interns voiced sometimes seemingly contradictory responses.

Martha: It was clearly a daunting experience, creating a portfolio. I didn't know where to begin. At first, we were asked to bring in one artifact that represented our growth as teachers. What could that be? And where did the standards fit in? Was the portfolio supposed to be a demonstration that we had met them? A tool for assessment? Or a record of our development?

Anna: The teams helped. They served as a coach to us. I liked the fact that we three interns worked together and had the help of school faculty, administrators, and previous interns. It was important— and consoling—to hear how we all were struggling. But what should the portfolio include? Someone suggested that we start with a statement of our philosophy. But I didn't have a teaching philosophy. At least I didn't think so.

Martha: But then we did bring in our artifacts. I could see that they were different but they made sense for each of us. Anna, you brought in a unit on an integrated math and language arts project that you had done with your elementary students. You had worked on integrated units all year. . . . Similarly, I wanted to show the artwork my high school students had done when they

were reading *The Scarlet Letter*. I had them embroidering the letter
"A." I consider that artistic experience ought to be part of students' experience of reading literature. I included some samples in
my portfolio along with student essays. Then, after we presented a
second portfolio entry, the whole project began to make sense. I
didn't relax, but I could see where it was going.

In the end, I came to see that the whole year of learning to
teach had seemed like a booming, buzzing in my head. Now I had
to make sense out of it. Consider a teaching philosophy? Think
about what was really important to me? I began to think about
times when my students had really responded to me, to what I
was presenting to them, to learning. I decided that is what I would
put into my portfolio.

Anna: And I started looking at my students' work, at their portfolios.
I was thrilled to find in them lessons and samples of the things we
had worked on together. The kids had deemed these things important enough to put into their portfolios. I decided that I would put
samples of their portfolios into mine. And suddenly I could see
that the portfolio was like a mirror. It was reflecting me, my teaching back to me.

Sarah: It was exhilarating, but daunting—constructing a portfolio. I
would even say at one time it was truly terrifying. I never felt so revealed: Who was I as a teacher? The portfolio was an answer.

Martha: But I know I am ready to teach. I am ready to have a class of
my own. It was the portfolio process that made that absolutely
clear to me. I am a teacher! We are teachers!

These teacher interns, students at the University of Southern
Maine's Extended Teacher Education Program, are participating in a
portfolio assessment process, what might be called an experiment in the
new teacher professionalism. Coming into teaching on the second wave
of school reform, these students are taking part in a re-imagined model
of teacher education: participating in an intensive internship in teaching; working for a full year in a professional development school site,
mentored by university and school faculty; and presenting the evidence
of their professional development through a portfolio process.

Portfolio assessment in the USM model, as with some other teacher
education portfolio experiments, involves what might be called a portfolio assessment process, a dynamic process with interacting elements that
become braided into the whole process of learning to teach. These include.

- *a set of goals or standards introduced early in the internship* by which the teacher intern will be judged ready to complete the program and be certified at an initial level, including, for example, understanding of one's subject matter, of child and adolescent development, and of how to connect with students' interests
- the construction of a portfolio, that is, *gathering a body of evidence of one's learning and competence* that constitutes the portfolio entries—for example, a statement of one's teaching platform or philosophy, classroom lessons, student work in written or video formats, and so on
- *critical conversations interrogating one's practice carried on* with mentors and peers as the portfolio is developed—usually over the course of a year or a semester
- *reflections* on the contents of the portfolio, triggered by collaborative interrogations and then written up, including which entries are included, why, what the teacher has learned from this experience about teaching and learning, and why that is important—the meaning of the person's own learning
- *a portfolio presentation* in which the teacher intern presents the portfolio to his or her mentors—university and classroom faculty and peers
- finally, *the decision about certification* based on the portfolio and other work of the intern.

Many portfolio makers talk about the difficulties they encounter with this process. Some come to feel overwhelmed at times by the sense of self revealed. Simultaneously they speak of the transformative power of it, the validation, the clarification of one's ideas, philosophy, and strategies for teaching that came out of their portfolio conversations. But some puzzles have emerged. Not all students easily engage in reflection (La Boskey, 1994, 1996; Lyons, 1997). What makes it possible for teachers to be reflective on their practice, to share their knowledge and understandings in ways that lead to professional development? How should mentors respond? While the chapters of this book offer current perspectives, these questions are clearly ongoing. They must be examined systematically and every day in the work of teachers and their mentors.

Many portfolio users warn, too, of the dangers of portfolios, of their being trivialized, and of their abilities to trivialize teaching. It is too easy to see them as a fad, or as elaborate scrapbooks. These tendencies must be guarded against. Shulman's notion that the portfolio is always an act of theory, a demonstration of one's beliefs about a vision of teaching and learning, is crucial.

PORTFOLIO POSSIBILITIES: THE FRAGILE CONSEQUENCES

> What matters most to America's future is finding the best teachers, helping
> them develop their skills to the greatest extent, and rewarding them for
> their work on behalf of children and youth. (National Commission on
> Teaching and America's Future, 1996)

If portfolios in teacher education are the hope of creating a new
vision of teacher professionalism, they have a heavy burden. This is in
spite of their expanded use by both the National Board, who now feature
portfolios as the central, organizing activity of their assessments of experienced teachers; and by INTASC and some 30 state departments of education who have similarly adopted the National Board standards and the
portfolio in their prototype assessments of beginning teachers. A cursory
perusal of the 1996 report of the prestigious National Commission on
Teaching and America's Future documents too well the still daunting
obstacles to the goal of professionalism:

> The Commission found a profession that has suffered from decades of
> neglect. By the standards of other professions and other countries, U.S.
> teacher education has historically been thin, uneven, and poorly financed.
> Teacher recruitment and hiring are distressingly ad hoc, and salaries lag
> significantly behind those of all other professions. This produces chronic
> shortages of qualified teachers in fields like mathematics and science, and
> the continual hiring of large numbers of people as "teacher" who are un-
> prepared for their jobs. (p. 5)

Arguing that after more than a decade of school reform, America is "still
a very long way from achieving its educational goals," the report acknowledges that the distance between "our stated goals and current realities is not due to lack of effort: "It is now clear that most schools and
teachers cannot produce the kind of learning the new reforms demand—not because they do not want to, but because they do not know
how, and the systems they work in do not support them in doing so. . . .
On the whole, the school reform movement has ignored the obvious:
What teachers know and can do makes the crucial difference in what
children learn" (National Commission, 1996, p. 6).

The sobering words of the report alert educators and citizens to the
challenging agenda for teacher education. Portfolio and other performance assessments can be only one part of the future agenda to transform teaching. But they are the heart of a vision of teacher education
for a profession. Portfolio assessment systems hold out standards of
rigor and excellence; require evidence of effective learning; foster one's

own readiness to teach, to author one's own learning; make collaboration a new norm for teaching, creating collaborative, interpretive communities of teacher learners who can interrogate critically their practice; and uncover and make public what counts as effective teaching in today's complex world of schools and learners. There are challenges to portfolios, but these are their clear possibilities.

This book, addressing these intriguing possibilities of portfolios, invites readers to look at them from several perspectives to make their own judgments.

REFERENCES

Carnegie Task Force on Teaching as a Professional (1986). *A nation prepared: Teachers for the 21st century.* NY: Author.

Darling-Hammond, L. (1986). A proposal for evaluation in the teaching profession. Elementary School Journal, 86, 531–551.

Haertel, E. H. (1991). New forms of teacher assessment. *Review of Research in Education, 17,* 3–27.

Haney, W., & Madaus, G. (1986). *Effects of standardized testing and the future of the national assessment of educational progress.* Chestnut Hill, MA: Boston College, Center for the Study of Testing, Evaluation and Educational Policy.

Haney, W., Madaus, G., & Kreitzer, A. (1987). Charms talismatic: Testing teachers for the improvement of American education. *Review of Research in Education, 14,* 169–238.

Holmes Group. (1986). *Tomorrow's teachers: A report of the Holmes Group.* East Lansing, MI: Author.

La Boskey, V. K. (1994). *Development of reflective practice.* New York: Teachers College Press.

La Boskey, V. K. (1996). *Reflection in teaching: Can it be taught?* Town meeting presentation at the annual meeting of the American Educational Research Association, New York.

Lyons, N. (1995). Teacher portfolio project. University of Southern Maine, Gorham.

Lyons, N. (1997, March). *Reflection in teaching: Is it developmental?* Town meeting presentation at the annual meeting of the American Educational Research Association, Chicago.

National Board for Professional Teaching Standards. (1989). *Toward high and rigorous standards for the teaching profession.* Washington, DC: Author.

National Board for Professional Teaching Standards. (1991). *What teachers should know and be able to do.* Washington, DC:

National Commission on Teaching and America's Future. (1996). *What matters most: Teaching for America's future.* New York: Author.

Sarason, S. B. (1982). *The culture of the school and the problem of change.* Boston: Allyn & Bacon.

Sarason, S. B. (1990). *The predictable failure of educational reform.* San Francisco: Jossey-Bass.

Sarason, S. B., Davidson, K. S., & Blatt, B. (1986). *The preparation of teachers: An unstudied problem in education.* Cambridge, MA: Brookline Books.

Shulman, L. S. (1986). Assessment for teaching: An initiative for the profession. *Phi Delta Kappan, 69,*(1), pp. 38–44.

Shulman, L. S.(1987). Those who understand: Knowledge growth in teaching. *Educational Researcher, 15*(2), 4–14.

Shulman, L. S., Haertel, E., & Bird, T. (1988). *Toward alternative assessments of teaching: A report of work in progress.* Stanford: Stanford University School of Education, Teacher Assessment Project.

Sizer, T. (1992). *Horace's school: Redesigning the American high school.* New York: Houghton Mifflin.

Sykes, G. (1986). Introduction. *Elementary School Journal, 86,* 365–367.

CHAPTER 2

Teacher Portfolios:
A Theoretical Activity

Lee Shulman

STANFORD UNIVERSITY

When I think about portfolios and their beginnings, I am reminded of a recent summer visit to a perfectly wonderful place in northern Spain, Santiago de Compestela. Until arriving there, we had not known that Santiago (the reputed burial place of the Apostle St. James) vied with Jerusalem and Rome as one of the three great pilgrimage destinations of the Middle Ages. As we toured the area, we began to realize that when you talk about a pilgrimage, you are not talking about a single path. Finding ourselves on an obscure road, we would be told, "Oh, yes, this is part of the pilgrimage to Santiago." When we said we thought the pilgramage followed a nearby freeway, we were assured: "No, no, some of the pilgrims made this side trip to this little convent and then they went on to Santiago." Apparently pilgrims from Hamburg even took side trips to Paris.

Somehow, even though engaged in some shared purpose, individual pilgrims and groups of pilgrims took very different paths—at times quite parallel, at other times simply intersecting. This feature of pilgrimages seems like a reasonable metaphor for some of the things I want to discuss about portfolios.

Key aspects of the trip that some colleagues and I have taken with portfolios can be captured in three stories. The first story recounts the work on teacher assessment that we began doing in 1985 with the

Teacher Assessment Project (TAP) and how that work drove us to the development and use of portfolios. That story continues in its own way today in the portfolio work of the National Board for Professional Teaching Standards (NBPTS). A second story is about the experiences that I have had and continue to have in the course that I teach at Stanford in the teacher education program, which uses portfolios as a central feature. The third is the Larry Cuban story, which I think is a very important instance of what happens when we take the portfolio notion and move it not only from students to teachers, but from teachers to teacher educators. After a few words of caution about some clear and present dangers in the use of portfolios, I conclude with my views on what I see as some of the virtues of the use of portfolios in teacher education.

THE PORTFOLIO AS A THEORETICAL ACT

A key point I want to stress at the beginning—and it is a theme that I will return to regularly—is that a portfolio is a theoretical act. By this I mean that every time you design, organize, or create in your teacher education program a template, a framework, or a model for a teaching portfolio, you are engaged in an act of theory. Your theory of teaching will determine a reasonable portfolio entry. What is declared worth documenting, worth reflecting on, what is deemed to be portfolio-worthy, is a theoretical act.

Let me elaborate. I am increasingly aware of the fact that the work we did in the TAP and the ways in which the teaching portfolio evolved there are really part of a continuing critique of theories of teaching. For me this critique first found concrete formulation in the creation of the Institute for Research on Teaching at Michigan State University. In 1975, when we created the Institute, we designed it as a powerful argument against the prevailing views of teaching as skilled behavior—the process–product conception of teaching that clearly reigned at that time. We argued then that teaching was a form of thought and judgment, that it was an act of an autonomous agent engaged in creating opportunities for students and adapting all kinds of goals and materials to the conditions of the moment and the students being taught. Therefore, we contended, an utterly new paradigm of research was needed for studying teaching, one that was much more cognitive and much more focused on the idiographic components of teaching, the uniquely local. That is why ethnographers—with their emphasis on concrete situations—became so important in our work. Rather than simply looking at what all teachers held in common, or considering effective teaching generically, we believed we had to talk about it in its contexts and intricate complexity.

What has become clearer to me is that this kind of theoretical and, if you will, ideological act—stipulating, "No, teaching is not really like that; it's more like this"—is also what we're doing when we design and conceptualize teaching portfolios. In all these discussions, it is important to keep in mind that the portfolio is a broad metaphor that comes alive as you begin to formulate the theoretical orientation to teaching that is most valuable to you. This became apparent with the work of the TAP and the emergence of the teaching portfolio.

NEW ASSESSMENTS FOR A NATIONAL BOARD FOR PROFESSIONAL TEACHING STANDARDS: THE EMERGENCE OF THE PORTFOLIO

The TAP, begun in 1985, was part of a continuing critique of the prevalent notions of teaching, which viewed teaching much too behaviorally, much too generically, and much too context-free. (A very important part of the missing context was what was being taught—the subject matter content.) At that time, two forms of teacher assessment were widely used, the National Teachers Examination and classroom observations. Neither had context or much thought associated with them. Classroom observations used exactly the same instrument, irrespective of whether one was looking at an eleventh-grade teacher teaching trigonometry or a second-grade teacher working with a reading group.

Dissatisfaction with these approaches produced this impossible dream: creating a National Board for Professional Teaching Standards. Toward that goal, we tried to invent a generation of assessments that would capture teaching in a much broader sense. I am not going to go into any of the details of those assessments. But what we created was an "assessment center" concept where we simulated various situations that teachers actually engage in. Some assessments required participants to look at textbook materials, critique them, and talk about how they would adapt them for use with particular groups of students. Videotapes of other teachers' teaching presented opportunities for participants to offer constructive, critical feedback. The champion simulation of all we called "Teaching a Familiar Lesson." In that situation, a teacher brought to the assessment center a lesson that he or she really enjoyed and was skilled at teaching. We first interviewed the teacher about the lesson: how it connected to the broader curriculum of which it was a part, what the teacher intended to do, and what kind of difficulties might be anticipated. Then we videotaped the teacher presenting the hour-long lesson to a group of students. Afterwards we interviewed the students about the lesson. We asked them deep, difficult questions such as, "What was that lesson about?" This turned out to be a very important question. In a separate interview, the teacher "candidate" had an opportunity to reflect on, critique, and analyze the lesson just taught, responding to questions such as, "What can you tell me about some of the individual kids you just taught?" Little questions like that.

This experience yielded good news and bad news. The good news was that as far as we could tell, compared with existing forms of teacher assessment, this was a winner. Both those doing the observation as well as those being assessed agreed that this was much more faithful to teaching than anything any of them had ever experienced before. One teacher examiner said at the end of 4 days, "I have watched more teaching and thought more about teaching in the last 4 days than I have in the previous 25 years." That was the good news.

The bad news was that the activity was still highly decontextualized. We kept asking ourselves, "But what are these folks like back in their classrooms?" Granted, we were putting them in situations that bore a much closer resemblance to the kinds of things they did in classrooms than a set of multiple choice test items did. And granted, there were virtues in basing our observations on a very systematic sampling of the work they did, not only in classroom-like settings, but in what I call kitchen table settings—where planning, analyzing, critiquing, and evaluating took place. But these assessments totally omitted classroom observation in a curriculum-specific way. With all those virtues, there was still this sense that something was missing.

At that time it was becoming clear that for the next generation of our assessments, we wanted to put more emphasis on some form of documentation, some way for teachers systematically to document what they were doing in their classrooms. We wanted that to become the core of the assessment. I don't remember when we began talking about such documentation as portfolios; it just sort of happened.

At some point I do remember my colleague Tom Bird engaged in what I would call a "thought experiment." He phoned some architects from the Yellow Pages, asking: "Do you have a portfolio?" and, if so, "Why?" We were just kind of mucking around trying to figure out how other professions document their work. Tom then wrote the first paper in our project on the teaching portfolio. It became a chapter in the Millman and Darling-Hammond volume on new approaches to the assessment of teaching. What is interesting is that Tom wrote that chapter before we had ever done a teaching portfolio. It was simply his attempt to describe what a portfolio would be like—if we did one.

And then we did. We tried to design portfolios with carefully speci-
fied entries that teacher candidates for National Board assessment
would complete over the course of a year, a large part of a year. These
entries would become the heart of their National Board review. In thinking of that sort of portfolio, we asked: "What would happen if you could
embody an assessment center concept in different kinds of exercises?"
Our mental image was the assessment center as a sort of rug that you
rolled up. You put it under your arm and you took it to a school and
into somebody's classroom and you unrolled it. What had been exercises
in an assessment center now became, in some sense, entries in a portfolio. So the conceptual structure remained, but now it was sited in the
real world and it was being done in real time, which meant weeks instead
of hours, perhaps months in some cases.

At that time one of our closest and most helpful advisors was the
Stanford University's already emeritus professor Lee Cronbach, the psy-
chometrician. Lee's job in our project was to give us permission to vio-
late yet another rule that he had written. We would come up with some
notion of a portfolio entry and we'd say, "Lee, can we do that?" He
would respond: "Don't worry. You create reasonable assessments and
let the psychometricians figure out how you can do it." That's very important advice. We have let the tail of psychometrics wag our work for
far too long.

Portfolio Entries: A Coached, Collaborative Activity

So we moved to this second generation of work on assessment in which
the portfolio, rather than the assessment center, became the heart of
the assessment. I recall vividly that the year we started our work, I was
approached by someone at the American Educational Research Association (AERA) annual meeting who took me aside and said, "Lee, I want to
save you a lot of trouble. We've tried portfolios in my state; they don't
work." I said, "Well, why don't they work?" And then in that wonderful way in which people tell little secrets they don't want everybody to
know, he just leaned over and said, "Teachers cheat." I said, "Oh, oh.
What do they do?" He continued: "They help each other out on their
portfolios. That invalidates it. It's like students copying from each other's test papers."

The underlying notion here is that what we were doing is testing
and, in testing, the individual working alone is the unit of analysis. It is
really quite a powerful orientation. In response, I suggested that the reason we had undertaken the National Board assessment project in the
first place was to help create the conditions under which teachers could

live lives that were more truly professional in the best sense of the word. One of the things that members of the professions did was work together and collaborate and talk to one another and advise one another and mentor one another, and isn't this what we have in mind? He shook his head, "That's cheating. It's cheating."

This conversation came to be repeated so many times that I composed a mini-interview. I came to say to these people: "Do you have a Ph.D.? Where did you get it? Did you have a committee? Who was your chair? Anybody else on the committee? They didn't give you any guidance, did they?" When each person recounted a story of interactions with dissertation committee members, I countered: "Then I can't take your dissertation very seriously as any kind of evidence of your competence, can I? You cheated!" The typical response claimed: "Well, that's different."

It isn't different: So many of the accomplishments we value are not accomplishments that we achieved in some kind of monastic solitude. Rather, they are the outcome of often extended periods of mentoring and coaching and deliberation and exchange. In the end, we feel pride in the achievement. Why, then, when teachers do it, even in a context of assessment, is this collaboration suddenly invalidated and seen as cheating?

In the assessment project, we literally turned necessity into virtue. (But again, I think it was ideologically driven.) In our design of portfolios, we mandated that every portfolio entry had to be coached. There had to be some evidence that some other person—teacher, mentor, whomever—had some chance to review, discuss, or coach an entry. Now it didn't always work. Some teachers never got that kind of help, so there was a source of variation that we were worried about. But the notion that teamwork ought to be commonplace, rather than be seen as some sort of idiosyncratic act of cheating, is really terribly important and it was important to us.

In 1994, with 1,500 portfolios being sent to teachers, the National Board had to confront the issue of teamwork again. They commissioned Sam Weinberg at the University of Washington to prepare a position paper on collaboration in teaching portfolios. I would like to share with you just the first page of Sam's position paper, called "Collaboration in Teacher Assessment."

Ezra Pound called it a masterpiece, one of the most important 19 pages in English. Conrad Aiken heralded it as "one of the most moving and original poems of our times." Even the trenchant I. A. Richards said that it expressed "the plight of a whole generation."

The Wasteland, T. S. Eliot's brilliant and infuriating critique of modernity, is known by anyone who has ever taken a college literature course. It is a jarring juxtaposition of classic and modern. Its magisterial allusions and disquieting meter have occupied and mystified literary critics for nearly a century, not to mention the untold hours spent by baffled freshmen trying to decipher its meaning. Published in 1922, the poem immediately thrust Eliot into the limelight. But the story behind his poem remained shrouded in mystery until 1968. In that year the original manuscript of *The Wasteland* was discovered and a facsimile edition appeared three years later. This edition showed a typewritten version of *The Wasteland* with whole stanzas crossed out with marginal comments such as, "Too loose, inversions not warranted by any real exigents of meter, dogmatic deduction and wobbly as well." When Eliot wrote "the cautious critics" in the section called "The Fire Sermon," the marginal note focussed on the word cautious, pointing out that, when speaking of London, this "adjective is tautological." In a handwritten section the critic drew a large X across the whole page and in a marginal squib issued this judgment: "Bad, but I can't attack it until I get the typescript."

The man behind the big X was none other than Ezra Pound. Ezra Pound, as Sam goes on to describe, had critiqued, suggested revisions, rewritten, and commented on all of *The Wasteland* in successive drafts. Sam raises the interesting question: So whose poem is it? Is it still Eliot's? Should *The Wasteland* be considered by Eliot and Pound? By Eliot with the assistance of Pound? Or is it still fundamentally Eliot's work because whatever your critics say, it is still your job to put it all together and take responsibility for the whole.

Sam Weinberg goes on to offer a whole series of analyses and suggestions for the role of coaching in teaching portfolios for National Board assessment. But he points out, again in the spirit of my previous argument, that all this work is theory. Since the mid-1980s, new psychological and anthropological theories have emerged to inform our work as educators—and these are not the same theories that we were using in the 1960s and 1970s. A Russian psychologist named Vygotsky is suddenly on the lips of almost every educator in the country. His sociocultural perspectives, and the idea of "distributed expertise" among learners, are studied by teachers across the nation. As the theoretical models that undergird our work change, activities such as portfolios will change in response. Both of those things have been going on with our work on portfolios.

One important point that drives all of our work in the TAP and continues to drive the National Board is a source of enormous tension: If you are going to introduce new forms of assessment, or argue for the continuation of older ones, you no longer can make arguments that are limited to the four great forms of validity—concurrent validity, predictive validity, content validity, and construct validity. The four kinds of validity have been the basis for determining whether a test either is or is not valid. But, in the past 4 or 5 years, even the psychometricians have changed their perspective. From Sam Messick to Lee Cronbach, to Ed Haertel, psychometricians write about the fifth form of validity. Some call it *consequential validity;* some call it systemic validity. The notion is rather simple: The claim that some form of assessment is valid requires that you offer evidence that when you deploy it, it has positive consequences for the entire system of which it is a part. The assessment cannot merely discriminate reliably, or correlate with some other indicator. In terms of teacher assessment, this new requirement means that any form of teacher assessment has to meet a new standard: that the manner in which it is deployed improves the quality of teaching and opportunities for becoming a better teacher. That's consequential validity for teacher assessment.

Again and again on the TAP, we kept asking what we called the "Stanley Kaplan question": Have we designed either a portfolio entry—or a form of assessment—that could be passed by somebody who had become test-wise, but who had not become a better teacher? Could you be trained to pass the test without having to become a better practitioner in order to do so? And if the answer was, "Probably," then we wanted to toss that one into the dustbin. If portfolios represented ways in which teachers had improved themselves, and if portfolios were having a positive impact on teachers' work in classrooms, then portfolios were beginning to meet the standard of consequential validity.

One other response to the critics who charged that teachers cheat was, in fact, a spinoff of the notion of the doctoral dissertation. Just as a doctoral dissertation ultimately is defended in an oral examination, so too do teacher assessments need a similar defense. The point is that somebody ought to be able not only to display their work, but to discuss it, to defend it, to engage in discourse about it. Therefore, the eventual design of the assessments that we handed over to the National Board in 1989 was a three-part assessment. The first part was a portfolio prepared by candidates in their own classrooms. These portfolios then were sent to the Stanford TAP project for review and the candidates came to Stanford for 2 days of interviews, discussions, and questioning. Through these interactions, candidates had a chance to elaborate, critique, and defend their portfolios—much in the spirit of a dissertation review.

So that was the story of the experience of the TAP.

PORTFOLIOS FOR TEACHER EDUCATION: THE STANFORD TEACHER EDUCATION PROGRAM STORY

In doing this assessment work, we came to understand more clearly that, whatever its effectiveness as an assessment form, the portfolio approach provided dynamite educational experiences. The teachers who have worked with us over the years continue to comment enthusiastically on their experiences. Their responses helped us to realize how rarely teachers have an opportunity to engage with somebody else in any piece of teaching or teaching-like activity and then to talk about it, think about it collaboratively. It was at this point that Grace Grant, then Director of Stanford's Teacher Education Program, and I began talking about introducing portfolios into the Stanford Teacher Education Program (STEP).

My teaching in this program reveals another connection to students' portfolios. Again, the theory-driven nature of portfolios becomes clear. Those who know me, know my obsession is with the intersection of pedagogy and content. Inevitably that is what the portfolio for this course is about: teaching particular ideas in one's field to particular students in one's classroom and how that plays itself out. So student teacher portfolios for this course include, for example, carefully written and re-written cases of their own teaching. You might ask: "What do cases have to do with portfolios?" A case written by a teacher is, for me, a supreme act of reflection, an attempt to capture an extended piece of one's own teaching, and of student learning, which then is transformed narratively so that it can be examined, looked at, and thought about.

The student cases, much inspired by the research of Judy Shulman at the Far West Lab, include an account of not only what the students did, but their interpretation and attempt to explain what they did, and to think about how it might be otherwise, what they might do the next time, and so on. They include, as appendices, artifacts that indicate what the materials looked like and what the students did. Every case is accompanied by two commentaries: one from a fellow student in the class and one from somebody who had nothing to do with the class, such as another teacher in the school or one of the children in the classroom. The case and the commentaries all become part of a portfolio entry. The entry also includes commentaries on cases presented by other students because these too are indicators of how a person is learning to think, act, and reflect as a teacher. Similarly, records of observations of one another's teaching—notes or interviews with the apprentice teacher and students—offer insight into student reflections on the teaching efforts of their peers. Again, the point is that this is a theory-driven portfolio. It is a reflective essay in which student teachers look back on the contents of the portfolio and analyze it from one of several perspectives.

As I reflect on this use of the portfolio, my most pointed critique is something that I intend to do something about. In some ways, the weakest part of our portfolio approach is the strongest part of an approach described by Nona Lyons in Chapter 7. Nona's portfolios are much less structured than mine, but they end with an extraordinary, in-depth debriefing interview—almost therapeutic in some cases. I am now beginning to realize that those portfolios only begin to scratch the surface of their potential if the only reflection that's done is by the student *in* his or her own portfolio. Somehow the portfolio needs to become the basis for what is now called supervision. Too often supervision is focused on classroom interactions and therefore becomes a form of crisis intervention and often true psychotherapy. Portfolios that include written cases and go beyond an individual episode offer extraordinary potential for critical reflection and for creative use as a central tool of supervision. That is the STEP story.

PORTFOLIOS FOR TEACHERS OF TEACHERS:
THE LARRY CUBAN STORY

Larry Cuban, my colleague at Stanford, is a very unusual historian of education. After 8 years as superintendent of schools in Arlington County, Virginia, like all great administrators, he was, as Clark Kerr put it, fired with enthusiasm. Larry Cuban constructed a teaching portfolio in unusual circumstances.

At the time of his promotion to full professor at Stanford, Larry asked if he could refuse tenure. This, of course, created a crisis in the provost's office. The prompt reply was, "No." Larry argued: "I don't want tenure because as soon as you give me tenure you give up your obligation to provide me with an intelligent review of my work. I refuse to work in an organization that does not take responsibility for reviewing the quality of my work regularly and providing me feedback on it." After an exchange of letters, Larry accepted tenure and, in turn, had a letter put in his file signed by the dean and the provost, saying that every 5 years, as a full professor, he would receive a careful review of his work by his colleagues.

At the first 5-year mark, Larry was president of AERA. His post-tenure review committee included Mike Smith, the Dean of Stanford at the time, John Baugh, a psycholinguist new to the faculty, Mike Atkin, chair of the committee, and me. At our first meeting, Larry proposed putting together a portfolio of his work, including scholarship, teaching, and service, and asked for a discussion of what ought to be included. Three months after that discussion we received a rather large box of materials: annotated copies of syllabi of courses he had designed and was teaching; a videotape of one or two sessions of courses he taught; and commentaries on how that videotape represented both the best things he did as a teacher and some of the enduring dilemmas he confronted as a teacher—ones he was still working on. The box also included copies of student evaluations of Larry's work and copies of student work that he thought particularly exemplified some of the best things that happened in his class. In addition, it held copies of essays that he had written, memoranda to himself about his teaching, and research documents. After reviewing the portfolio materials, we met with Larry for an hour and a half, talking about stuff that was in the portfolio, raising questions, challenging him. After that, Larry said, "Well, I clearly have to think about this some more and do some more writing." In a subsequent memo, he tried to respond to our questions and the process continued. We met three times in all. At the end, I made a brief report to the faculty, at a regular faculty meeting, about the whole process.

What was clear, was that it was not only Larry Cuban who profited from the experience; each of us benefited. John Baugh reported that he learned more quickly about teaching at Stanford than he ever would have learned in the normal ways in which new faculty could possibly learn. When do we get a chance to peer into the window of our colleagues' teaching?

My insights were somewhat different. I realized that as colleagues in the teacher education program, Larry and I both taught the same students. I came to see some aspects of my students through Larry's eyes and through Larry's course, and in ways I never saw them before because we were doing different things. The students were performing in different contexts and, suddenly, a two-dimensional view of students became three dimensional. I became much more sensitive to Larry's teaching and he to mine, and that is also very important. One of the reasons that my own portfolio has remained incomplete, although I've got all the parts around, is that I am not part of an ad hoc community organized to discuss my portfolio. It was Larry who was thoughtful enough to make sure that we provided such a community, created a group to discuss his portfolio. I am left with the question: What would happen if we as teacher educators organized ourselves to review each other's work in this way? If we supported each other in this way, what would that do for us and our students?

When we began this work on teaching portfolios for assessment purposes, we did not have a glimmer of an idea that it might have consequences for teacher development quite independent of assessment. I don't think any of us anticipated how rapidly this perspective would blossom in higher education. In both state and private universities there are efforts to find better ways of evaluating the quality of teaching than current reliance on student evaluation forms. The American Association of Higher Education is encouraging the development of teaching portfolios as the basis both for pre-tenure and tenure reviews. In the long run, however, portfolios may be more important as a professional development activity through peer review—another kind of Larry Cuban story.

The consequences of these initiatives are very hard to predict. But, in a nutshell, my argument for the importance of peer review of teaching at universities goes like this: I don't accept the complaint that teaching is valued less than research in universities. In principle, I don't think that's true. I think what universities and colleges value are those things that become community property. Research becomes community property. The word *publish* and the word *public* come from the same root. They become part of the community's discourse. While research becomes part of the community's discourse, teaching has remained for most of us a private act. Of course, it is not strictly private if our students come to class. But teaching is still seen as private in the same way that doing medicine is private—as long as the only people who see you do it are your patients. The argument for peer review and portfolios in teaching is that they contribute to making teaching community property in colleges and universities and, therefore, put teaching and research into the same orbit. We will see whether that argument or hypothesis works.

PORTFOLIOS: SOME DANGERS, SOME VIRTUES

Because all promising practices can be misused or abused, I would like to mention five dangers quickly. The first danger, one that Tom Bird many years ago dubbed, "lamination," is that a portfolio becomes a mere exhibition. If the notion of exhibition dominates, then style or how glossy it is begins to take control rather than substance. This potential for mere "showmanship" explains some of the resistance to teaching portfolios that I find from university faculty and I suspect exists among K–12 teachers as well. People are uncomfortable—and justifiably so—if they are simply asked to do some sort of advertisements for themselves, to show off.

The second danger is what I call "heavy lifting." Portfolios done seriously take a long time. They are hard to do. Teaching is a job that occupies every waking and some nonwaking moments of good teachers. (Some of those nonwaking moments are at night, some while teaching.) Given such demands, the question is: Is that much work worth it? And, if it's worth it, is there any chance in the world of reorganizing the life of teachers so that they can do this hard work without killing themselves? Heavy lifting.

The third danger is trivialization. As we learned with multiple choice tests, once you've got a mode of assessment, you start asking the kinds of questions that best fit that mode. Then follows a shift to lines of least resistance and to the increased trivialization of what gets documented. If this happens with portfolios, people will start documenting stuff that isn't even worth reflecting on.

A fourth danger is perversion. If portfolios are going to be used, whether at the state level in Vermont or California, or the national level by the National Board, as a form of high stakes assessment, why will portfolios be more resistant to perversion than all other forms of assessment have been? And if one of the requirements in these cases is that you develop a sufficiently objective scoring system so you can fairly compare people with one another, will your scoring system end up objectifying what's in a portfolio to the point where the portfolio will be nothing but a very, very cumbersome multiple choice test?

A final danger of portfolios is misrepresentation. With such a heavy emphasis on portfolios as samples of a teacher's best work, at what point do we confront the danger that these isolated samples of best work may be so remote from the teacher's typical work that they no longer serve the purpose—any of the purposes—that we have in mind?

But this litany of dangers needs to be balanced by a listing of the virtues of teaching portfolios. First, portfolios permit the tracking and documentation of longer episodes of teaching and learning than happens in supervisory observation. Too, much of our work as teacher educators is organized around the lessons or lesson fragments that we can observe when we make school site visits. Yet, most of the embarrassments of pedagogy that I encounter are not the inability of teachers to teach well for an hour or even a day. Rather they flow from an inability to sustain episodes of teaching and learning over time that unfold, accumulate, into meaningful understanding in students. This becomes especially pertinent with the current renewed emphases on higher standards, higher-order thinking, and so forth. You don't get higher-order thinking in an hour. If portfolios have the virtue of permitting students to display, think about, and engage in the kind of intellectual work that takes time to unfold, then certainly we need something parallel in teaching. That is one of the virtues of a portfolio.

Second, portfolios encourage the reconnection between process and product. I am a great critic of process–product approaches to teaching, except for one thing: They are fundamentally moral in their perspective. They affirm that the end of the teaching is learning. Yet, often in our work we so focus on the practice of teaching, that we don't ask, "But what do the students learn?" Portfolios of the best kind include not only the documentation of teaching, but the documentation of student learning. In the ultimate nirvana, the very best teaching portfolios will consist predominantly of student portfolios. If you want to see my teaching portfolio, I will quickly produce my students' dissertations. And if you're smart, you'll say, "How about the ones that never got finished?" We can structure portfolios that way: to document not only the successes, but the failures, and talk about why that happened and what role you might have played.

Third, portfolios institutionalize norms of collaboration, reflection, and discussion. A research group for the National Board discovered that teachers preparing portfolios were forming video clubs. They began regularly discussing videos of their own teaching for the purpose of eventually putting them in their portfolios. The video became almost epiphenomenal; it was discussion and collaboration that became the core.

Fourth, a portfolio can be seen as a portable residency. The typical student teaching or internship experience that we all value so much has a great achilles heel. Once you send interns out there, you don't have a clue about what they're doing. Once interns are in classrooms, they become part of whatever happens to be going on in that teacher's classroom or in that school, with that particular group of students. A portfolio introduces structure to the field experience. The candidate, the supervising teacher, and the faculty supervisor share some joint sense of what the student is supposed to learn during that period and what's supposed to be documented and reflected on. I see this as a possible virtue.

Fifth, and really most important, the portfolio shifts the agency from an observer back to the teacher interns. This is a sharp contrast to classroom observations, student evaluations, and most other forms of assessment. Portfolios are owned and operated by teachers; they organize the portfolios; they decide what goes into them. It was Tom Bird who asked us to think about the distinction between the teachers' filing cabinet and the teachers' portfolios. As teachers, we accumulate a great deal of documentation of our work. But depending on the case we have to make, we draw from the filing cabinet and create a particular portfolio. I suspect that that is true of artists and architects as well. In taking charge of their portfolios, teachers select materials to illuminate concepts of teaching and learning that undergird their work.

The three stories I have recounted traced different paths I have followed or observed for constructing and using portfolios. In subsequent chapters, other authors present similar journeys and outline the paths they followed. Although my rubrics for a portfolio change over time, I would like to conclude with my current working definition of a portfolio: A teaching portfolio is the structured, documentary history of a set of coached or mentored acts of teaching, substantiated by samples of student portfolios, and fully realized only through reflective writing, deliberation, and conversation. I think all of those parts are necessary—but I may be wrong.

PART II

Emerging Portfolio Practices: A Sampler

"WHAT IS GOOD TEACHING?"
GENERATING A FORUM FOR PUBLIC DISCUSSION

Through a sampling of portfolio practices, Part II of this book presents actual adaptations of the teacher portfolio. These chapters uncover, too, the core portfolio process: the gathering of evidence of one's growing competency in teaching and understanding student learning; the participation in conversations with critical friends about portfolio entries that help surface knowledge and values of practice; and the presentation to colleagues and mentors of the completed portfolio with its entries and all-important reflections on what one has learned. What emerges in this process is discussion and debate about what until now has remained nearly hidden from view, that is, public dialogue about "What is good teaching?"

Foundational issues of a portfolio process are addressed here. Dennie Wolf argues for the necessity to develop an appropriate school culture that allows portfolio experimentation to flourish no matter where portfolios are initiated. As samples of student work become critical entries in a teacher's portfolio, Steve Seidel urges the usefulness of gaining skill in looking at and interrogating student work, asking what the work means to a student. The focus then shifts to examining diverse practices of portfolio makers in a variety of teacher education programs.

In these chapters, teacher educators discuss their practices and trace the changes in the thinking of teacher interns and their mentors as the portfolio-making process takes life. The complex development of an interpretive community takes shape as mentors and teacher interns struggle to articulate for themselves what constitutes effective practices, meaningful philosophies, and student learning. The vulnerability of the self, so profoundly implicated in the act of teaching, is revealed as interns reflect on and question their own notion of good practice. The rarely observed intersection of personal development and learning to teach is captured, made public, and laid open to scrutiny.

CHAPTER 3

Creating a Portfolio Culture

Dennie Wolf

HARVARD UNIVERSITY

I want to explain why I see portfolios as more than minor disturbances
in the field of education. To do that I draw on my experiences and those
of my colleagues at Harvard's Performance Assessment in Collaboration
for Education Project (PACE) creating in some urban middle schools
what I call a "portfolio culture." Then through some examples, vignettes
of teachers at work in these schools helping students construct their own
portfolios, I suggest implications of this portfolio work for teacher education.

BUILDING A PORTFOLIO CULTURE

Our first learning experience came as soon as we entered schools with
the label "the portfolio project." Many saw us as people who were going
to buy manila folders, get milk crates to store them in, and then produce
a shrink-wrapped list of the 12 things to put into a portfolio. We learned
from this that we really wanted to be seen not as a project about portfolio
assessment, but as a project about creating what I call a "portfolio culture."

A portfolio culture means developing a kind of learning environment of intense expectations, care, and richness. In the context of urban
middle schools, this creation requires a major shift away from minimum
competency education. Achieving such a shift means students would
leave middle school with capacities that would guarantee that they
would not end up in general math, that they could move on to algebra,
and that they would have access to being in foreign language classes.

Such expectations create "more than minor disturbances." They ask schools to move away from a curriculum characterized by coverage; away from responding to the question, "How do we know that the kids have understood math? with the answer: "We got to the end of the book." We are trying to move down a different path where students have access to sustained work, to larger projects, and to more demanding arenas in which they can demonstrate or exhibit that "they understand what they know." This new way, however, requires a new culture.

In encouraging this shift from minimal competency education to a richer, more complex approach to learning, our project tackles three other not-so-small revolutions: (1) making public the standards for doing good work; (2) seeing revision of work as a path to success; and (3) accepting collaboration as a part of students' performance assessment.

Public Standards for Good Work

Eunice Greer, one of my colleagues at PACE, poses a trenchant question: "Are the kids who are failing, or getting Cs, or in the counselor's office all the time, in these situations because they are C people or failing people, or because they have never seen what B and A actually look like?" Too often in American public schools, the difference between C and A is a profound secret. Too often an A is the private property of those students who happen to be able to perform because of personal grit, or personal skills, or because they get it at the breakfast table. The most fundamental mandate of American public schools ought to be to make that kind of knowledge—knowledge of what it takes to succeed—a common property of every child who crosses their thresholds. In a large and sustained project such as ours, we have found at least one way to address this problem. At the beginning of each year, students who performed well last year come in and show what they did. They talk about all of the things that went into their success: the resources tapped, the people talked to, the books read, the kinds of revisions done. Presentations such as this take the mystery out of a way of working.

Revision as a Path to High Performance

We've discovered that our project is doing enormous damage to what some like to call the harsh regularities of nineteenth-century schooling. Most schooling, for example, is organized without second chances. If I fail my long division test, I have forever a 52 on my record. If I get a 76 later, then the 52 and the 76 can be averaged together. The whole concept of revision is absent; most public schools do not address the question: How do I get from failing to middling to better?

Collaborative Performance Assessment

The third "not-so-minor revolution" emerging from our project struggles to break the lasting stranglehold of highly individualized notions
of performance. Most teachers easily recall their classroom experiences
during test taking. Most of the time, the higher the stakes, the more
vigilantly we require teachers to walk up and down the rows and make
sure that there is no conversation. Think of that famous phrase, "Put all
books and papers away!" Yet, who would trust a scholar who put all
books and papers away? Who would trust a scholar who had not passed
a piece of work around, who had not suffered the slings and arrows of
review? But solo performance continues as an iron-clad rule in most
schools.

In the urban middle schools in which we work, we are trying to work
these three not-so-minor revolutions. For teachers, the consequences of
a portfolio process are both powerful and disruptive. The following two
vignettes, of project teachers working with students, focus on the implications of the portfolio process for teachers and their ongoing development.

PORTFOLIOS FOR LEARNING AND TEACHING:
DRAWING LONG THREADS OF CONNECTIONS

Learning from Students: An Interview with NL

Carol Barry's school in San Diego has a very harsh heritage. The school
itself is located in a kind of paradise where bougainvillaea blooms. Nevertheless, it is a middle school that is one of the peculiar artifacts that
Brown v. *Board of Education* created: Even in a racially balanced school,
opportunities to learn can be unevenly distributed. No longer under a
court order, the school draws half of its student population from surrounding palatial homes; the remaining students are bused every day
from inner-city San Diego. Through the years, a firmly entrenched
Gifted and Talented Education Program has produced a pattern of
classroom segregation by economic class. But a set of extremely "brassy"
sixth-grade teachers see portfolios as a way to break that pattern. They
want to demonstrate to the rest of the school that, given an opportunity
to learn, many "bused" kids have capacities that would entitle them to
the same kind of education that has been the private preserve of a selected few students.

Here, Carol Barry, a sixth-grade classroom teacher, is interviewing
NL, a bused student, about a history project that he did. NL is a great,

typical sixth grader: He wanders from topic to topic. In the social studies classroom of sixth graders, the assumption is that all students should be learning the basic tools of doing social science rather than copying out textbook facts. Students are expected to do history, for example, by examining some building, asking what the evidence is in a building and what kinds of inferences can be draw from the arrangement of rooms and furniture— that kind of thing. An oral history project requires students to formulate questions, carry out an interview, transcribe it, and then write it up.

This is the particular project that NL is talking about with Carol Barry. Carol is helping NL to put together the portfolio that he will send to his seventh-grade teachers as a kind of message that he is a wise, smart, capable student. Carol is helping NL pick from several stacks of his work folders, to see what pieces of work will send the message of who he is. Carol guides the conversation as NL sometimes wanders from topic to topic.

Carol: Could you find me your favorite piece of work in here, in your portfolio?

NL: Yah, here it is. It's my interview with my grandpa.

Carol: Why is it the best?

NL: Hmmm, I learned things I never knew before.

Carol: Like what?

NL: You know, about a lot of things, mostly about the Mexican Revolution and about how America is the land of opportunity, only it's hard to find work here, how families have to move around a lot and take chances.

Carol: It sounds like you learned a lot of history.

NL: Yah, I guess so.

Carol: Can I ask you a question? You're going to have American history later, right? [NL responds, "Yah. Mrs. Wazney in eighth grade."] So what did you learn about interviewing your grandpa that you think is important for American history?

NL: Well, my dad, he's a history teacher. He had to show me his books for me to learn about it. 'Cause it isn't a revolution that happened here, so you don't learn very much about it.

Carol: Well, so what did you learn from your dad?

NL: Well, like about how my great grandfather was in Poncho Villa's army. Like, I mean, he was one of his men. But they forced him to come here afterwards. (What? Tell me about that.) Well, see, a lot of them had to leave the country because the government didn't want them staying on making trouble. My grandpa had to come here and he moved to Texas and then to Michigan where there was more work. And see, one time he was working on a farm and he came to get his money and the man who owed it to him had gone and he had done all this work and didn't get anything for it. So after that they had to leave because they couldn't pay the rent and went to Denver. So that's how come I have a lot of family there, that's why my mom's sister is there.

Carol: What else about the revolution?

NL: Poncho Villa has this gold suit, really, a real one.

Carol: Okay. I have another question for you, maybe a hard one. Not everybody has a dad who has all those books or a grandpa they can interview to tell them all those kinds of things about the revolution, so what if you were a history teacher?

NL: Oh good, good, my dad's a history teacher.

Carol: Great. So maybe this won't be such a hard question. Imagine you're a history teacher and you want kids to understand about the Mexican Revolution, what would you do?

NL: Well, um, I would do a big project, you know, like the ones we've been doing. Remember when you wanted us to understand about the ancient world, like the project we did together? Well see, my dad showed me lots of pictures, I mean like photographs, they tell you about the old times. So I'd make sure there were photographs in it. And like Poncho Villa made movies of the revolution, even afterwards, like "Poncho Villa Returns" and "Poncho Villa Rides Again," with him leading everybody and winning. He made millions of dollars that way. (So what about those movies?) Well, I'd want to show them to kids.

Carol: Well, why would you want to show them to kids?

NL: Well, because it's important for them to know all about the revolution, the exciting part like Poncho Villa movies and then the ordinary part, like the lives of families. So I would give them the photographs, I would give them the Poncho Villa movies, and then I'd give them things like what I wrote about my grandpa.

Carol: How come?

NL: Because they have to understand how many different stories there are about the revolution. Like there are more than two sides. Maybe even more than three sides. Okay?

Here is a teacher talking to a student about work that wasn't conducted in her class; yet she is pursuing with him—through a sixth grader's maze—a line of questioning. Her questions, I would argue, transform what that student originally would have thought about simply as exciting little bits of anecdotes—gold suits, Poncho Villa movies. By drawing these anecdotes, these threads into a larger picture, she has helped to integrate the pieces—photographs, films, the information from the oral interview—into his own view of different stories about a revolution. What otherwise would exist as little flecks on an educational landscape are now brought together into a larger whole.

I have come to think that teachers must have this kind of ability to go through portfolios and do more than say, "First I want you to find two math pieces. Now I want a social studies piece. . . ." I have come to believe that unless teachers can actually turn those materials into a much more continuous fabric, help kids to draw connections across them, find the meanings embedded in their work, then what we have invented is simply a new collection technology. It is no better than what we had before.

But this vignette has a second episode. Excited about what she has heard and seen in NL's interview, Carol Barry brings NL's oral history project interview with his grandfather to a colleague, Mrs. Wazney, the eighth-grade teacher. Together they work on a piece of curriculum for eighth graders that grows out of NL's interview. One assignment in the new curriculum for eighth-grade American history asks students to select a paragraph from their textbook and, in a sense, explode that paragraph. They are being asked to take a monologic account, one delivered in print, and choose an event, a personage, a period, and do some research. The research may involve oral discussion, additional reading, or looking at artifacts, video records, photographs. The assignment is to rewrite that usually fairly compact monologic paragraph and, in that way, to understand something about the all-too-smooth surface of the usual historical account.

This raises a second perspective on drawing connections. For the teacher, NL's face-to-face interview first posed the challenge: "Can I draw the threads together here from NL's comments?" But equally important is another challenge: "Although this is a sixth-grade project, can I understand that what's going on in sixth grade should have long-range implications for what else is happening in the context of the educational institution in which I'm working. Can we as teachers, as colleagues, work together in that way to create, in a sense, even longer threads, so that the kinds of things that my sixth graders are working on have some payoff in eighth grade? Can there be a kind of long thread developing here about the multiplicity of sources in history, about the multiplicity of historical accounts?"

Seeing Students in Their Own Terms: Transforming Teaching Strategies

My second vignette comes from the Ben Franklin Middle School in the heart of San Francisco. In the span of some 15 years, a student population of docile, English-speaking, middle-class children has been changed entirely, replaced by students of different social, cultural, and economic backgrounds. Because the teaching staff has not changed, there was a long period of yearning for the old days. Right now the school is trying to forgive, forget, leave off that yearning and think about the children who actually sit in front of them. Part of that is to think of students not as non-English speakers, but as children who already speak one language fluently and who are learning English—children who eventually will be bilingual in a way that many of the children they used to teach never dreamed of being.

Nadine Bagel, a mathematics teacher in the school for 25 years, has seen the landscape of mathematics teaching change dramatically. As a young teacher, she felt competent when her kids could do times tables, some even in less than 3 minutes. That was teaching practice. Willing and able to weather all of the dramatic changes that the National Council of Teachers of Mathematics (NCTM) would have her make, she has not abandoned the times tables. Instead she uses them as a tool, usually linked with a calculator. Currently she's exploring concepts of measurement and of pattern to encourage pre-algebra thinking in students.

Nadine teaches the "newcomer" class—classes for students who have been in the United States less than 3 months. Moreover, they come into schools in waves. If something disastrous happens in Haiti, within a month there will be a wave of Haitian children in Nadine's classroom. In another month it might be a wave of Russian children. There is literally no common language in her classroom. Moreover, some children may come from a country like El Salvador where families had no particular access to schooling. The children are not literate, not because they are deficient, but because there is no history of literacy—for them, for their siblings, or often for their fairly young parents. On the other hand, some children who do not speak English may have a mother who was a neurosurgeon and a father who was a physicist in Bejing. The range of student backgrounds is enormous.

Situations such as this expose one of the tragedies of second-language English teaching in this country. Too often we have created English speakers at the cost of teaching children in their native languages in which they could have gone on developing conceptually as scientists, as historians, or as mathematicians. We have traded away that possibility in order that they learn English grammar or English vocabulary.

Nadine's challenge was to reconfigure a mathematics class so that it was not "a holding tank," or simply a pretext for learning English. She faced the task of substantially rethinking a piece of curriculum—to adapt it to her students in their different contexts—without trading away high expectations for academic performance. She had to consider which aspects of mathematics were most valuable—with long-term payoffs for students—and which of those could be taught with a minimum of language.

For instance, for an opening curriculum sequence, Nadine deals with pattern, which can be taught visually. Gradually she can ask for the translation of these patterns into other kinds of symbolic languages. So, for instance, you can walk into Nadine's classroom and see pinned up on the front of her desk a huge piece of Hmung cross-stitch embroidery. Students are working on detecting the pattern in the piece of embroidery and translating that into a numerical representation, not unlike knitting patterns. Then, they attempt to make much more elegant and much more condensed numerical statements. Instead of writing for each row, students find an equation or a mathematical representation that will account for the fact that there are alternating rows, and so on. A colorful piece of embroidery has provided students with a common experience and introduced them to important mathematics concepts and skills.

Students in this class keep a mathematics journal and write in their own first languages. Although Nadine cannot read what is written there in Haitian, or Creole, she does put the students' mathematics work and those journals together and send them home. Students are asked to explain their work to their parents in their first languages. The bet here is that even though this work is not monitored in the typical way we think of schoolwork having to be monitored, the very real need of students is to develop mathematical ideas in the language in which they are conceptually fluent. The teacher is working that fundamental fluency in a first language, against the emerging fluency in English, making the joining place the language of mathematics, at first visually rendered and then numerically rendered and increasingly captured in English.

As these students begin to develop a kind of mathematical English, Nadine is doing the same thing for them that Carol Barry is doing for NL. She's insisting that they use their emerging mathematical English to draw some long threads in their learning. So, for instance, as they go from pattern to measurement, they engage with students in their own classrooms and also with younger children at a neighboring elementary school. They derive, for example, mathematical statements that describe the proportion of arm to trunk or foot to leg. Once they have the data, they create graphs and detect the patterns in the graphs. Then they are asked to think across those two projects about detecting patterns in mathematical data and about the role of numbers in making those patterns clear. Here again, students are writing in their first language. Nadine then begins to build moments when students write in their first language most fluently, then attempt to write the same idea in English. And they talk out loud about what it is to shift information from a first language to English, where they have difficulties. They make legitimate what has been suppressed in classrooms, which is how to move information from a first language into English. That becomes a part of the classroom conversation.

IMPLICATIONS FOR TEACHER PORTFOLIOS

These two examples highlight, for me, two key considerations in building teachers' portfolios: presenting evidence of these two kinds of abilities, that is, learning from and building upon student work; and adapting curriculum and instruction to meet students in their own contexts. These skills demand making a new kind of clinical judgment, not the usual one of looking across a body of student work and determining if it meets some standard or fails to meet it. This kind of clinical judgment asks: Can I listen to a student and capture something of tremendous worth here and, then, use it to feed my own professional development? Moreover, can I extend this professional activity to other people in my teaching community? Carol Barry answered these questions first through her interview with NL and then answered the last question by literally running across the courtyard to find Fay Wazney to say, "I have this great idea. Let's think about it in the context of eighth-grade teaching."

The second piece of evidence that I think we should consider looking for in teaching portfolios is this ability to adapt a piece of curriculum to one's own students. To take something as pressing, for instance, as the NCTM standards and say, "How do I make these available to students whose own educational histories, whose families' educational histories, and whose first languages may not make this a straightforward translation?" Teachers' portfolios need to reveal the ability to make clinical judgments of this new kind, to carry the work of students to show how this is done and with what effect.

Our work in these urban schools has made me aware of some harsh realities that, I believe, need to enter this discussion. One of the things that we've learned is that student portfolios work very well in contexts where children have continuous lives. Those continuous lives can come from being middle class, from living in a safe community, or from a grandmother who picks a child up at school and walks him or her past what otherwise would be a dangerous bus stop. But many children lead discontinuous lives: Their families move often and fast; basic supports for physical or psychological safety may be nonexistent. We have to think very carefully about this. If we're going to look to student portfolios increasingly as being the measure of student achievement or student growth, or the health of an educational system, to the extent that we have children who have very discontinuous lives, we're either going to have to create a safety net for those children, or we're going to have to think about whether we can make this a system for all children.

One of our project schools has addressed this problem by extending school hours until 6 p.m. From 3 to 6 the computer lab is open and eighth-grade mentors provide assistance with homework. These are clear and concrete signals that the school is serious about student performance.

I think the same thing applies to teacher portfolios. The strongest and the most dedicated teachers I know working in these urban settings have taken on a set of responsibilities for the welfare and the well-being of their children that leaves them a very small margin of professional time. At Jefferson Middle School in Rochester, New York, when the final bell rings and children start walking home, teachers get in their cars and follow large groups of their children home—just because walking in the neighborhood is dangerous. They have accepted a level of care and social responsibility that is different from that in other communities. I would call driving home watching those children professional time, although I don't know that it adds up to a portfolio entry. But if we mean for portfolios to be avenues for teacher growth, for access to mentor teacher status, and so on, it means that in these urban settings schools are going to have to be organized in somewhat different ways.

So, for instance, we're going to have to press building principals and superintendents to do such things as invest in cluster subs, ones who can be attached to a building. Good teachers are not crazy about leaving their children with just any old sub. So what you really have to do is create that margin of possibility within a school building by making a known and decent professional available. I want to be very clear here. Building a professional portfolio is extremely important, and perhaps even wildly important to teachers who make the commitment to teach in these kinds of situations. They need and want care and feeding. I'm talking about the kinds of structural changes we'll have to make in order to make that possible.

Similarly, I think we're going to have to think much more seriously about things like professional development schools where schools themselves become the site of teacher training and where teachers themselves teach intern teachers. This could give teachers the extra hands that make it possible to do this kind of portfolio work with their children; otherwise it becomes an impossibility.

Creating a portfolio culture for students and teachers demands new skills, new visions of being a professional, and the commitment of each school community to its students and teachers. It is a necessary challenge holding great possibilities.

CHAPTER 4

Mentoring Portfolio Development

Helen Freidus

BANK STREET COLLEGE OF EDUCATION

*The desire to teach in a certain way does not magically erase all of my own
negative experiences. We are a product of our experiences. We tend to teach
the way we were taught. Struggling against this tendency is an exhausting
and yet exhilarating effort. It means, on my part, a long-term commitment
to reworking me.*

—W.T., Fall 1993[1]

Learning to engage in learner-centered practice (Darling-Hammond,
1992; Darling-Hammond & Snyder, 1992) involves more than acquiring a new set of learnings. It also, to a great degree, involves unlearning,
that is, reconceptualizing one's image of self and other, genuine questioning of what is and ought to be, and re-imagining the relationship
between authority and education (O'Laughlin, 1992). The task is often
frustrating for both teachers and teacher educators; in many ways, it
runs counter to traditional ways of acquiring knowledge. Change, for
adults, as well as for children, emerges over time through a process of
construction, a process, both experiential and dialogical, that is transformative (Burbules, 1993; Greene, 1978, 1994).

The construction of portfolios to document professional growth
and development enables teachers to experience the complexity of a
constructivist pedagogy. It engages them in an open-ended process that
pushes them to revisit their own knowledge and express it in personally
meaningful ways. In so doing, they often pause in their search for the

"right way" as they define and redefine the implications of their own tacitly held beliefs and their actual classroom practices.

This chapter describes this process in the use of portfolios in teacher education at Bank Street College of Education. It pays particular attention to the role of mentoring within the portfolio process, examining ways in which mentoring creates possibilities for dialogue and a concrete context in which both teachers and teacher educators may examine and extend their personal and professional constructions of knowledge. Drawing upon interviews with students and faculty, this chapter examines three kinds of mentoring that takes place in the portfolio process: mentoring between faculty and students; mentoring among students as peers; and mentoring within students themselves (that is, self-mentoring).

PORTFOLIOS AT BANK STREET COLLEGE

Since the fall of 1993, portfolios have been used at Bank Street College of Education as an option for the culminating project for the masters degree in education. When portfolios were first considered, a great deal of thought was given to the question of whether they would be consonant with the educational vision of Bank Street. A report to the faculty made in June 1993 concluded that after reviewing portfolios, faculty "were eager to see how they might work for us and our teachers." The promise was great for the following reasons:

- The theory behind portfolios meshes with a basic Deweyan idea that learning involves an experiential continuum in which new knowledge is built upon and mediated by prior knowledge and values. In portfolios, conscious reflection on one's teaching experiences serves as a vehicle for professional development.
- Portfolios are consistent with Bank Street's constructivist vision of learning. Portfolios allow students opportunities to build their own educational vision through active engagement with content.
- Portfolios hold promise for expanding the traditional structures of education in order to allow more diverse voices to be heard.

A subsequent report, reflecting upon the completed portfolios of the first cohort of portfolio candidates, concluded that the portfolio was consistent with the mission of the institution and its goals for a process and product that would serve as a culminating study for a graduate degree. The pedagogy would support institutional goals; the institutional vision would support the pedagogy.

The Portfolio Process Today

The Bank Street portfolio process documents the unique professional journey of each student. Students are asked to: (1) identify and discuss the artifacts that they find most significant in their personal and professional development (representing understanding of theory and practice in the domains of human development, curriculum, history and philosophy of education, and social context of learning); (2) identify connections between and among artifacts; (3) reflect upon these connections in order to identify a unifying theme; (4) examine artifacts and theme from both personal and theoretical perspectives; and (5) participate in public presentations of the portfolio. The completed portfolio includes

1. An articulated theme: It is a requirement of the portfolio as defined at Bank Street that there be an articulated theme. In most cases the theme emerges from common threads running through artifacts; the theme does not dictate the selection of artifacts but highlights patterns within them. Over the years, themes have included such titles as *"Race, Class, and Outsider Status," "The Teacher as Builder of Community," "Understanding Difference,"* and *"The Politics of Literacy."*
2. Artifacts: Six artifacts are included in the portfolio. These document understanding of or competency in four domains of teacher education, that is, human development, educational history and philosophy, the social context of teaching, and curriculum. The artifacts are personal representations of the student's professional knowledge base. Artifacts are represented through diverse media, including but not limited to audiotapes, videotapes, picture collages, charts, graphs, and a variety of writing genres.
3. Captions: A one- or two-page caption accompanies each artifact. Terse captions, informed by theory and reflection, provide a rationale for the inclusion of the artifact in the portfolio and relate the artifact to an emergent theme that connects the artifacts. Captions provide responses to the questions: What have I learned from the experiences represented by this artifact? How does this artifact represent my personal and professional values? How does the artifact bring to life the theory I have studied? What implications does this artifact have for my classroom practice?

4. Framing statements: An introduction of three to five pages articulates the theme and relates it to the individual's philosophy of teaching.
A concluding statement, also three to five pages, synthesizes the work
included in the portfolio and, with references to relevant theory, discusses the educational implications of the theme and the student's personal journey.

The requirements define what is to be addressed. How these requirements are to be addressed—what is to be included and how it is to be
represented—is open-ended and differs from portfolio to portfolio.

Portfolios are seen as bridges connecting personal knowledge, academic knowledge, and knowledge of the field. Individual students develop their own portfolios, but in the process of doing so, they are actively engaged in a community of faculty and peers. They participate in
the portfolio process as a cohort, beginning their work in early fall and
concluding with a formal presentation in the spring. The work of each
student is scaffolded by individual meetings between students and faculty portfolio mentors. An additional scaffold is provided by a series of
required monthly meetings in which small groups of students engaged
in the portfolio process meet to discuss their progress. These monthly
meetings, facilitated by faculty mentors, have proven to be an extremely
rich forum for peer mentoring that supports and extends the faculty
mentoring process. This multifaceted approach encourages students to
articulate the meaning that the study and practice of teaching hold for
them as individuals, creates a context in which they are helped to ground
this meaning in theory, and enables them to recognize and respect the
similarities and differences between their own constructions of what is
professionally significant and the constructions of their peers who are
going through the same process.

THE SIGNIFICANCE OF MENTORING

From the earliest discussions exploring whether the use of portfolios
would mesh with Bank Street's educational vision, mentoring was seen
as an important component of the portfolio process. Lee Shulman's
story—reported in Chapter 2—describing his own "failed" efforts to
construct a portfolio representing his teaching, was taken as a sobering
lesson. Shulman attributed his lack of success to the absence of mentors,
colleagues who could become a community for conversation about his
own teaching and research. Consequently, at Bank Street, each student
is assigned a faculty mentor who serves as an advisor throughout the

process. The portfolio process takes place over the course of a year as students participate as a cohort, beginning their work in early fall and concluding with a formal presentation in the spring. There are individual meetings between students and faculty mentors and required monthly meetings of students facilitated by faculty.

The mentoring process has, however, taken on new meaning over the years. Today, it is recognized that portfolio mentoring involves faculty mentoring, peer mentoring, and the self-mentoring that emerges from the structure of the portfolio itself. This tripartite approach evolved as students were encouraged to voice their responses to the portfolio process and to make suggestions as to how it could be improved. Students' suggestions helped faculty to see things from new perspectives, identify problems in the process, and articulate priorities. As faculty listened and responded to students' questions and critiques, students increasingly became collaborators both in their own learning and in the design and implementation of the portfolio process itself. As the portfolio process became more and more refined by the insights offered by students, faculty became increasingly aware of how cognizant students were of their own strengths and needs, and how much they, like their students, could learn from a dialogical process.

Faculty–Student Mentoring: Bridging the Disequilibrium of Open-Ended Learning

When portfolios were first introduced at Bank Street, the role of the mentor was traditionally envisioned. With an open-ended portfolio process new to the field of education, it was easy for faculty to anticipate that students would need support. Implicitly or explicitly, existing educational processes often encourage students to look to teachers, and teachers to look to administrators, for confirmation of a job well done (Apple, 1986; Darling-Hammond, 1992). This was immediately confirmed by students participating in the portfolio process.

> Portfolio seemed the best possible option to culminate my time at Bank Street. . . . Yet my traditional education has been hard to shake, and at times I have been paralyzed by fears of my work not being good enough. I think that I spend a good deal of energy teaching myself, reminding myself to embrace the chances I get to represent myself *as I am,* as I have discovered myself as a teacher and learner, rather than allowing an imposed structure or standard to guide my process and my sense of self. (A.B., 1995)

Constructing portfolios that are both reflective and substantive involves both learning and unlearning. In the portfolio process, students learn to look for patterns and connections within and among the educational experiences they have found meaningful for themselves and their students. They learn to look for connections between their personal constructions of meaning and the theory they have studied in graduate and undergraduate programs. Constructions of meaning inevitably are influenced by students' own cultural, linguistic, and epistemological background as well as by their individual learning styles and personal experience. It is not expected that the connections and constructions made by one student will be the same as those of another. However, this process occurs within the context of an educational institution, the same context, at least nominally, in which they, as "good students," learned to identify and comply with the external standards consonant with the dominant canon of classroom knowledge and expectations. In order to be free to identify and discuss what they truly believe and value, students first must unlearn many of the ways of being they have learned in their more than 16 years of school-related experience.

When the portfolio process first was implemented, these challenges were not fully understood. Nonetheless, it was recognized that portfolios represented a less commonly experienced way of learning and documenting one's work. Consequently, from the beginning, each student was assigned a faculty mentor whose role was to create a relationship in which the ability to make choices was nurtured and the language for supporting these choices was developed personally and professionally.

> You asked what helps make this process work. I think for me it is sitting down with my mentor and shooting ideas back and forth with her and having her say, "Pick out what is important to you. Don't worry about how things come together until you lay them all out." Talking about this with someone who doesn't say, "Oh, that's crazy. That's not relevant," is really important. Constructing a portfolio is a constant, complex and big process; it's often hard to know if you're on the right track. (A.B., transcript, February 7, 1995, p. 7)

The mentoring relationship, initially, was seen as a supportive structure that would focus primarily on the cognitive components of the task. Soon, however, it became apparent that the need for emotional support during the early stages of portfolio construction is quite intense. As students begin to document and share their own personal and professional development, they feel an enormous sense of risk. What they know, how they think, how they may respond in times of comfort and in times of stress are open for scrutiny—first privately by self, then more publicly by others. They grapple with whether they should assume a posture of self as expert or self as novice, revealing the vulnerability they feel while struggling to meet the complex needs of children in today's classrooms. As a result, the first 2 to 3 months of participation in the portfolio process frequently are accompanied by extreme anxiety. There appears to be a pervasive "worry that you won't be able to pull together your conceptualization of self quickly enough, articulately enough, or thoroughly enough" (D.H., 1996). The need to support students through this early stage of anxiety pushes the boundaries of the traditional role of mentoring in higher education and gives new meaning to the challenge of teaching the "whole person."

There is yet another anxiety that some students experience as they embark on the process of creating portfolios to document their professional development. This anxiety emerges in part from the tensions surrounding revelations of personal constructions of knowledge but also from the ways in which these constructions are valued within the academic world.

A.B.: There are risks involved when you're presenting a culminating project that starts with yourself. I kept wondering: "Is this really legitimate? Is it as rigorous as a thesis or is it something softer?" Out in the world we frequently hear that projects that involve the self are less highly regarded.

Portfolio as a form of evaluation is fairly new at Bank Street; it's quite new in academia. I never really felt that portfolios were less legitimate, but I felt a certain tension. Explaining the process to people outside the Bank Street community was difficult. . . . It wasn't so difficult that I ever regretted it, but it complicated the process. Even here at Bank Street, people have said, "Oh, the portfolio is so easy. If you've been working and you have a bunch of projects, you can just put them out there and there you go." And by some definitions of portfolio, they are just a collection without any real strand of the connection between theory and self.

Interviewer: Do you mean that you were concerned that your choice of portfolio would keep you from being perceived as a serious scholar, that you were actually choosing a less scholarly option for your final project?

A.B.: Maybe 20% of myself felt that I had to go out of my way to make portfolios sound more legitimate to the world. The rest of

me felt that portfolios are the cutting edge . . . exactly what I
should be doing, absolutely appropriate for my experience here.

Contrary to common perceptions, most students coming into the
field of teaching view themselves as professionals. They want to learn as
much as they can; they recognize the impact that public perception of
their knowledge and skills can have on the realities of classroom life.
They learn the traditional role of "good students" in elementary school
and high school and begin to learn the role of "good scholars" in their
undergraduate experiences. For most, this means learning to separate
personal from professional funds of knowledge. In order to use portfolios to document their professional expertise, they need to depart from
external standards of evaluation, to articulate standards that are consonant with their belief systems, and to document the ways in which their
performance measures up to these standards. While such performance
is consonant with current educational discourse (Clandinin & Connelly,
1992, 1995; Darling-Hammond & Goodwin, 1993; Garcia & Pearson,
1994), there is no certainty that it is deeply honored within the academy or, for that matter, throughout the general population. Ultimately,
most portfolio candidates become articulate advocates for portfolios and
other forms of learner-centered assessment, but the initial stages prove
traumatic for many.

> I wanted a right and wrong. I really felt that I was swimming
> alone out there without definition or structure when I was not
> told, "This is good," or "This is no good." I had to put much
> more of myself into the process, observe more carefully, and learn
> to embrace complexity. (A.B., June 1996)

Mentoring, then, becomes the nexus of trust building and accountability. Mentors seek to validate students' experiences on both professional and personal levels without being judgmental. They also help students to identify benchmarks of professional development within the
context of personal experience and to evaluate and critique their own
performance by these benchmarks. To do this, they articulate not only
the strengths of students' work but also the ways in which they see the
work as professionally substantive.

> This has evidently been a complex and special journey for you. It's
> clear from your written material that the process of developing a
> portfolio has helped you to sharpen and integrate your thinking
> about education—and to look ahead. In general, the sections are

clear, well-focused, theoretically rooted, related to the required do-mains as well as to your organizing theme. (L. O., May 1995)

Mentors also let students know when their work needs to be extended or clarified:

The video tape of adolescents and senior citizens working together is terrific. It clearly illustrates the value of collaboration and co-operative learning. The caption needs some elaboration. For ex-ample, it is important to clarify what is meant by "layers of collab-oration." (M.V., May 1995)

or when the material that is submitted is incomplete:

While each artifact is powerful, it does not seem to reflect your growth. Where are you in this portfolio? (C.C., April 1995)

Wentworth (1980) describes a model of "socialization as interac-tion" in which the novice plays an important role in constructing the content of the socializing experience and, as a result, the socialization contributes to the formation of the community as well as the individual. This description is a valuable lens for making sense of the nature of mentoring within the portfolio process. In each of the cases referred to above, both the mentor and the portfolio candidate possess a body of expertise; each "mentors" the other in understanding the relevance of this expertise and its connection to professional knowledge. Each teaches and is taught by the other, both individually and collectively. The words of the mentor validate the student's work, strengthen the na-ture of the collaborative relationship, and contribute to students' work-ing and reworking the portfolio in order to best represent the linkage of personal and professional knowledge. As students come to trust their mentors, they drop the traditional defenses assumed within the world of academia and allow mentors to see what is truly meaningful to them and the impact their constructions of meaning have on their classroom practice. Student openness enables mentors to engage in a dialogical relationship in which they, like the students, "begin to see more possi-bilities and become more flexible both cognitively and emotionally" (D.E., June 1996). As mentors become more cognizant of and better attuned to diverse ways of knowing, they gain a broader knowledge base on which they can draw in their roles as faculty instructors, field supervi-sors, classroom consultants, and researchers.

Peer Mentoring

> The monthly meetings were wonderful . . . the angst, the pain, . . .
> we supported each other. (audiotape, May 1995)

When portfolios were first implemented at Bank Street, there was
no vision of a need for structures to encourage collaborative work among
peers; it was assumed that this would evolve informally as needed. In the
debriefing session following the first year of the portfolio pilot project,
students commented that the support relationships they had established
among themselves had been helpful but had been late in coming. They
described ways in which they had mentored each other and suggested
that it would have been valuable to have had regularly scheduled, organized peer meetings from the beginning of the academic year. Their suggestion was enacted the following year. Monthly meetings in which
faculty and students might elect to share their work were scheduled.
Student attendance was dismal. Yet, at that year's final debriefing session, a similar request was made.

When faculty pointed out that meetings had been scheduled but
few participants had come, students responded: "We wish we had."
With these responses in mind, a decision was made to require the meetings for the next cohort. If the sessions proved fruitful, they would become a formal part of the requirements. If not, there would be no more
attention paid to the call for institutionalized forums for peer dialogue.
During this year of required sessions, attendance was excellent; dialogue
was rich. Students valued faculty input but, as their predecessors had
suggested, appeared to gain special strength from the feedback of their
peers.

> Having an opportunity to talk about all the things we're scared
> about and finding out that other people are scared about them too
> was invaluable. Portfolio is a process that has to involve conversa-
> tion. Constructing portfolios is so foreign to most people that you
> can't just call someone up to talk about it. Through the meetings,
> our little group became both friends and colleagues working and
> growing together. (A.B., transcript, February 1995)

Students found the feedback of their peers particularly meaningful
as they struggled to bridge formal and informal knowledge systems. Peer
critique contributed greatly to students' abilities to articulate their beliefs and practices, their growing understanding of the significance of

these beliefs and practices, and their understanding that beliefs and practices that differed from those commonly found in schools could be valid. The actual content of the peer meetings frequently overlapped the content of individual mentor meetings. However, rather than being redundant, opportunities to discuss problems and successes in diverse forums appeared to be reinforcing and affirming.

While relationships with faculty mentors were seen as validating and stimulating, peer support was seen as equally if not more so. The bonds that were formed within the group created a haven within the academic context in which students gradually could lay aside all facades and comfortably say, "This is too hard," "I don't know," or simply, "Help." They used each other as models, resources, and sounding boards.

> Portfolio is a path, but it is a bit of a maze. I couldn't have done it by myself. I needed to see and hear what others were doing. The process can be perceived in so many ways. In the meetings it was possible to see how other people interpreted the task; that would stimulate me to come up with my own new ideas. At the end, probably because I was relaxed when it was almost over, I felt increasingly able to conceptualize and demonstrate my own interpretation of literacy at work. (A.B., interview, June 1996)

The role of faculty in these groups was strictly facilitative. The meetings provided them with the luxury of observing their students in more informal settings, settings in which students assumed active roles both as teachers and as learners. In the debriefing sessions that concluded each monthly meeting, students discussed the ways in which the meetings helped them to bring to consciousness the significance of their practice and to confirm what they did, indeed, know.

Faculty Mentor: How, if at all, was tonight's experience helpful to you?
Student S: I came thinking I was totally off the mark and now I feel that I am on target after all.
Student J: One of the things that helped me was to find out that my theme and my artifacts really were meshing together.
Faculty Mentor: . . .and how did you get that? Did you get it from talking among your peers?
Student J: Exactly. I mentioned an artifact that I wasn't sure was fitting in. . . . It was like a brainstorming session. People bounced it around and helped me to see that it worked.

Student M: And it's really nice to know that everybody's in the same
   boat you are in. Working alone with your mentor, you often think,
   "What am I doing?"

(February 1995 peer group meeting)

These group experiences document a social-constructivist interpretation of teaching and learning. As students shared their artifacts and
captions with each other, they frequently referred to the abstract concepts they encountered in their coursework and connected the concepts
to their life experience. They learned that there were many ways to construct meaning from commonly shared experiences and that these constructions were directly related to personal funds of knowledge. As they
began to recognize how much they could learn from each other, they
began to value diversity viscerally as well as cognitively. Faculty mentors,
observing and participating in the process, were able to confirm and
extend their beliefs about the value of peer learning for students of all
ages.

> Somehow I hold the students in my group in awe right now. I see
> them as a kind of intellectual giants. Being a portfolio mentor was
> an important experience for me. My teaching will be changed
> because of it. I can't pin down quite how, but I know there is an
> effect. I will most likely have more open-ended, more creative,
> more synthesizing assignments and believe that many students will
> have a really positive experience with them. (S.G., June 1996)

Self-Structural Mentoring

> The more I am a part of making change, the less resistant I am. I
> didn't realize this till I finished my last artifact. Portfolio is unique
> in the individualized way it allows us to bring ourselves to the pro-
> cess. (R.C., Spring 1995)

There is yet a third form of mentoring that emerged as part of the
portfolio process. This is the metacognitive awareness that develops as
students engage with the articulated structures of the portfolio process.
When students work to complete the requirements of the portfolio project, they come to know more about themselves and the personal and
professional thinking that drives their practice. The requirement that
students include artifacts documenting their work over time encourages
them to view learning as a process shaped by diverse experiences and
contexts. The forums for public sharing elicit thoughtful responses from

faculty and peers, responses that stimulate students to probe for the meaning behind their beliefs and practices. These same forums enable students to see that others, engaging with them in the portfolio process, construct responses to the requirements that are very different, but equally valid. The connections made between students' own experiences and those of their peers help them to develop a schema of professional knowledge and experience through which they can more readily make sense of theoretical knowledge.

Portfolios submitted at Bank Street conclude with an essay designed to facilitate students' ability to synthesize the learning documented in the portfolio and to articulate its implications for their future growth and development. The question that frames this section is: "How does the work I have completed to date establish the groundwork for my future growth and development as an educator?" This requirement encourages students to add a forward thrust to the process of reflection and thus to develop a habit of mind that makes future professional development a more conscious process. In the words of one student:

> Portfolio helped me to create my voice. It helped me to understand who I am and where I want to go. (M.D., transcript, final debriefing, May 1995)

In the first 2 years of our pilot study, students were asked to begin the portfolio process by identifying the theme they wished to develop. They then identified artifacts, meaningful to themselves, that were connected to the theme. For some this worked well. Others, however, appeared to be frozen by this process that worked from the outside in. In the third year of portfolio implementation, students were encouraged to reverse the process. They were asked to begin by identifying documents and objects that were currently or had been significant markers of their professional growth and development and to provide an explanation of their significance. They then were asked to identify connections between and among artifacts and rationales and to reflect on these in order to identify the unifying theme for the portfolio. This change has facilitated and deepened the overall experience for many students. It appears to nurture reflection by providing experiences that encourage inductive and synthetic thought processes within a safe context.

We discussed this procedural change with the 1994–95 cohort of students during an early peer group meeting. They responded:

Student M: It's better to get as many artifacts as you can and then see how they fit together. (murmurs of agreement)

Faculty Mentor: Tell us more, because this was an experiment. It was a hunch. Why do you think this works better?

Student M: I chose a few pieces that were really important to me. Then I said: "Oh, I'm looking at this, and I'm looking at this and if I am, what kinds of other things should be included? Well, I should really put in a research piece, because that's important to the way I see myself as a teacher-leader."

Student A: . . .If you give yourself enough time to reflect as you go along, things emerge.

Faculty Mentor: What you say is important. A goal of the portfolio process is to encourage teachers to see patterns in their own work and to help them understand what practices they really value. It sounds to me as if you are also saying: "If this is meaningful to me and this is meaningful to me, what else fits in with these? What makes it all meaningful? What do I value in my teaching?"

Barbara Biber, in an article entitled *Premature Structuring as a Deterrent to Creativity* (1958), discusses how the didactic nature of traditional education places blinders on the learner's sense of possibility. She speaks of the importance of "the repeated initiation of each of us at all stages to new raw materials of sensation, expanded awareness of unorganized facts, and the unresolved contradictions inherent in the physical or the human universe" (p. 3). When students were asked to begin the portfolio process by identifying a theme to which all artifacts would be related, they looked at their experience through only one lens, limiting their opportunities for constant comparison and critical thought. The time between identifying the theme and completing the portfolio was then devoted to developing one's thesis rather than "deepening the capacity to wonder" (Biber, 1958, p. 3).

Implicit in the dialogue cited above is the notion that by placing the initial emphasis of the portfolio on the personal, more students are able to enter into the process at a point of comfort. They then are able to use what they know to scaffold their growing knowledge base by making *ongoing* connections between personal and professional understandings. As students become more comfortable with the inductive process of recognizing previously unidentified patterns, they become more prepared to find meaningful patterns amid the complex realities embedded in the world of teaching. The process of making meaning from complexity does not stop with the portfolio but becomes a way of thinking that shapes practice throughout one's career.

I perceive portfolio as an ongoing conversation. It begins with a mentor and is extended in a group meeting. It continues and flourishes there with the added voices of advisors and portfolio candidates with diverse perspectives. The process then continues through the presentation at which point still more people join in. I think that all this dialogue is what made portfolio so successful an experience for me.

This portfolio conversation has never ended for me. When I went out into the field, I took not one thesis but six artifacts that reflected myriad processes I had gone through. As a result, I feel equipped to discuss things in multiple ways. I continue to ask the questions that I started to ask while doing my portfolio. I keep looking at issues and interpreting research, because the process is so connected to so many pieces of my life as a teacher and as a student. It is the kind of thing that prepared me to keep going. There wasn't an ending. There was no stopping point at the presentation or at graduation; the process continues.

The portfolio prepared me for the strands of complexity that I keep finding in my work. For example, I have discovered over the last year that when I have a problem in my practice as a reading specialist, I come up with solutions, but I do not really consider them solutions until I reflect upon them and try them out. I began to think this way during the portfolio process. Because that process was so fluid, I experimented with things and reflected upon them, looked at what happened and discussed the implications. There was no simple right or wrong. Now, I am a little bit less phased when things keep getting more complex. I see myself as still in process. (A.B., June 1996)

CONCLUSION

Portfolios show great promise as a pedagogy of transformative teaching within institutions of teacher education. The portfolio process helps teachers to construct a professional knowledge base meaningful within the context of their own diverse cultures and diverse experiences, a knowledge base that they can identify and adapt to meet the exigencies of today's classrooms. The potential of portfolios appears to be greatest when the process incorporates a densely textured model of connected learning including:

• faculty–student connections (mentoring relationships) in which faculty scaffold students' understandings of the professional knowledge base of teaching and learning, and students, in turn, scaffold teacher educators' understanding of the significance of this knowledge base within the context of diverse cultures and experiences

• student–student connections (peer mentoring) in which students as fellow wayfarers on a professional journey support and extend each other's constructions of knowledge

Both of these forms of connection promote personal and professional growth within the context of community. Voicing their own stories and listening to the voices of others, teachers and teacher educators alike make new connections between their own constructions of knowledge and the constructions of others. In so doing, they develop habits of mind that respect and value divergence, while identifying the common goals and standards that often are embedded in seemingly diverse practices.

In addition to these socially constructed connections, there is another, more individually constructed set of connections that appear to be nurtured within the portfolio process. These include:

• the connections individuals make as they link personal funds of knowledge derived from experiences as teacher and learner with the academic knowledge base developed within the academic institution

• the connections individuals identify between the beliefs they hold and the social context within which those beliefs were constructed

• the connections individuals identify between the theory they study and the classroom practices they implement

• the connections individuals make as they identify links between their own experiences as learners and the experiences of the students they teach

• the connections individuals make as they examine the development of their own beliefs and practices over time

• the connections individuals articulate between their current beliefs and practices and the goals they set for their own personal growth and development.

Each of these threads of connection is holistic in nature, involving both cognitive and affective learning, individual and social constructions of knowledge. Portfolios that make a difference involve complex processes that are not always consonant with the current structures and practices of educational institutions. From preschool to university, we are far more comfortable with educational models that are efficient, replicable, and efficient in terms of both time and money. A portfolio process that is transformative in nature is unlikely to gain high marks in these areas. Nonetheless, it appears that the benefits of the portfolio process are extensive. There are few forms of pedagogy in which so much learning occurs for both students and participating faculty. Portfolios appear to generate both a broader knowledge base and a network of caring that is pervasive.

Many years ago, Dewey (1902/1959) wrote:

> Learning is active. It involves reaching out of the mind. It involves organic assimilation starting from within. Literally, we must take our stand with the child and our departure from him. It is he and not the subject-matter which determines both quality and quantity of learning. (p. 95)

The experiences of teachers and teacher educators who participate in the portfolio process suggest that if we are interested in the quality of the teachers we prepare, teacher education also must be active, take its point of departure from the personal knowledge base of the students it prepares, and provide contexts in which habits of mind conducive to lifelong learning are experienced by both students and faculty.

NOTE

1. Initials and dates refer to Bank Street students or their mentors and the time of year that a conversation or interview took place.

REFERENCES

Apple, M. (1986). *Teachers & texts: A political economy of class and gender relations in education.* New York: Routledge & Kegan Paul.

Biber, B. (1958). *Premature structuring as a deterrent to creativity* (Monograph No. 67) New York: Bank Street College.

Burbules, N. (1993). *Dialogue in teaching.* New York: Teachers College Press.

Clandinin, J., & Connelly, M. (1992). Teacher as curriculum maker. In P. Jackson (Ed.), *Handbook of research on curriculum* (pp. 363–401). New York: Macmillan.

Clandinin, J., & Connelly, M. (1995). *Teachers' professional knowledge landscapes.* New York: Teachers College Press.

Darling-Hammond, L. (1992). *Standards of practice for learner-centered schools.* New York: NCREST.

Darling-Hammond, L., & Snyder, J. (1992). Framing accountability: Creating learner-centered schools. In A. Lieberman (Ed.), *The changing contexts of teaching* (pp. 11–36). Chicago: NSSE Yearbook.

Darling-Hammond, L., & Goodwin, L. (1993). Progress towards professionalism in teaching. In G. Kawelti (Ed.), *Challenges and achievements of Ameri-*

can education (pp. 19–52). Alexandria, VA: Association for Supervision and Curriculum Development.

Dewey, J. (1959). The child and the curriculum. In M. Dworkin (Ed.), *Dewey on education.* New York: Teachers College Press. (Original work published 1902)

Garcia, G., & Pearson, P. D. (1994). Assessment and diversity. In L. Darling-Hammond (Ed.), *Review of research in education, Volume 20* (pp. 337–391). Washington, DC: American Educational Research Association.

Greene, M. (1978). *Landscapes of learning.* New York: Teachers College Press.

Greene, M. (1994). Epistemology and educational research: The influence of recent approaches to knowledge. In L. Darling-Hammond (Ed.), *Review of research in education, Volume 20* (pp. 423–464). Washington, DC: American Educational Research Association.

O'Laughlin, M. (1992, November–December). Engaging teachers in emancipatory knowledge construction. *Journal of Teacher Education, 43*(5), 336–346.

Wentworth, W. M. (1980). *Context and understanding.* New York: Elsevier.

CHAPTER 5

Learning from Looking

Steve Seidel

HARVARD UNIVERSITY

You can observe a lot by watching.
—Yogi Berra

SERIOUS WORK, SERIOUS ATTENTION

When she was in second grade, Sofia and her classmates were given the assignment to paint as many pictures of a "starry night" as they could. They had already studied constellations and mythology. They'd taken an evening class trip to observe the night sky. They looked through a book of paintings by Vincent Van Gogh and came across his painting, "Starry Night." They were interested in, and had much to say about, the way Van Gogh created his painting. Their teacher, Cathy Skowron, thought this would be a good moment to encourage these children to explore the challenges of capturing this complex visual experience with paint.

Over the next 3 weeks, Sofia produced nine paintings of night skies. She painted on newsprint sheets, 14″ × 20″, using poster paints, brushes of various shapes and sizes, knives, and pencil erasers (which turned out to be effective for creating small and very round stars). Each day, Sofia filled out a "work receipt" in which she described what she did, the materials she used, and the problems she was working on. At the end of day seven, for example, she wrote, "I panted my 7th starey night picksher. I mixed blue read yellow to make brown and I mixed blue and black to make darck blue. I trid to make brown but it didn't come out the same way." Upon completing this project, she displayed her work proudly and was happy to talk at length about her accomplishments: the specific problems she took on, her various solutions to those problems, and her opinions about the results of her labors.

This substantial body of work—the series of paintings, the work receipts, her comments when interviewed by her teacher about the whole project—certainly would take an important place in her portfolio. But what would a reader of Sofia's portfolio make of all of this material? What would readers look for? What would they see? And what would they learn about Sofia—or anything else—in this process?

The fundamental premise of this chapter is that seeing—taking something in visually and truly considering that thing—is not necessarily a result of looking. Rather, seeing is the result of deliberate work: noticing, considering, comparing, and wondering. It is serious cognitive activity, demanding full attention and engagement.

Most of our schools provide few, if any, opportunities for teachers to engage in this kind of looking at students or student work. Even if teachers spend individual time in more careful observation, it is rare that they are afforded the benefits of looking *together*, with all the variety that various people can bring to this activity. This chapter explores why seeing is so critical to assessment of student work. It is also about a protocol for engaging teachers in close study of pieces of student work and provides accounts of conversations between teachers using that protocol. This chapter is about the learning that can come from thoughtful looking.

Looking (and Maybe Seeing)

Henry David Thoreau, in a passage from his *Journal* (1858/1982) entitled "On Seeing," discusses intentional looking as a prerequisite for seeing.

> Objects are concealed from our view not so much because they are out of the course of our visual ray as because there is no intention of the mind and eye toward them. We do not realize how far and widely, or how near and narrowly, we are to look. The greater part of the phenomena of nature are for this reason concealed to us all our lives. Here, too, as in political economy, the supply answers to the demand. Nature does not cast pearls before swine. There is just as much beauty visible to us in the landscape as we are prepared to appreciate—not a grain more. The actual objects which one person will see as from a particular hilltop are just as different from those which another will see as the persons are different. The scarlet oak

must, in a sense, be in your eye when you go forth. We cannot see anything until we are possessed with the idea of it, and then we can hardly see anything else. (pp. 214–215)

Imagine that Thoreau was talking about "the phenomena of" children's writing, rather than aspects of the natural world. Seeing student work isn't a case of simply looking it over or "giving it a read." As for Thoreau in noticing nature, the "supply" of complexity in children's work answers to our "demand"—how long we spend with it, how much we ask from it. Truly seeing student work is about becoming engaged and entering into the work—naming what we see, noting questions that come to mind, speculating on what the child was working on.

Most teachers become adept early in their careers at determining whether assignments are done thoroughly, neatly, and on time. In addition, teachers train themselves to notice whether the particular skills or concepts that have been emphasized in recent lessons have been demonstrated and mastered. But what about the other dimensions of the work they have been handed—the creativity, interests, intention, concerns, questions, aesthetics, insights, and efforts that may be present in the work, dimensions that may exist quite apart from the specific requirements of the assignment? Given serious assignments, as Sofia was, children will do serious (and often seriously playful) work, work worthy of extended and rigorous examination. Certainly there is much to be learned about children from studying their work, including clues to ways to help them make the most of their opportunities for learning.

Michael Armstrong (1992), a member of the Bread Loaf School of English faculty, engages his students in group investigations of children's writing and, through those sessions, has come to similar conclusions about the seriousness of looking closely at young children's writing.

It became obvious to all of us that the only way in which we could begin to understand why children wrote in the way they did, or make any kind of sense of their writing let alone hope to help them was to assume that they were indeed genuine storytellers and poets, even at the very beginning of artistic enterprise. We came to see that to write a story is to engage in a practice, whether you are five or whether you are fifty. . . . The more closely I looked at children's stories or painting or speculations, the surer I grew that what children were doing was not radically different from what mature artists and thinkers do. They were engaged in the same enterprise, only at an early point in development. (p. 2)

The regular, rigorous, and sustained practice of observing and describing what one sees when looking at student work inevitably will expand each participant's repertoire of things to look for and notice in student texts. It is the same work one would engage in when entering a complex text by a mature writer (Wolf, 1988). It requires the same mental activity and effort to make sense of the text and a willingness to try to understand it on its own terms. The practices of collecting, examining, and assessing student work make enormous demands on teachers. There are, of course, the demands of time. But there are also demands on the teachers' ability to "read" this work carefully enough to see beyond what is quickly or easily noticed.

Teachers always need more practice to meet this challenge. This statement is not meant as an insult to any teacher's capacity for rigorous reading of student work. It simply recognizes that the task of reading is one of meaning making, a serious endeavor and one that calls for and deserves lifelong practice. The opportunity for discussion about specific pieces of work is a critical element in the development of these sophisticated reading skills. Time and structures for this kind of conversation exist in no more than a very small handful of American public schools.

DEVELOPING SOPHISTICATED READING SKILLS

In 1994, I explored some of the complexities and difficulties of using a phenomenological approach to reading children's works with a group of 10 elementary teachers and professional staff at an elementary school in Gloucester, Massachusetts. We used a protocol for discussing student work, developed through a project called Arts Propel, as both an approach to assessment and a form of professional development (Winner, 1991).

I met with the Gloucester staff over five sessions for a total of 18 hours. The staff's responsibilities covered the spectrum of K–5, special education, and curriculum development. In each session we discussed two or three pieces of work brought by the participants. The protocol we used for looking and talking—"collaborative assessment conferences"—was designed to influence habits of reading, assessing, and thinking about student work that could never be altered in one session. Intrinsic to the design of the collaborative assessment conferences was the idea that it was, indeed, a professional practice, a way to practice looking, seeing, reading, and discussing, that would have greatest effect if it were a regular feature of the school year throughout a teacher's career.

The collaborative assessment conference is not unique in establishing observation and description as a starting point for group discussion of student work. The "descriptive review process" developed by Patricia Carini and her colleagues at the Prospect Archive and Center for Education and Research has, as the name suggests, observation and description as essential elements of the process.

> An underlying assumption of the process is that each child is active in seeking to make sense of her or his experiences. By describing the child as fully, and in as balanced a way as possible, we begin to gain access to the child's modes of thinking and learning and to see their world from their point of view: what catches their attention, what arouses their wonder and curiosity, what sustains their interest and purpose. (Prospect Center, 1986, p. 1)

Another process employing careful observation and description of children's work is the "Biographic Literacy Profile Project." This effort, designed, led, and documented by Denny Taylor, involves teachers in long-term examinations, or "digs," into extensive collections of children's early efforts at symbolic representations and writing. Taylor (1990) articulates a challenge to observing that becomes a fundamental purpose of all of these practices.

> Our task is to try to describe children's personal understandings of the forms and functions of written language that they develop as they participate in the problem-solving environments that we create for them. To achieve this aim, it is essential that teachers are supported in their own explorations of the many functions, uses, and forms of written language, for we cannot observe what we have not learned to see. (p. 11)

How can we develop this sensitivity and rigor? The kinds of carefully structured protocols mentioned here have demonstrated promise for building the capacity to "notice." Through detailed accounts of conversations during the Gloucester sessions, I examine some of the challenges and rewards of observing and describing student work in group discussions, as each person brings distinct perspectives and various forms of expertise to the conversation.

Starting with Observation and Description

The collaborative assessment conference protocol begins with description of a piece of student work. The instruction to the participants is to "simply describe some aspect of the work." As discussed earlier, judgments are discouraged. But, if participants were not allowed any judgmental comments, what *could* they talk about?

> Having only the vaguest ideas of what I was looking for, I merely gathered my materials, looked at them carefully, and wrote descriptions of the

words, rhythms, content and themes of the children's writing. What happened then, in the process of my own writing, seemed almost magical to me. As I examined the children's work and described it as accurately as I could, the material seemed to yield its own meanings. The more closely I concentrated on the details of the writing, always linking them back to the whole piece and other pieces by the same child, the more I could understand about the work and the writer. Instead of starting out with theories about the children, I was being led by the work itself into succeeding levels of perception that gradually brought me deeper into each child's thinking. (Martin, 1983, p. 4)

Anne Martin, an elementary school teacher who has worked with Carini and the descriptive review process, is talking about her own investigations into children's writing, but aptly describes the experience we had during Arts Propel as we focused the conversations on our own observations and descriptions of the student writing we were reading. Through successive meetings, we found that the more we opened the discussion of the students' works with descriptions of what was striking to us, the more complex and intriguing the texts became to us. Our conversations lengthened. We began to have more questions about the works and fewer quick answers. We began to make the kind of connections and discoveries Armstrong (1992) describes, again from his work with teachers at the Bread Loaf School of English.

Often we begin with no more than a banal detail. We were looking at a piece the other day and noticed how suddenly, half way through the child's manuscript her handwriting, which had previously been confined to the center of the page, began to spread out across the paper on either side. It's the apparently casual detail that offers a clue to what's going on. We began to wonder why that change took place. We examined the text again and realized that the narrative had undergone a sudden but unobtrusive transformation. And so it goes on. (p. 3)

COLLABORATIVE ASSESSMENT CONFERENCES:
A STRUCTURE FOR LOOKING CAREFULLY IN GROUPS

The collaborative assessment conference protocol has a series of distinct sections and some basic guidelines. Briefly, the protocol has the following structure:

1. Reading the text. In silence, everyone reads a student text that has been brought to the session by a participant who has agreed to be the "presenting" teacher for the conference.

2. Observation and description. All other participants discuss the work, focusing first, as strictly as possible, on a description of the piece.

3. Raising questions. Description is followed by articulation of questions about the text, the author, or the context of the writing.

4. Speculation on what the child is working on. Finally, these readers speculate on what they think the child was working on as he or she created this text.

5. Response of the presenting teacher. Throughout this discussion, the presenting teacher has been silent. At this point, though, the presenting teacher adds any observations she has of the text and answers as many of the questions as she can.

6. Teaching moves and pedagogical responses. Together, the readers and presenting teacher consider possible teaching moves any of them might be inclined to make to encourage and challenge this writer.

7. Reflection. When all of this is complete, the entire group, including the facilitator, reflect on the conference, considering its satisfactions, frustrations, confusions, and ways to improve the next conference.

In addition to prescribing when the presenting teacher should speak and when to listen, the protocol has two major guidelines or rules. First, that there is to be no expression of any individual's judgments of the work in question—judgments of taste ("I like or don't like this about the work . . .") or of quality ("This is good or this isn't . . ."). Second, the initial phases of the conference are conducted with as little information revealed as possible about the writer and the context of the writing (assignment, grade, materials provided, etc.).

Collaborative assessment takes time. An individual conference on a single piece of work easily can take 45 minutes to an hour. This has seemed like a very long time to some teachers and strikes many as impractical. In time, though, most teachers start to find a sense of purpose and degree of satisfaction in the conferences that initially were elusive. To be useful, these conferences should be a regular practice in schools. In other words, participating in these conferences once or twice is inadequate to the larger purpose of the protocol. They must be practiced time and again.

Several features of the protocol make collaborative assessment conferences quite different from forms of assessment that are more regularly practiced by teachers. Perhaps the most unusual feature is that teachers are asked to refrain from making judgments or expressing opinions about the quality of the work. There is also no attempt to compare, rank, or rate the works. Few teachers in America have sustained opportunities to look at what a child has produced, while withholding critical judgment. In contrast, many more teachers participate in scoring sessions (holistic or otherwise) sponsored by the state, a district, or private companies.

Furthermore, most teachers never experience any form of structured or regular professional conversation about specific pieces of children's work. It is not part of regular staff discussion, inservice programs, or most teacher training courses. In this light, the Gloucester workshops, focused and structured as they were, were an extraordinary professional experience for these teachers. Without making specific claims for their value, I can say with certainty that these workshops were a radical departure from the ordinary.

From early on in these sessions, participating teachers indicated that they saw it as their responsibility to determine the implications of these considerations of one child's work for the assessment of other children's work. These teachers seemed to accept the idea that insight into the learning experiences of other children could be gathered from insight into those of one child. While one must be careful in drawing conclusions about one child from the situation of another, this belief is at the foundation of the design of the protocol. The protocol is not proposed as a practical approach to the assessment of every child or, even more preposterous, every piece of every child's work. But it is useful for drawing attention to the complexity of even apparently simple work and as a reminder of how much more might be seen from looking longer and dwelling with a work.

Looking More and Seeing More

Within the first 10 minutes of the first Gloucester session, I suggested that we start right away to look at student work and I handed out copies of a piece of work I brought for this first conversation. (See Figure 5.1.) (The reader is encouraged to look carefully at this work before reading the following account. Frequent reference to the work should help in understanding the conversation and in engaging one's own process of noticing.)

In this first conference, the group spent 20 minutes observing and describing this work. I include much, but not all, of the transcript of that phase of the conference to share the process of this conversation. This opening discussion was typical of the later conferences in one crucial way—one person's observation often led another person to see something he or she hadn't noticed before. Observations also gave rise to questions and interpretations. The transcript of this conversation provides an example of that process.

FIGURE 5.1. A Student's Work.

There are sequences in this transcript in which it almost feels as if the comments are a series of nonsequiturs. I believe this is the result of having 10 people intensely engaged in looking and listening. They often blurted out their observations as they noticed some new aspect of the picture. The new observation may have been stimulated by something commented on minutes or moments earlier. Although there are also sequences in which each comment follows coherently on the previous one, this is, overall, not a neat conversation.

After the group had looked in silence at "Adam is for applles" for about a minute, I asked them to start by simply describing some "aspect of what is on the page." There was a moment of silence, and then Annette asked the age of the child. I noted her question, said that I would answer it later, and asked again for descriptions of what could be seen on the page.

Liz: Can you read the word that is under the "A"? I can't read that . . .
Margaret: Yes, I can't read that.
Alyce: It's A-D-A-M going down . . .
Liz: Okay.

There was silence for almost another minute.

Steve: Okay, any time . . .
Annette: It raises a million questions . . .
Steve: Start with description . . . just describe any aspect of what you
    see.
Annette: It's very creative and offbeat.
Alyce: It's a Bart Simpson-type boy.
Cherylann: Yeah. The drawing is more sophisticated than the writing.
Alyce: Yes, definitely.
Annette: I don't agree. I don't agree. I think the writing is very sophisti-
    cated.

Suddenly the contemplative tone of the previous comments was broken and at least half the group jumped in to express their opinions on the "sophistication" of the writing. Some people actively agreed with Cherylann and others argued that Annette was right. I heard these comments as judgments and wanted to move toward more descriptions.

Steve: Before we leap into this argument, let me try to bring you back
    even further. I want to maintain a focus on description even if it
    seems you are describing the most obvious and mundane things.

Annette: Okay, he had three magic markers.
Liz: I see a poem. There's a poem with the child's name.
Alyce: Loves to make stars.
Liz: Almost the whole page is full with a combination of drawing and writing.
Annette: I'd love to know if he means to say "A dam" or "Adam."
Alyce: Is that a gun in one hand and a balloon in the other?
Cherylann: Or a hatchet?
Liz: Or an apple?
Steve: Describe what it looks like.
Alyce: It looks like a . . . a hatchet. With a happy balloon.
Steve: Wait, where's the hatchet? I'm sorry.
Cherylann: Yeah, where is it?
Liz: Whoa, I didn't even see it.
Alyce: In that hand.
Steve: (pointing to the boy on top of the apple) In the right hand?
Margaret: Except if that's a hatchet, what is the thing coming around . . . ?
Alyce: Coming out of the hatchet?
Margaret: Is it air or wind?
Cherylann: Is this a firecracker?

Someone started to offer another opinion of what was "coming out of the hatchet," but stopped. Three people said, "Yeah," very quietly and the conversation came to a brief pause.

Cherylann: (pointing to the bottom left corner of the picture) And then is this a sun rising over the mountains?
Alyce: Or setting.
Cherylann: The stars are going around him. It's like this circular . . .
Annette: The apple is huge. It's 10 times the size of either person.
Cherylann: The thing I noticed about it when it was being read is that a lot of my kids wouldn't be changing the verb tense. They would go, "Adam is for apples, Apples *is* for Adam." Or, you know . . .
Ellen: Yeah, it changes . . .
Julie: I like the repetition of the words. Adam, apples, apples . . .
Liz: Yeah . . .
Julie: . . . and the two boys.
Alyce: Are they both Adam? One who is Adam who is for apples and the other is . . . (laughter from the group) . . . the one the apples are for. (more laughter)

Cherylann: It looks like he's dancing on the stem.

Steve: Describe in more detail what the figure is actually doing.

Cherylann: He's actually tip-toeing on the stem of the apple. It's almost as if he were doing a little balancing act there. And then the figure down below is almost doing (She imitates the move and sings) . . . Ta Da!

Liz: I'd like to see the face on that figure.

We moved the picture closer to Liz. There were several short comments murmured at her end of the table and then laughter.

Steve: I didn't hear what you all were talking about . . .

Julie: The top figure is doing a "ta da" kind of thing and the figure at the bottom is holding back the apple or holding it up . . . or holding it . . .

Alyce: . . . away . . .

Annette: This character is all colored in. This one is not.

Liz: The stars are sort of . . . it's as if the stars are framing the apple. And then on the left side of the paper, the stars are . . . well, it's not really random but . . .

Liz: They're almost like a frame around the whole thing.

Nancy: The writing is excluded . . . separate . . . from the drawing . . . except for his name.

Sheila: It's not embedded in the picture—except for the name.

Ellen: It's interesting how he used his name. The name, "A-D-A-M," going down one side. And he used the "D" for one line and the "A" for another. I don't know if he thought of that by himself but if he did, that's pretty sophisticated.

Alyce: Or they were given a lesson like that to do and that's what he was doing . . .

Nancy: Maybe they were making an alphabet book.

Liz: That's an acrostic.

Julie made some observations about differences in the way the artist formed his letters, and the group proceeded to make numerous observations about letter formation, spelling, and erasing, and then speculated about whether he had used pencil, marker, crayon, or some combination.

Margaret: What is that thing that looks like a torch with a handle and right next to it . . . I can't see clearly . . . is that a heart with a little dribble hanging down?

Steve: Just describe what you do see.
Margaret: I see something that is orange and gray and brown with a stem . . .
Cherylann: Oh, I thought they were balloons.

There was a murmuring of general agreement and then a short pause as people looked and thought.

Julie: The figure on the bottom is really quite sophisticated. It's not like a head with hair. It's a whole outline including the hair. . . .
Alyce: But kids went through that period of attempting to draw Bart Simpson.
Cherylann: But it's not exactly Bart Simpson. I mean, the hair is much more creative than Bart Simpson's hair.
Liz: I keep thinking of *James and the Giant Peach*. (Several people chimed in with their agreement.) This is almost like "Adam and the Giant Apple."
Alyce: I'm thinking the opposite. I'm thinking this kid has been to Sunday School. (big laugh from the group)
Annette: Yes, yes, religion did come into it. The very first time I looked at it I thought, "Adam and apple!" I did think it was biblical.

The laughter continued and a number of people started talking among themselves. I couldn't tell if they had exhausted their observations. I did feel that they certainly had had a productive discussion. Their tendency to stray from description didn't surprise or dismay me. On the contrary, I expected it. The spontaneous statement of theories, questions, and interpretations seemed a perfectly natural impulse. I didn't want to criticize those comments but I did want to try to gently nudge them back to description, to a focus on what the child had put on the page. In this way, I hoped to anchor interpretations and questions in the observable specifics of the work.

The group was quiet for a moment and I made one more observation about the nature of their recent comments on the child's religious background and the "biblical" imagery of the drawing and the text. "We've probably moved from description." Most people laughed and Cherylann declared, "Into interpretation!"

Steve: Have we exhausted description?
Margaret: The idea—this probably isn't description—the idea is very sophisticated. "Adam is for applles. Apples are for Adam," is not something that many children would think of.

Alyce: Both boys have the same kind of shirts too. The lines going
down, colored pants . . .

Liz: The one on top to me . . . the face just seems much happier than
the one on the bottom . . .

Annette: What's he got in his hand?

Alyce: Is that a star gone bad? (considerable laughter)

Liz: Actually, just drawing all those stars . . .

Annette: It's interesting, too, how he has got the ground here. It's not
just like kids usually scribble a straight line.

Margaret: That's why I wonder if it is *James and the Giant Peach* influence.

Sheila: Would you think those boys are characters he has practiced
a lot?

Several people said, "Yeah."

Cherylann: And those stars. They [kids] go through phases where they
finally learn how to make stars and then stars are all over the
place.

More people murmured their agreement.

Liz asked to see the picture more closely and I handed it to her. She
looked at it intently and then pointed to the boy on top of the apple.

Liz: The stem is extraordinary too.

Steve: Tell us out loud about what you are seeing because it is good to
see it close but we need you to share it. Say what you see about
the stem.

Liz: The stem is very real as though he were looking at an apple when
he drew it.

Steve: Say what detail it is that makes you think that.

Liz: The little leaf, the green leaf on the edge of the stem. It looks
very lifelike, realistic.

The conversation moved into a bit more discussion of distinctions
in the drawing of the two boys. Annette noted the direction the bottom
boy's feet were pointing and wondered if they were meant to suggest
motion. Margaret commented that the single piece of green in the stem
was the only green in the picture. Alyce suggested the artist/author may
have only had a few markers. Several people began a short conversation
about whether the artist was exercising conscious "choices" in the use
of colors or whether he was making almost random use of the markers
that were available at the moment. Having noticed a new detail, Sheila

added her observation to the discussion. "It just occurred to me that the only thing that is anchored on the ground is the one boy. The stars go under the apple. Everything else is floating in the air. I wonder if that one hand is holding it secure."

I felt the group was beginning to slow down. Some people looked a bit tired and sat back in their seats. Perhaps I had become tired. Discussion turned to a question of whether the writer had deliberately left a space in his name so as to make the words, "A dam." Ellen was quite certain the author had meant for the reader to read the "A" on top of the "D" as the beginning of the name "Adam." While this debate continued a bit longer, I decided that, indeed, this part of the conversation had yielded a significant number of observations that had not been immediately obvious to everyone. Although they probably could have discovered more to "see" in the piece, I was concerned about time and wanted to stop while the group still felt they were being productive. It seemed time to move to articulating the questions that the work had raised for people. I asked, "If you were to go back now and look, what questions would you like to raise about the work—the piece, the child, the context?"

There were over a dozen questions. They asked if the child's name was Adam and how old he was. They wanted to know if he drew the picture before writing the text or vice versa. How does the artist feel about the work? Does he consider it finished? Was he influenced by *James and the Giant Peach* or Bart Simpson? How long has he been drawing stars and this figure of a boy?

I explained what I knew about the child and the creation of this work. Adam was a first-grade boy who drew this during "journal" time, which was a regular classroom activity during which children could write and draw anything they wanted. He had attempted an acrostic and, when I spoke with him about this piece, he explained that the writing was a "mess-up." The writing had been done before the drawing, and his journal had other earlier examples of this figure of a boy.

While this information seemed to satisfy some of the group's curiosity, it also seemed to provoke more questions. Were acrostics modeled in the class? Did he like his work? Did he feel any "looser" drawing than writing? Did his markers go dry?

Altogether, this conversation had lasted nearly 45 minutes. Finally, it seemed to be slowing down and someone asked, half seriously and half in jest, "Can we meet Adam? We're fascinated by him." Everyone laughed and I, pleased that they had become interested in this child through his work, suggested that we move on to a reflection on the conference.

Immediately there were comments about the difficulty of "describing without interpreting." Alyce noted the effect of this as a collaborative practice. "It made me see a lot more than I would just sitting alone." And Julie added, "And the more you looked at it, the more you saw." A few minutes later in this discussion, Alyce suggested that "to know the kid is to know the work." And I commented that I felt one of my central questions about collaborative assessment was the inverse of Alyce's comment—if one knows the work, does one know the child?

CHALLENGES AND REWARDS OF OBSERVING AND DESCRIBING

As I began the Gloucester sessions, I suspected that, of all the steps of the protocol, the opening phase of observing and describing would be most difficult for new participants. I had always found description difficult, especially when working with student writing. It is challenging to me to do the descriptions and it certainly has appeared difficult for many of the groups I have worked with. Models, drawings, and other forms of visual art are usually somewhat easier. Temporal performances (dances, plays, etc.) have their own inherent difficulties, related to the necessary reliance on memory. (Video, of course, helps with the memory problem but also distorts the specific qualities of the performance and is therefore unreliable.)

My thoughts on why description should be so difficult are entirely speculative. I suspect that two tendencies in our culture mix dangerously and make what should be a simple act of description far more difficult than one might anticipate. First, we tend to move very quickly and rarely stop to dwell at length on what is before our eyes. A trip to a museum to watch people looking at the art often confirms that most of us spend very little time looking at a single painting. Face to face with a Rembrandt, an extraordinary opportunity to observe the work of a master, to dwell on what many consider a major accomplishment of Western culture and to allow one's own specific and unique response to begin to form in relationship to this work of art, most of us spend little more than a minute or two. In a curious way, we seem *not to be* in the habit of looking closely at what is in front of us.

Further, we seem *to be* in the habit of making very quick judgments, even of things that might benefit from some reflection. We often expect of ourselves and our companions that we will know our thoughts, feelings, and opinions of a film before we've even crossed the street outside the theater. Exemplified by the film critics Siskel and Ebert's "thumbs up" or "thumbs down," there is a "let's look at it once, declare it good or bad, and get on to the next" mentality that dominates our behavior perhaps a bit more than we might like to admit. Maybe it is not so surprising that if asked to "simply describe" a piece of student writing, most of us will find ourselves at something of a loss.

Description of any student work has, I believe, two sources of difficulty. First, it is not easy to state the obvious. And yet, that is the initial challenge—simply to say what you see. The second difficulty is to limit your comments to description. All kinds of other statements enter the discourse in this phase, including judgments, opinions of various sorts, questions, and interpretations. In a child's painting, for example, many people will say that there is "a sun in the sky" rather than describing, a "roughly 2-inch diameter circle of yellow surrounded by blue which covers the entire top half of the paper."

Why is this rigor about language so important? I'm making a distinction between interpretation of what the painting represents and description of what is there on the page. To one person, the yellow circle represents the sun. But to another, it represents the moon. They have each interpreted the blue on the top of the paper differently. One sees day, the other night. Neither may have any doubt about the appropriateness of the interpretation. Indeed, both interpretations are certainly appropriate. Neither is more correct than the other. Both people, however, can agree that the child created a ". . . circle of yellow surrounded by blue . . . ," and so on. Descriptions are statements that a group can generally agree on with relative ease. Interpretations are highly individual and often controversial.

Inevitably, participants intermingle descriptive and interpretive comments in these conferences. I find I have to encourage the descriptions since they seem to be considerably more difficult for participants than interpretive statements. I encourage the descriptions as a way of establishing a common base of perceptions about what the child has put on the page. The descriptions help everyone in the group to notice things they may have missed in their looking.

Everyone sees and therefore comes to know an object from his or her own point of view—and, necessarily, only partially. Montessori (1966) refers to William James in her consideration of this point:

> A true observer acts from an inner impulse, a kind of feeling or special taste, and consequently he is selective in his choice of images. This concept was illustrated by James when he said that no one ever sees an object in the totality of its particulars. Each individual sees only a portion of it, that is, he views it in the light of his own sentiments and interests. Thus the same object is described in different ways by different individuals. (p. 76)

It is exactly this infinite variety of description that makes collaborative assessment such a potentially rich activity. Each participant sees different aspects of a text and will describe what he or she sees differently. It is through words, the translation of what we see into descriptive language, that we share our observations. As Maxine Greene (1987) points out, it is hearing others articulate their perceptions that allows us to see, hear, and know an object or a text in ways otherwise unavailable to us.

> The individual sees profiles, aspects of the building entered in the morning, the school or the agency. He/she, similarly, grasps aspects of the novel being read, the painting being looked at; there is always more to be discovered, each time he/she focuses attention. As important, each time he/she is with others—in dialogue, in teaching-learning situations, in mutual pursuit of a project—additional new perspectives open; *language opens possibilities of seeing, hearing, understanding.* (p. 21, emphasis added)

In the course of the Gloucester workshops only two teachers spoke of professional experiences in which collaborative description was the foundation of a study of children or children's work. Margaret Wilmot, a curriculum coordinator on the verge of her retirement, spoke of her work with holistic scoring and her preference for the design of the collaborative assessment conferences. "I've had the experience sharing ideas about children's writing when doing holistic scoring . . . and I hated it. I hated every minute of it. I never felt it was really either worthwhile or true. This [workshop series] seemed to me so reality-based. Even though there was speculation, it was based on real evidence."

Annette Boothroyd, a fifth-grade teacher in mid-career, remembered her experience, 17 years earlier, discussing children in a professional workshop that used "a medical model and you weren't allowed to say anything that wasn't description. No interpretation. It opened your mind so much it was incredible. It allows you to open your mind to what is really there."

Multiple Perspectives

Sharing interpretations is an essential part of the experience of these conferences. The Gloucester group came to recognize that the range of interpretations can be literally shocking. Often, someone will understand some aspect of a picture or a text in wildly different ways from others. Once the unusual interpretation has been explained, the group often can follow where it came from, although it may not be adopted generally. My purpose as facilitator of these sessions is not to validate any of the interpretations or encourage agreement or disagreement. Rather I am interested in the sense participants make of the variety and range of interpretations in the group. I do ask people to explain what in the picture or the text has suggested an interpretation. Always, there is a return to the specific, describable details of the text. Meaning is arguable but, at least, rooted in what the child has put on the page. Often, people change their interpretations in the course of the discussion or, at least, begin to entertain multiple possibilities for the meaning of the work.

Of course, the major role for most people was that of reader, and that proved to be a major source of satisfaction and somewhat unexpected reward. Reflecting on the first conference, Alyce said, ". . . it was neat to hear other people's statements. It made me see a lot more than I would just sitting alone." There were several agreements from the group and someone added, "And the more you looked at it (Adam is for applles), the more you saw!"

Throughout the sessions, there were frequent comments about the pleasures of sitting together, talking, and listening to each other's various perspectives on the writing. Readers saw new possibilities from each other's descriptions. One person's questions would spark another's insights. It seemed as though this kind of thoughtful give-and-take was, in itself, a pleasure. Certainly the benefit of multiple perspectives is one of the purposes of the design of the protocol. It may be only through the exploration of so many perspectives that the ambiguity of meanings in these texts can be discovered and examined. At the end of the third session, Margaret said, ". . . I loved the ambiguity today. I loved the feeling that because there wasn't any punctuation . . . I loved it . . . having everybody's interpretations."

In addition, the conferences gave everyone a chance to contribute and there was no way of predicting who might make a significant contribution to the next piece. Expertise came by virtue of a fairly wide variety of characteristics. Some teachers had worked extensively with children of a certain age and therefore were familiar with particular sets of writing issues. Other teachers had special interest in certain genres of writing. Others simply had life experiences that allowed them special insight into the content of the writing.

In the End . . .

The final moments of the last of the Gloucester sessions were dominated by discussion of the teachers' appreciation of these sessions as opportunities to "learn to observe." They focused on this as the thing they most valued from this experience and most wanted to bring back to their students. Quickly, several people in the group became quite involved in a conversation about the possibility of getting parents to become careful observers of their own children's writing.

What I came to see is that this kind of careful examination of "the actual work itself" can be a bit like stepping through Alice's looking glass into a room at first familiar, but one in which further exploration reveals remarkable surprises. In this case, looking at the object not only allowed us to see the child presented in a unique fashion, but also provided views of the classroom with its complex of materials, ideas, pedagogy, and approaches to writing.

David Hawkins, in his essay, "I, Thou and It" (1974), talks about teaching and learning in terms of a triangular relationship with teacher, student, and object of study as the three points of the triangle. I had wondered for some time where the things children make might go in this diagram. Often, I'd pictured them outside and just off the point that hosts the student. But this never felt quite right.

In the course of this study, I began to see the things children make in school as resting solidly in the middle of the triangle. They deserve that place, I believe, for an important reason. They are the product not only of the child but of the alchemy of teacher, student, and object of study (poetry, for example). Each exerts an influence on the making and learning processes. In turn, the final product also reflects all of these influences. In this way, the things children make in school are remarkable artifacts worthy of extensive study, as they can provide those interested with great pleasure as well as extraordinary information about child, teacher, object or focus of study, and the domain in which the product is fashioned—that is, if one has had the time and opportunity to develop the inclination to see these things.

NOTE

1. Thanks to the Lilly Endowment, Pew Charitable Trusts, and Rockefeller Foundation for support of the research discussed in this chapter. Grateful acknowledgment, also, of the teachers and administrators at Fuller Elementary School in Gloucester, Massachusetts, and Veterans Memorial Elementary School in Provincetown, Massachusetts, who supported and participated in this work: Annette Boothroyd, Bill Bruns, Sheila Callahan-Young, Pamela Card, Julie Carter, Ron Eckel, Cathy Skowron, Alyce McMenimen, Elizabeth Parillo, Cherylann Parker, Nancy Rhodes, Ellen Sibley, Elliot Tocci, Margaret Wilmot. Thanks to Kim Powell for assistance in this research, and to Sara Hendren for her excellent editorial advice. Also, special thanks to the young artists and their families for permission to use their work.

REFERENCES

Armstrong, M. (1992). Children's stories as literature: An interview with Michael Armstrong. *Bread Loaf News, 5*(1), 2, 4.

Greene, M. (1987). *The dialectic of freedom.* New York: Teachers College Press.

Hawkins, D. (1974). *The informed vision.* New York: Agathon.

Martin, A. (1983). *Reading your students: Their writing and their selves* (Teachers & Writers Think/Ink Book 3). New York: Teachers and Writers Collaborative.

Montessori, M. (1966). *The secret of childhood.* Notre Dame, IN: Fides.

Prospect Center. (1986). *The Prospect Center documentary practices.* North Bennington, VT: Prospect Archive and Center for Education and Research.

Taylor, D. (1990). Teaching without testing. *English Education, 23*(1), 4–74.

Thoreau, H. D. (1982). *Great short works of Henry David Thoreau* (W. Glick, Ed.). New York: HarperCollins. (Original work published 1858)

Winner, E. (Ed.). (1991). *Arts propel: An introductory handbook.* Cambridge, MA: Harvard Project Zero and Educational Testing Service.

Wolf, D. (1988). *Reading reconsidered: Literature and literacy in high school.* New York: College Entrance Examination Board.

CHAPTER 6

Reflections on the Use of Teams to Support the Portfolio Process

Carol Lynn Davis
UNIVERSITY OF SOUTHERN MAINE

Ellen Honan
YARMOUTH PUBLIC SCHOOLS

For me, the value of the portfolio exists as a tool whereby I can celebrate my growth and my passion in being a lifelong learner. I feel the portfolio has little value as a definitive evaluative tool. At first I felt as if this was the purpose for constructing them [portfolios]. The process was difficult, uninspiring, and without foundation, in my opinion, but I pressed on . . . until, at my final portfolio team meeting, they [portfolio team members] released me from this ball and chain and suggested that I be me, and that I represent this in my portfolio.

Terry, ETEP intern, 1996

This chapter focuses on the process of developing and using teams to structure conversations about teaching portfolios. The chapter describes how interns in a fifth-year teacher education program experience the teaming approach to portfolio development. It also presents the perspectives of mentors who served on the portfolio teams. Implications for using teaming in the portfolio development process are discussed. Most important in this story are the shifts in thinking about the portfolio process that took place for both interns and their mentors. One of the learnings, as illustrated by the quote above, was that developing a teaching portfolio could and should be considered as both a celebratory experience as well as an evaluative one.

The context is the University of Southern Maine's Extended Teacher Education Program (ETEP). ETEP is a fifth-year, innovative, professional development school model, teacher education program designed for liberal arts graduates that leads to teacher certification after a one-year internship. During the year, interns work as a cohort group at one of five school sites dedicated to school renewal and reform in the southern Maine area. The use of portfolio teams occurred with interns in the Yarmouth School System, which has served as an ETEP site since 1992. In the ETEP model for teacher education, a school-based faculty member and a university-based faculty member serve as program coordinators and mentors for the interns. The authors of this chapter currently serve as the coordinators and mentors for interns at the Yarmouth site.

With the integration of theory and practice as the basis of ETEP, the interns take graduate-level university courses during the year that connect closely with their year-long work in the classroom. At the Yarmouth site, interns usually have two classroom placements during the year—one from August to December and the other from January to May. The teachers with whom the interns are placed serve as mentors for the interns and are referred to as cooperating teachers. Successful completion of the internship year and recommendation for teacher certification are, in part, determined by the demonstration of 11 ETEP outcomes (Figure 6.1). Teacher interns at all ETEP sites are required to document this growth and development through a teaching portfolio that serves as one forum for the demonstration and review of intern performance.

The Yarmouth ETEP site has used peer/mentor teams as part of the portfolio development process since the 1993–94 internship year. The idea of using teams to support the portfolio development process was formulated during a presentation by Lee Shulman at the Portfolios in Teacher Education Conference in Cambridge, Massachusetts, in January 1994. Listening to Lee Shulman share the rewards and excitement of being on the portfolio team that served as Larry Cuban's peer review committee (described in Chapter 2), prompted Nancy Austin and Ellen Honan, Yarmouth ETEP site coordinators at the time, to create a similar learning environment for the portfolio development of their teacher interns that spring. A search of the literature found that little had been written about the specific procedures of establishing and conducting peer/mentor teams for portfolio development. Bird (1990) and Wolf (1994) discussed the importance of working with colleagues to examine

1. *Knowledge of Child/Adolescent Development and Principles of Learning.* The teacher demonstrates respect, concern for children, and an understanding of how they continue to develop and learn. She or he uses this knowledge to plan and guide instruction and to create a challenging, supportive learning environment.

2. *Knowledge of Subject Matter and Inquiry.* The teacher understands the framework of the subject matter(s) that she or he teaches and makes accessible to students the discipline's tools of inquiry, central concepts, internal structure, and connections to other domains of knowledge, in a manner that promotes the learner's independent inquiry.

3. *Instructional Planning.* The teacher consistently plans and evaluates instruction based on knowledge of the learner, the subject matter, the community, the intended student outcomes, and the curriculum.

4. *Instructional Strategies and Technology.* The teacher understands and uses a variety of teaching strategies, including appropriate technology, to promote learning and independent inquiry for all students.

5. *Assessment.* The teacher enhances and documents learning through continuing use of formal and informal assessment strategies, communicates feedback, and promotes guided self-evaluation in learners.

6. *Diversity.* The teacher models respect for individual differences among students and coworkers. She or he plans and creates instructional opportunities with sensitivity to individual learners.

7. *Beliefs About Teaching and Learning.* The teacher clearly communicates his or her beliefs about learning, teaching, assessment, and the role of education in society, and demonstrates practices that support those beliefs.

8. *Citizenship.* The teacher understands principles of democratic community and plans instruction to promote ideals, values, and practices of citizenship.

9. *Collaboration and Professionalism.* The teacher demonstrates professional responsibility to school and community. She or he works collaboratively with colleagues, parents, and community members to improve the conditions of learning for all students and adults.

10. *Professional Development.* The teacher recognizes that she or he is, above all, a learner. She or he continually reflects on and evaluates choices and actions, and seeks out opportunities for professional development as well as ways to improve teaching and learning.

11. *Classroom Management.* The teacher understands and implements classroom management techniques that support individual responsibility and the principles of democratic community.

FIGURE 6.1. ETEP Outcomes.

and refine the portfolio through sustained conversations about teaching and learning, and Shulman (1992) suggested that a teaching portfolio reached its full value when it provided an opportunity for conversations about one's teaching. Shulman's definition of a teaching portfolio offered a model for the portfolio development process at the Yarmouth ETEP site: "A teaching portfolio is the structured, documentary history of a set of coached or mentored acts of teaching, substantiated by samples of student portfolios, and fully realized only through reflective writing, deliberation, and conversation."

The use of teams to support the portfolio development process at the Yarmouth ETEP site was implemented during the spring of 1994. During the first 2 years of the project, the structure for the use of the teams included the following:

1. At a seminar class in February, interns were provided with examples of teaching portfolios when interns from the previous year shared the portfolios that they had developed.
2. Portfolio teams then were created consisting of two or three interns, a university faculty member, a cooperating teacher, an administrator, and a former intern.
3. These teams met in March and again in April for an hour each time.
4. In May, interns presented the portfolios they had developed.

The purpose of the teams was to provide support and guidance for the interns throughout the portfolio development process. Each team member was encouraged to play the role of a compassionate listener for the interns. During these team meetings, interns shared potential artifacts, reflected on the significance of these artifacts, and received feedback from the team members. The portfolio presentation session was designed to celebrate the accomplishments of each intern.

The process and structure for using the portfolio teams have evolved over time. Based on observations as well as in response to oral and written feedback gathered through seminar discussions, free writes, journal prompts, surveys, and interviews, the Yarmouth site coordinators made changes in the use of portfolio teams to better address the needs of the program and the interns. Modifications made for the most recent cohort of interns include:

1. Beginning the portfolio teaming process earlier in the internship year
2. Increasing the number of times that the teams meet
3. Clarifying the roles of both the interns and the mentors on the teams
4. Comparing the teaming process for portfolio development with a writing conference

5. Designing and designating the portfolio presentation sessions as both celebratory and evaluative.

(Figure 6.2 presents a more detailed account of how the portfolio teaming process was structured most recently at the Yarmouth site.)

INTERN AND MENTOR EXPERIENCES OF THE TEAMING PROCESS

Intern and mentor reflections illustrate the scope of support that the teams contributed to the portfolio development process.

Interns

The experiences of the interns as they engage in constructing their portfolios using the teams as a supportive structure continue to inform the teaming practice. Overall, these experiences have been most positive for all the interns. However, the process is not experienced in the same manner by all the interns. Each intern has a unique personal perspective of the process.

Tamara, an intern at the elementary level, looked forward to the portfolio team meetings, anticipating that the team would provide her with valuable insights. Her response to the process exemplifies that the intended support, feedback, and questioning by team members occurred in her case. She writes:

> The entire portfolio process was very important to me. Right through the final presentation, I found myself reflecting and thinking what I could change to capture my philosophy of teaching. Working in the portfolio groups was helpful to me. Portfolio members were supportive and they gave [me] concrete suggestions to strengthen a particular artifact ot to make the portfolio a more cohesive reflection of my beliefs. . . . The team helped me learn "why are you including this artifact?" and "what does it say about you as a learner and a teacher?" Paul and Naomi (two team members) asked very probing questions which got me identifying my core beliefs. That was critical—I am appreciative of their astuteness and valued their questions and comments.

The role of reflection in the portfolio process itself was highlighted by Nathan, a secondary intern who was most reflective about his teaching practices. In one of his journal responses, he wrote:

1. SPECIFIC LEARNING EXPERIENCES such as journal writing, a personal artifact share, goal setting, formal and informal feedback sessions related to teaching episodes, and the creation of teaching videos were designed to provide the interns with a valuable foundation for the development of their portfolios during the fall.

2. IN JANUARY, A panel of former ETEP interns shared their portfolios with the current cohort group of interns and offered advice regarding the creation of a teaching portfolio; the process of using the team approach for portfolio development was described. The portfolio team meetings were characterized as structured, supportive forums for conversations and feedback regarding potential portfolio artifacts and were portrayed as an extension of the existing cohort team, one that would include different voices and perspectives. Peers and mentors on each team were described as fulfilling the role of compassionate listeners and critical friends.

3. MENTORS FOR THE teams were chosen based on their expressed interest, their proven ability as reflective practitioners, and their availability to attend the team meetings and portfolio presentations. Five teams were established, with each team consisting of three interns, a university faculty member, a school administrator, one or two teachers, and a former ETEP intern.

4. THE COMPOSITION OF the teams were determined by the coordinators, with input from interns as to which interns they would prefer on their team and which they would not prefer on their team. The three interns on each team met as a group in February (prior to the first team meeting) to discuss effective group dynamics (e.g., active listening, time management) for their portfolio team meetings. The intent of this discussion was to provide the interns with a sense of ownership and responsibility for their own learning throughout the portfolio development process.

5. THE TWO COORDINATORS met with the mentors for an hour prior to the first team meeting to describe and discuss their roles on the teams. Mentors were briefed on the work that the interns had been doing throughout the year in preparation for constructing their portfolio. The role of the team mentors was outlined as being all of the following: a critical friend, a compassionate listener, a coach, a support person, an active listener, and a questioner. It was pointed out to the mentors that although their role was an important one, the ownership of the team ultimately belonged to the interns and that the mentors needed to be aware of their own voices within the team as well as the voices of others—voice getting and voice letting. The portfolio team meetings were compared with the structure of a writing conference (Awell, 1987; Calkins, 1985; Graves, 1983) where the author shares his or her work and asks for feedback. Mentors were reminded again of the scheduled team meetings and their commitment to attend each one.

6. THE PORTFOLIO TEAMS met once in February, once in March, and twice in April for 1-hour sessions. Each intern brought to the meetings potential artifacts accompanied by written reflections that demonstrated some aspect of the intern as a teacher, learner, and individual. As each intern presented an artifact and reflection, the mentors and other interns asked key questions, such as: Why is this important to you? Why is this important to your students? What does this show about you as a teacher and a learner? How have your beliefs about teaching and learning been changed or strengthened as a result of this lesson? What can we expect to see at the next meeting?

7. THE FOURTH TEAM meeting, at the end of April, was designed as a presentation practice session. Interns received feedback from team members and continued to revise their portfolios and/or their presentation format.

8. EACH TEAM WAS allotted a 3-hour presentation session during the first week of May, with 1 hour designated for each intern's portfolio presentation and feedback. The audience for each intern consisted of all team members, site coordinators, and the intern's cooperating teachers. Each member of the audience was encouraged to give oral and written feedback to the intern.

FIGURE 6.2. Structuring the Teaming Process.

> The portfolio process worked best when it helped me to reflect on what I can improve on and what I did well. I have found that when I am in the process of something I become convinced that I will remember it—including all the details. But I don't. . . . I have found that when I reflect and create my portfolio, I reinforce the event in my memory so that I am less likely to forget about it. The process of reflection imprints the event in a unique way. . . . What this points to is the need to create portfolios contemporaneously with the [teaching] process.

Nathan suggested that requiring each intern to write a weekly reflection on a potential portfolio artifact would be most helpful as additional foundational work. He explains that "in the end they [the weekly reflections] could be refined, but it would be very helpful to create them as you go along." Nathan stated that he "would not change the free form nature of [portfolio] design" since "every portfolio was unique *and* very high quality." He would not have wanted a "structure imposed" on the portfolio itself.

Michael, an intern who enjoyed working with early adolescents, agreed with Nathan concerning the individuality of each portfolio. He wrote:

> Portfolios are so unique and personal. Yes, I can say what I wanted [to say] in a better way, and my team helped me towards that goal. However, there is no correct portfolio. It would stifle creativity if there were; for the criteria would have to be the guiding force, and not the person. . . . I found the entire portfolio process to be positive in every way. Right from the beginning members of the portfolio team brought diverse perspectives to people's artifacts. Each individual gave creative, constructive criticism to all meetings. . . . Because it was a continuous process, adaptations and refining took place to enhance the power of the portfolio. Most importantly, ETEP interns were always encouraged to keep developing [the portfolio] even up to the final portfolio presentation. That's what made it so powerful. The portfolio continues to grow and improve as people do. To think that there is a standard or finality to a portfolio compares in absurdity to a teacher knowing everything about being a teacher.

Not all interns were initially as positive as Tamara, Nathan, and Michael about the portfolio development process. One elementary intern, Emily, was hesitant about the entire process of using teams. Before the first team meeting, she expressed concern that the mentors on her team, whom she perceived as "strangers," would be "judging" her work and "directing" the development of her portfolio in a manner not in line with her wishes. However, after the first portfolio team meeting she wrote in her journal:

> [I] got my first portfolio class "under my belt"—what an interesting week. Yes, my biggest surprise was the portfolio meeting. It was invigorating! The atmosphere, in my mind, was not threatening at all, just helpful and welcoming.

She was pleased that not everyone on the team had attended the meeting, stating that, "We were a couple of people short, so we ended up being just six people all together—just perfect." In her final reflection on the portfolio process, Emily wrote:

> The process itself was great, only, due to the wonderful "idea pool" on my team. Also I was quite closed to the whole idea of meeting with "all those people," [but] it became something that I valued. I am, however, grateful that at no time were all team members present. The group would have been toooo big for my comfort level. The "intimate" circle we became was inspiring.

Emily continues with some thoughts about the unique nature of each portfolio.

> Perhaps the portfolio is a question of ownership.—Who owns the right/privilege of saying what my most valuable moments are, created by ETEP, created by me? Then, again, perhaps you may want a clearer connection from the portfolio to the outcomes . . . a more directed and less creative portfolio. Well, does "directed" cancel out "creative"? I'm not sure. This, I guess, could be a hot topic.

Terry, a self-identified "reluctant reflector," struggled with some of these issues as he developed his portfolio, and it was the advice of his team members that finally allowed him to take ownership of his portfolio, as noted in the quote that begins this chapter. He wrote:

> I must say that the portfolio process was one that I enjoyed greatly. As my site coordinators could attest, reflecting to the degree required in ETEP was not something I enjoyed. . . . However,

the portfolio became a wonderful way for me to reflect upon all of growth, learning, and accomplishments.

When his team members convinced him that a portfolio should showcase the uniqueness of its author, he found that

> The experience instantly gained value. "Show yourself," they said. "Show us who you are and why this makes you an exceptional teacher," and so I did. I constructed, I cut, I pasted, I reflected, I reflected, I reflected, and in the end I gained more from this experience that I ever thought possible. My portfolio is a "work in progress" because I am a work in progress. I am a lifelong learner. . . . The portfolio process allowed me to celebrate who I am and how I have grown.

Erica, a secondary intern who had used portfolios in her own teaching practice during the year, reiterated some of the learnings shared by Terry.

> I value portfolios as a valid learning tool. Designing my portfolio helped me to clarify and articulate visually and in writing my teaching philosophy. It is the actual process that I value: collecting artifacts, organizing, reflecting, and receiving feedback at the portfolio evaluation.

She described her response to the portfolio presentation session as well.

> I found my evaluation extremely rewarding. The theme and goal of Yarmouth ETEP has been to promote the lifelong learner. By receiving positive feedback and constructive criticism, I concluded that my portfolio is a continuum of my learning as a teacher, i.e., it will *never* be done. My learning will continue beyond ETEP. . . . Instead of my portfolio presentation being a final, pass/fail assessment, it was a learning experience in and of itself.

Mentors

Mentors were asked to describe how they had experienced their roles on the team. Their impressions corresponded to the experiences that the interns reported. Laurie, an elementary teacher, reported that she perceived her role as follows:

It was just giving some feedback, helping to brainstorm some ideas, talking over and wrestling over ideas about what was important about the person . . . and that became really clear that first you had to know who you were and what you wanted your portfolio to reflect about you and your thinking . . . we were more of a sounding board, . . . pointing out what was well done and perhaps where they might want to add things to it, at least that was my role. There were other people within the group who were from the university level and administration and I think my role as a teacher meant encouragement.

Tricia, a university faculty member, described the teaming as follows:

To some of them it was a new experience, and it was clearly for some of them, a little bit unsettling. They weren't totally sure of what they were going to do and I think we . . . our role was to try to help them see that what they were doing was really fine. . . . They were working through some questions of why was this meaningful for their portfolio. So, I think that is kind of what we were doing during those sessions, just trying to help them articulate why they chose something, allay their fears that this is an impossible task.

Steve, another university faculty member on a portfolio team, stated:

I was trying to be a critical friend and someone who brought other perspectives, not necessarily better perspectives, but other perspectives on what might be in a portfolio and how it might be organized. So . . . I was trying to provide honest and courteous and supportive feedback to the exhibits. At the same time I was trying to stretch the thinking of the people who were doing it as to what else was possible, not that what else was possible was more desirable, or even desirable, but so that they would have it as part of their consideration.

These reported experiences from the interns and mentors about their involvement with portfolio team meetings confirmed the expectations that the peers and mentors on the portfolio teams provided support, gave feedback, were active listeners, asked questions, offered different perspectives, and strengthened the portfolio development process. The value of teaming during the portfolio development process is evident from the feedback received from the interns and mentors involved. By providing the structure for portfolio-based conversations, the teams foster reflection about teaching and enable interns to better articulate their beliefs about teaching and learning.

IMPLICATIONS FOR THE FUTURE USE OF PORTFOLIO TEAMS

As with any effective teaching practice, the use of teams for the portfolio development process at the Yarmouth ETEP site has changed with every new group of interns and will continue to evolve. Some of the shifts in thinking have included using the term *critical friend* as well as *compassionate listener* to describe the expectations of the role of a team member. Initially, it was thought that a supportive, nurturing environment was the best setting for constructing a portfolio. Observations over time have led to the realization that a balance needs to be created between a strictly supportive environment and a setting where the interns also can look at their work more critically and be more reflective in their thinking. Thus, one of the improvements in the role of team members has been the creation of a balance between the team members' roles as compassionate listeners and their roles as critical friends.

Another major change has been in the recognition that the portfolio presentation could serve both a celebratory and an evaluative purpose. Several aspects of the structure of the presentation sessions were restructured during the most recent year. At the portfolio team meeting prior to the presentation session, each intern was given an opportunity to practice the presentation of her or his portfolio and to receive feedback from team members as to how the presentation or the portfolio might be improved. Portfolio revisions continued as many interns took copious notes during this feedback session and some interns made major revisions before the final presentation.

The presentation sessions were designed so that each team was allotted a 3-hour time period in which interns had 1 hour to present their portfolio and receive oral and written feedback from the audience, which consisted of all the other members of their team, the two ETEP coordinators, and the cooperating teachers with whom each intern had been placed during the year. The length of each portfolio presentation was approximately 30 minutes. The remainder of the hour was filled with discussion and feedback concerning the intern's portfolio and the presentation of the portfolio, as well as the development of the intern's teaching style and philosophy over the year. In addition, the participants at each portfolio presentation were encouraged to fill out written feedback forms, which were given to the intern at the presentation. The portfolio presentation sessions were intended to provide an opportunity for interns to showcase themselves as teachers, demonstrate some of their learnings during the internship year, and continue to reflect on their teaching.

In previous years, the celebratory nature of the portfolio presentations appeared to leave the impression that the portfolio at that point was a final product and revisions were not necessary. With the changes, however, feedback was expected, welcomed, and internalized to the point that many portfolios were revised several more times after the final presentation. The interns appeared to understand that, like a piece of writing, the portfolio is a continuous work in progress.

It was confirming to the authors to read the recent work of Wolf, Whinery, and Hagerty (1995), which delineated specific procedures for establishing and conducting peer/mentor teams for portfolio development. Wolf and colleagues provided guidelines for structuring portfolio conversations, which paralleled the portfolio team process created by the authors. Based on observations, feedback from interns and mentors, and a recent review of the literature, further revisions for the teaming process included:

1. Introducing teaching portfolios early in the fall with a portfolio share by former interns.

2. Making the portfolio process, guidelines, and expectations more explicit during the fall placement.

3. Providing opportunities for portfolio conversations in the fall with peer teams sharing classroom artifacts.

4. Strengthening the connection between the writing process and the portfolio development process, as suggested by Wolf and colleagues (1995), to include the expectation that the portfolio author would bring specific requests for feedback to the portfolio team meeting.

5. Establishing the team meeting dates in the fall to ensure attendance by all team members.

6. Continuing work leading to an appropriate type of assessment for the portfolios.

It is expected that other changes might occur as necessitated by the needs of the interns. It is also the hope of the authors that by providing a supportive learning environment for these teacher interns, they will, in turn, help their own students develop portfolios and encourage collegial conversations within their own school faculties.

REFERENCES

Atwell, N. (1987). *In the middle: Writing, reading, and learning with adolescents.* Portsmouth, NH: Boynton/Cook.

Bird, T. (1990). The schoolteacher's portfolio: An essay on possibilities. In J. Millman & L. Darling-Hammond (Eds.), *The new handbook of teacher evaluation: Assessing elementary and secondary school teachers,* (2nd ed.; pp. 241–256). Newbury Park, CA: Sage.

Calkins, L. M. (1985). *The art of teaching writing.* Portsmouth, NH: Heinemann.

Graves, D. (1983). *Teachers and children at work.* Portsmouth, NH: Heinemann.

Shulman, L. S. (1992, April). *Portfolios in teacher education: A component of reflective teacher education.* Paper presented at the annual meeting of the American Educational Research Association, San Francisco.

Wolf, K. (1994). Teaching portfolios: Capturing the complexity of teaching. In L. Ingvarson & R. Chadborne (Eds.), *Valuing teachers' work: New directions in teacher appraisal* (pp. 112–136). Victoria: Australian Council for Educational Research.

Wolf, K., Whinery, B., & Hagerty, P. (1995). Teaching portfolios and portfolio conversations for teacher educators and teachers. *Action in Teacher Education, 17,* 30–39.

CHAPTER 7

Constructing Narratives for Understanding: Using Portfolio Interviews to Scaffold Teacher Reflection

Nona Lyons

UNIVERSITY OF SOUTHERN MAINE

The young woman, Martha Martinez, had just completed a semester of student teaching. Invited to participate in an interview, to talk about her experience of learning to teach, she had come to the interview with artifacts as well as experiences she considered markers of her own development as a teacher—entries for a teaching portfolio. Later, Martha reflected on this "portfolio" experience.

> The idea of putting together this portfolio helped me . . . organize my thoughts and organize what the experience of student teaching was . . . to sort of put these things down and to be able to have a reason to put something into the portfolio, to play that through your mind. . . . "Okay, this does fit in. This doesn't fit in, because it's interesting, but it didn't really contribute to my overall feelings about teaching . . . and growth in teaching." That sort of thing.

In a second interview and, importantly, after she had read the transcript of her first interview, Martha distinguishes between putting a portfolio together and the conversation of the portfolio interview. She discussed the surprising discoveries she made about herself as a teacher.

> As I was looking through the interview transcripts, what came to me—sort of the overall big idea—was that the content of the portfolio itself really showed the *how* of my student teaching experience: how I went about things, how people saw what I did, how I viewed what other people did and more or less the mechanics of things. And those seem to be what we get to talk about in our classes. . . . Sort of on the *how* level.
>
> Through the [interview] . . . I was able to get to the *why* of my teaching, because it's that level that we never seem to get to in the classroom. . . . In the portfolio interview we got to more of a personal teaching philosophy. . . . And that was interesting for me to see because I really never thought of myself as having a personal teaching philosophy.

Martha went on to elaborate elements of this philosophy.

> It struck me that the things that I found important [in our conversation] are the things that I would call the cornerstone of whatever my personal teaching philosophy is. [For example] . . . talking about the importance of culture and how it affects what I do in the classroom and how I think it would affect any teacher in thinking about the culture of the class. [Or] talking about sharing information with the students. That was another thing we talked a lot about [in the interview]. The teacher shouldn't always present things as "this is the right way," but should allow students to have their opinion, to make it more of an uncertain thing. That learning is a process of uncertainty. . . . And I think this is an important cornerstone of what I believe in.
>
> These things sort of struck me. I knew that I have thought about [them], but to put it all together and say this package is what I think teaching should be, that was very important.

Thus, Martha finds in a conversation an opportunity to look at and reflect on her experiences, to go beyond the entries of her portfolio, to see and make connections about her teaching, her students' learning, and her growth and development as a reflective practitioner.

When in the late 1980s school reformers at last realized that there could be no school renewal without the reform of teacher education, there was little agreement about how reform should take place. There was, however, a clear consensus that teachers had to be educated to be reflective practitioners. Without the ability to reflect, to be able to see and interrogate their practices, to question their own learning and that of their students, teachers would never be willing or able to relinquish a role as tellers and join their students as collaborators in constructing knowledge.

The idea of reflective practice as a goal for teacher education was not new. John Dewey articulated the concept earlier in the twentieth century and it gained renewed currency in the 1980s through the work of Donald Schön. Across North American, teacher educators took up the challenge to make reflection a goal of teacher education programs. In the 1990s as new modes of teacher assessment were developed, especially portfolios and other performance assessments generated by Lee Shulman's research and the work of the National Board for Professional Teaching Standards, the ability to engage in reflective practice became an increasingly important skill that both new and experienced teachers needed to demonstrate. Constructing a teaching portfolio became one possible mode to demonstrate that skill. However, as reports of the efforts to educate teachers in reflective practice began to reach scholarly journals and conference tables, a puzzle emerged.

Reflection was not uniformly achieved. Indeed, while some teachers grasped the idea, it seemed to elude others. In 1995, the National Board for Professional Teaching Standards reported results of the first round of portfolio reviews for Board certification. They revealed that experienced teachers found constructing a teaching portfolio one of the most profound reflective experiences of their careers. Simultaneously, the Board reported, these teachers had trouble making distinctions among description, analysis, and reflection (Baratz-Snowden, 1995). Similar findings are confirmed by teacher educators of beginning teachers. This contradictory feedback raises compelling questions: What enables some teachers to engage in reflective practice while others are unable to do so? How—if at all—do culture, epistemology, learning style, or developmental stage affect one's ability to demonstrate reflection? Can reflection be taught? How? In what circumstances? What is the role of the portfolio? Finally, what meaning do teacher interns themselves make of their experience of learning to be reflective practitioners?

A review of the research on reflection reveals that reflective practice is defined in a variety of ways and employed in teacher education programs with equal diversity (see Clarke, 1995; Grimmett, Erickson, Mac Kinnon, & Riecken, 1990; La Boskey, 1994; Zeichner & Liston, 1987). Most of these definitions have been influenced by the work of Dewey or

Schön. Dewey (1933) believed that reflective thinking involves: "(1) a state of doubt, hesitation, perplexity, mental difficulty, in which thinking originates, and (2) an act of searching, hunting, inquiring, to find material that will resolve the doubt, settle and dispose of the perplexity" (p. 12). Reflective thinking for Dewey is "deliberation," a kind of thinking close to scientific thinking. For Schön (1983, 1987, 1991), thought is embodied in action. Reflective practice comes into play in thinking in action, calling up all previous knowledge to address the particular situation of practice. There also can be reflection on action, but, for Schön, reflection may not necessarily involve problem solving. Schön eschews a notion prevalent in teacher education, that rational processes and universal laws can guide teaching practice. Both Dewey and Schön view the world of practice as a world of "complex, unstable, uncertain and conflictual" practice. Inquiry into this world must be carried on in it. Context and setting are critical.

For some, Schön's idea of "knowledge-in-action" and Dewey's idea of "deliberation" have become critical conceptual components for thinking about the education of teachers and the knowledge of reflection. For others, they have become points of departure. Yinger (1990) sees reflection as "contemplation"; Fenstermacher (1988) describes it as "practical arguments"; and, Zeichner and Liston (1987) emphasize "values and morals." In experiments with teaching Schön's ideas, some refinements have emerged. Most recently Anthony Clarke (1995) argues that mentors of teachers do not always act in quite the modal ways Schön describes. Clarke reports that reflection is not found in the course of a single incident or conversation, as Schön suggests. Rather, for student teachers, reflection is born of incidents thematic in nature, occurring over long periods of time, "interwoven across multiple classroom and personal interaction contexts" (Clarke, 1995, p. 259). There are two significant points in this research: the focus on reflection occurring over time, rather than in a single incident and/or context; and the focus on the student teachers and their own construction of meaning.

This chapter explores the usefulness of a portfolio interview as one mode of fostering teacher reflection. It supports Clarke's idea of reflection as thematic constructions of meaning taking place over time and drawn from multiple experiences. It also points to a refined conception of reflection: that is, that reflection ought to be considered as a drawing together of long strands of connections, the weaving together of experiences, theory, and practices into meaning for the individual teacher and a kind of construction of knowledge— a knowledge of teaching practice.

When I initiated this project using portfolios in teacher education, I intended to focus more generally on the portfolio as a method for assessing beginning teachers' professional development. The project began in the early 1990s with a series of interviews with teacher interns who constructed and then presented their portfolios. But over time, as the interviews accumulated, my focus shifted to the interview itself. It seemed that something important was emerging in the interview process. Through the narratives teachers told of their teaching experiences, and then through their comments and reflections on the portfolio process itself, these new teachers were articulating the meaning of their experiences. This usually occurred in a two-step process: the presentation of the portfolio and the discussion of it in an interview, which was tape-recorded; and, then, reading or listening to the transcripts and engaging in a second interview. What became significant to me as a teacher educator was that it seemed in this process teachers were simultaneously constructing the meanings of their experiences and making them available for their own learning—and, importantly, for their teacher educators as well.

This chapter presents examples of this process. It first describes the experience of one teacher to illustrate how the portfolio interview structured a conversation about the teacher's own learning. Then the experiences of other teacher interns are presented. Finally, the chapter considers implications that follow from this work: for refining a conception of teacher reflection; for considering the portfolio interview both as an instrument of assessment and a scaffolding for learning; and for the use of narrative in the portfolio interview process as a mode of knowing, given the narrative nature of the stories teachers tell in portfolio interviews and the role of narrative in the construction of knowledge (Bruner, 1986; Coles, 1989; Connelly & Clandinin, 1990; Elbaz, 1983; Mishler, 1990; Mitchell, 1981; Polkinghorne, 1988; Witherell & Noddings, 1991). Indeed, the data presented here suggest that without the portfolio interview—also called the reflective interview—some significant aspects of teachers' knowledge of practice, and their ways of constructing it, might remain hidden from view.

THE PORTFOLIO INTERVIEW: THE CASE OF MARTHA MARTINEZ

To illustrate the way in which the dialogue around a portfolio interview becomes a moment of reflection for an apprentice teacher, consider the case of the young woman, Martha Martinez, introduced earlier. In the course of a series of portfolio interviews, 24-year-old Martha Martinez presented several observations about her experiences as an intern teacher, ones that at times were surprising to her. Three incidents were particularly powerful. One already presented was her way of thinking about her teaching philosophy, her concern that students see learning as a process of uncertainty and not assume there are only right answers to questions. Another involved an instance of how Martha linked theory and practice; and a third concerned how her own cultural background, her Mexican-American heritage, was a part of who she is as a teacher.

This last, critical discovery came in midyear at the end of a semester of student teaching. Reflecting on how she describes herself as a teacher, Martha begins by characterizing herself as "formal." But it is only in elaborating this idea that she connects this description of herself to her own cultural background and then reveals how that, in turn, influences her teaching.

> I'd describe myself I guess as pretty formal in terms of the way I run a class and in terms of the way I go about doing things in class. I think I much more follow sort of an established pattern than other people that I know, even in this program, who are sort of more free-spirited and willing to try experimental ways of running a classroom. And I think that's just because I feel more comfortable being formal. I mean I still think that within those lines of formality we can do a number of things but I *don't* think I'd feel very comfortable trying something completely different, until maybe I got the hang of it. And I think that has to do with the way I was brought up. . . . And I think it also has to do a lot with culture. Coming from a Mexican-American background, things follow a very formal pattern. And to stray from that formality depending on the situation, can show a sign of disrespect. Or can show that you're sort of leaving the culture. And so being brought up in that environment, we always learned that there's a certain way you do things and that's the way you do them. And so that's sort of been drilled into me. And to stray from that, for me, would feel like I was trying to be something that I'm not. It would be sort of assimilating in a way that I wouldn't feel comfortable assimilating.

For Martha, her way of being in the classroom is not arbitrary. It is a part of who she is, deeply connected to her sense of herself, her past, and her culture. Although observed in her student teaching and characterized in reports as "formal," the deeper connection to her own personal, cultural identity may have been unknown to her supervisors. It also seems it became available to Martha herself through the discovery of her teaching philosophy. In her portfolio interview, Martha identified how culture affects "what I do in the classroom" and her belief that it would affect any teacher in thinking about the culture of her class. That such an important aspect of who she is as a teacher could have remained hidden is curious in its own right. But its importance in how a teacher experiences other aspects of her teacher education is significant to understand. Visiting an out-of-state high school to observe classes, Martha comments on her observations of a class.

> It was a great class, but it seemed very white to me in the way that it was being run. And I didn't mean that as a bad thing. I just meant it as an observation. . . . It wasn't a classroom [setting], it was just a very comfortable looking room . . . and the students were on the floor and in the chairs and sort of flopped around. But the discussion was very on-task, a very high level of discussion. It was very intellectual and I wrote down all these things. But I said, just the way that this is set up . . . the casualness of it. It said to me that seems like a very light way of teaching because a person of color would be more formal in the presentation. Because usually just coming from those cultures, that's the way we're brought up, to be formal. School is a formal place and so you present things in a fuller way. And I think that people sometimes put value judgments on those things. Like one way is better than the other or worse than the other. And I don't want to do that, I mean because there was certainly a very good conversation going on, and many colleges function that way. But it's not the way I would do it.

Martha Martinez thus finds that her cultural background influences her understanding of her own and others' classroom practices.

DISCOVERIES OF THE INTERVIEW

The Developing Teacher's Sense of Self and Cultural Background

Although Martha Martinez never found a place to discuss her cultural background in her teacher education classes, these issues became connected to her own teaching. When Martha entered an all-white junior high school for her student teaching, she found herself surprised.

> I had never been in a school before that was so much, it was just so white. I walked into my classroom and I probably had this look

of shock on my face because of everybody there. And they had the
same look when they looked at me, like "Who are you?"

And so it became very clear to me that all these students came
from a certain sort of background, that I might not be as familiar
with as someone else. But I never felt uncomfortable with it, and I
don't think they ever felt uncomfortable with me. I tried to make
them feel very open about talking about things like that, if they
wanted to, and at one point they asked, "Well, just what are you?"
And whenever I tell people that story some people say, "Oh, that's
awful that they didn't know what ethnicity you were." Well, given
where they lived, how are they going to know? But I actually felt
good that they felt comfortable enough to ask. And that they were
honest enough about it to ask, and that when I told them that,
they were curious, they wanted to know more and that made me
see it as a positive experience.

Another student, Ramon Hildago, also talked about his working-
class and Costa Rican cultural backgrounds and how these entered into
his sense of self as a teacher. Commenting in his portfolio interview
about his student teaching, he talks about his own learning as a highlight
of student teaching.

How much I learned—not so much about them [the students] but
about myself . . . it sounds selfish in a way. But every teacher
wants to communicate with the students and I felt [in doing my
student teaching] as if I really have had a true test because of my
background. I know a lot of [my high school] students grew up in
a similar [situation to mine] . . . so this was really a test of whether
I had forgotten my past, so to speak, or whether that was still
there, you know, and [whether I would only be seen as a university
student, which I am]. . . . I found out that I do have something valuable and *that* was valuable. So knowing that about myself . . .
that really changed things around and made me realize that these
students had that there too . . . something valuable in their culture. [But] that's what made it so difficult in the beginning [of student teaching]. It wasn't just your teaching methods that may have
failed . . . *but also I'm talking about my past being irrelevant here, you
know.*

Cultural and social heritage that interacts with who the teacher is,
may be hidden in the ordinary ways teacher educators know their student teachers. Yet this heritage lies at the core of who a teacher is and

will become. The vulnerability of the self so clearly involved at all stages of teaching, yet little documented, may be greatest at the beginning of one's career, difficult to untangle, yet in need of understanding.

Connecting Theory and Practice

Other aspects of the experience of new teachers similarly became available to students through the portfolio interview. Returning once again to Martha Martinez, she recalls how in one instance she came to connect theory to practice.

> The other thing that struck me about the portfolio, not just the portfolio but the reflection on it, was that it gave me a chance to bridge practice and theory. I think teachers are so tied to practical things in their day-to-day [experiences that they are] not as tied to studying other theories or even theorizing about what they are doing.

Martha elaborates an example:

> As I was looking at things [in the portfolio] and putting things together, it reminded me of certain readings I had already done either in psychology or methods classes. And at the time that I read those articles, they did not have a great deal of meaning for me because there was nothing I could attach them to. My mind works more like a teacher than a researcher in that I think more in terms of the practical. But by looking at these [interview transcripts], I said, "This is like an article I read. It said that these things can happen . . ." One example would be [discussions] about moral development in [my psychology class]. [The professor] in my class was talking about stages of moral development. I couldn't even tell you the names of the authors who wrote the articles, but they were about how children at different ages are at different stages of moral development.
>
> At the time we read those things, . . . I found them interesting but couldn't place [them] in any framework. And I found that frustrating.
>
> But going on to student teaching—first of all, I was with two different age groups—different stages. Eighth graders are 13 years old and they are just starting the real pains of adolescence and I was with tenth graders who ranged from 14 to 18. And in that

one class I got to see a range of levels. And then what was in those articles started to make sense to me.

And the whole incident with my tenth-grade class, having the class fall apart. Well, the class did fall apart but the class is made up of individual students. And talk about any given, individual student, I think they would all be at different levels of development. And part of the difficulty in teaching that kind of a class is trying to address all of those levels. And I didn't know how to do it at first. And I took full responsibility upon myself and I said I have to meet everyone's needs in some original way and it would work. And I finally decided, "No." The students are a source of help in this case and they should be responsible for some of their development. And I sort of oversee the whole thing.

Some of the problems of the class could have stemmed from the fact that in not succeeding in helping different people in whatever stage they were at, I was not helping anyone. And particularly with this group of students, they are not very patient. They are in school because they have to be. They are not very happy about it. And their experience in school has not been good. So unless we can catch them and say we can make this experience, this 45 minutes in class a good experience, it is not going to work.

Well, [in reviewing the portfolio interviews] that just brought all the ideas of moral development to mind, not when it was happening but when I was reading over the interview. That's when that came to me.

This kind of connection happened for the intern only after the event, not in the heat of a crisis when things fell apart. Only after the event—one Martha did successfully rescue—and after telling the story of what had happened and then seeing it in the written transcript, does the connection take place. Then Martha sees how the idea of different stages of development offers an interpretive lens for a puzzling, nearly disastrous experience. She sees too the real dilemma of a teacher trying to meet the range of developmental needs of students 14 to 18 years of age. But these discoveries come only through her reflections. Another student teacher offers a hypothesis of why this may be so.

There is a tension built into student teaching. You must do so much of the mechanical stuff. But the learning that you want to come from student teaching can't come at that time. In the blitz-krieg of the teaching experience—dealing with teachers, students—you cannot get perspective on it. It is almost impossible to integrate, to be reflective. I've done a lot more thinking since that time. The Wednesday afternoon seminar—Analysis of Teaching—was one little respite during student teaching. One chance to sit back. But it was only 2 hours a week. [And] you need to be reflective. . . . In student teaching we are so busy with the minutiae of it all—and it is so difficult to draw back from what seems so important; from the lessons you need to write, from the kids you see each day but can't really get to know.

Thus it may be that a certain kind of reflection can happen only after an event. These students demonstrate that the portfolio interview raises important issues and suggest, too, that it allows them to draw together these experiences, their interpretive frameworks of theory as they construct tentative hypotheses about their actual teaching practices. They suggest, too, that this kind of reflection may not even be possible at the time of student teaching. Or that may depend on the nature of the student's experience of learning to teach and the opportunities to develop as a reflective practitioner.

Uncovering the Ethical Dimensions of Teaching

Finally, student reflections suggest one other observation: The happenings of a class are intricately connected to a teacher's ethical sense, to what counts as good or bad, right or wrong. Martha presented an example in her discussion of her tenth-grade class, the class that fell apart. The incident happened shortly after the start of her student teaching. The tenth-grade students, characterized by a tracking system as having minimal abilities, had been increasingly disruptive, calling each other names and interrupting the flow of classroom work. Things reached a head one day for Martha when her cooperating teacher walked out of the classroom because she was so angry with the rudeness of the students. Martha took radical action, reprimanding her students and managing to make the class work. We listen to Martha tell of the failure she encountered with this class and of her construction of its meaning.

At the lowest point, I felt that I was failing them, certainly I wasn't giving them anything to learn. They weren't helping, but I had to take some of the blame. And I was failing myself because I felt I could be better than that and I wasn't doing something right. I don't think anyone could have told me what was the right thing to do. I had to find that myself, and it took me a while to do it, it

took until it almost reached a crisis point for me to find it. But
I did.

What is immediately apparent is the ethical language the teacher
uses: the "oughts," the quest for something "right." The teacher finds a
moral dilemma in the very interactions of learning about her students,
her own actions as a teacher, and her beliefs about her students. She
characterizes these beliefs and their impact on her and her class:
"Towards the end I was thinking that whatever I gave them to do, they
wouldn't be able to do, so why try it. . . . They had already painted
themselves as failures, and I had sort of painted them as failures as well
and sort of painted myself as a failure as well. And we were going down
together." When asked if this situation presented itself as an ethical issue,
she responds:

> I do see it as that to the extent I wonder if it is right for the
> teacher to make those assumptions. On the one hand you can't
> help but make those assumptions when you come into that kind of
> situation and see that the kids are not willing to help themselves
> out of their predicament. On the other hand, it just leads to the
> whole issue of self-fulfilling prophecies. If you act like failures, and
> I see you act like failures, and then you see that I see you act like
> failures, you will be failures.
> *The real question for me . . . is if I were to walk into a classroom like*
> *that again, how would I approach [it], get these students to learn, and not*
> *only learn material, but to come away with a sense of self-esteem, that they*
> *can learn.*

Remarkably, what Martha questions here is not the abilities of her
students but the harm her own assumptions about their abilities may
bring to them. For the teacher, the development of her students is
central.

Ethical dimensions of teaching are so daily and so intricately tied to
teachers' work. Yet opportunities to discuss these are rare, as are frameworks for interpretation. Most educational delineations of the ethical
are in terms of rights and fairness—rights or responsibilities, the central
concepts of an ethic of justice. But the ethical dilemma in the situation
reported here comes from issues of the good and of the centrality of the
relationship of student and teacher to each other, and concerns about
harm. These notions of care and harm in one's relationships, including
those with students, are central concepts of an ethic of care, one that
is not always identified in the education of teachers and needs to be

(Lyons, 1983, 1990; Noddings, 1986). The language of the ethical underscores the personal values of the teacher and how easily and daily ethical dilemmas may be encountered by a teacher in enacting teaching practices (Lyons, 1990).

Using Reflection to Change One's Practices

What begins to come into focus in considering the experiences of Martha Martinez and the other student teachers is that what they are about is nothing less than authoring their own learning and professional development. Armed with the insights of reflection, seeing the implications their own beliefs have to influence their students, they shape and reshape their practices over the course of their professional experiences. Ideals, values that come into focus in a portfolio interview are carried across time and space.

One example comes from Martha Martinez. In the second year of her teaching, Martha confronted a situation eerily like her student teaching experience. She was again asked to teach a low-tracked class. This time, however, she was determined "not to make those assumptions about the students that I had made about the class that failed during my student teaching." Recalling that "in the last portfolio interview, we talked about making judgments on kids, I determined to go into that class assuming that these students can succeed and that I would go down fighting to make that happen."

> So I thought this time I'm going to do it differently, I'm not going to have those assumptions. I'm going to go in just like I would with my other two classes, with a very upbeat, positive attitude and say, "These kids can do something and whatever it is, we're going to do it. We'll find a way to do it."

Happily, Martha reports that the class did succeed. This teacher, drawing long strands of connections between her experiences of student teaching, her understanding of her teaching philosophy, and the existential situation she encountered in a new school and with a new class, tailored her practice to the needs of a particular group of students and found success. Clearly, the teacher is in command of her developing learning. Thus, through a process of reflection on her own experience, begun with a portfolio interview, carried over across 2 years, Martha Martinez scaffolds her own practice and her professional development.

IMPLICATIONS

Several implications emerge from this work. The first concerns the concept of reflection. Reflective thinking has been conceptualized largely as the justification of teachers' actions, of giving why's, of offering reasons, rationales. The work of Schön (1983, 1987) and Fenstermacher's (1988) and Zeichner's (1991) critical reviews point to this conception of teachers' reflective practice. But the interviews presented here suggest that reflective thinking—as Clarke's (1995) research indicates—is more like a weaving, a threading together of experience, of making connections. This construction of meaning is in part directly in the service of making conscious a teacher's knowledge of practice—a teaching philosophy, the sociopolitical or cultural contexts that influence the understanding of teaching or learning, and the understanding that the ethical may be a daily aspect of teaching. This takes place over time. Thus, this work suggests that a more adequate definition of teacher reflection needs to include these dimensions.

Second, reflection on practice needs a scaffold; it may always need a scaffold. The portfolio interview may usefully provide one kind of scaffolding. The two-step process offers a way to organize for reflection: first through constructing and presenting the portfolio, selecting entries, and presenting the portfolio evidence; and then, in a second interview, reflecting on the portfolio process, saying what meaning one gives to the experiences of learning to teach. A review of interview transcripts is one method that can facilitate this process. The process of reflection, usually coming at the end of student teaching or an internship in learning to teach, looks both backward and forward: backward by weaving together a knowledge of what one has learned; and forward through a new consciousness of one's goals and purposes for teaching and student learning.

This process can be costly in both time and money. Interviews need to be conducted. Taped interviews need to be transcribed. But there may be alternatives. Most recently, a post-portfolio interview tape was used alone without the transcript analysis. It appeared equally important in revealing the process of constructing meaning for interns. This work also makes clear that the portfolio development process alone does not reveal the process of meaning making. As Martha Martinez articulated, it reveals how the teacher intern approaches things. Only in reflecting on "why" may a person's own interpretation of meaning be made evident.

Third, narratives may constitute the critical element of the portfolio process. What are teachers learning when they tell the stories of their experiences, when they construct the narratives of their professional lives as they do in portfolio interviews? Teachers use narratives frequently in their discussion of teaching practice. What role does narrative itself play?

Psychologist Jerome Bruner offers one way of thinking about this. Bruner argues that there are two modes of knowing: the more traditionally acknowledged "paradigmatic" or logical-scientific mode; and a narrative mode. Bruner (1985) characterizes the differences between the two as irreducible.

> Each also provides ways of organizing representation in memory and of filtering the perceptual world. Efforts to reduce one mode to the other or to ignore one at the expense of the other inevitably fail to capture the rich ways in which people "know" and describe events around them. As Rorty has recently put it, one mode is centered around the narrow epistemological question of how to know the truth; the other around the broader and more inclusive question of the meaning of experience.
>
> The imaginative application of the paradigmatic mode leads to good theory, that is, logical proof, and empirical discovery guided by reasoned hypothesis. The imaginative application of the narrative mode leads instead to good stories, gripping drama, believable historical accounts. It deals in human or human-like intention and action and the vicissitudes and consequences that mark their course. It is essentially temporal rather than timeless. And we know much less about it. (pp. 97–98)

Bruner identifies two aspects of narrative knowing: the focus in narrative on the dual landscape of action and of consciousness. These two compelling aspects of narrative may be what makes the portfolio interview important to teacher educators. The stories teachers tell in the portfolio presentation narrating the events of their experiences seem to make possible several things: They create texts that bring things into view—one's actions and values, what is important in teaching—and they bring into consciousness the teacher's own beliefs, ones he or she may have acted upon even subconsciously—for example, that a teaching philosophy ought to involve student opinion, that learning is a process of uncertainty, that there is not one right way. Through the reflective portfolio interview, these insights and learnings become accessible both to the teachers and, importantly, to their teacher educators.

Narrative may well have another importance connected to teaching, portfolio making, and understanding the construction of teacher knowledge. Narrative—story—carries both events and the interpretation of their author's meanings. Portfolios are filled with the evidence of the events of lives in classrooms. Interpretation, at the heart of the portfolio-making process, is also intricately a part of teaching and assessing what one has learned. Teaching is a supremely interpretive activity taking place on many levels: in determining how children will learn a particular subject, how a subject needs to be presented, and so forth. To the degree that portfolios mirror teaching, portfolio making is also an interpretive act. What one puts into a portfolio is, as Lee Shulman argues in Chapter 2, a theoretical act, an act defining one's assumptions about teaching or learning.

The work presented here offers a preliminary set of observations, ones that seem important to pursue in a next round of research. Of particular interest is the idea that reflection of one kind seems like making long strands of connections. These interviews also suggest that in constructing narratives, telling the stories of practice, conversation and dialogue are significant to the reflective process. The role of the listener comes into play. A teller always needs a listener. But in this case the listener also engages in the dialogue. In the conversation, both speaker and listener find new meanings. Indeed, some researchers argue that one can never understand the meaning or the nature of the kind of knowledge revealed except by considering the relationship between interviewer and interviewee, between a teller and a listener, and the dialogue of the two (see Freeman, 1996; Mishler, 1990).

REFERENCES

Baratz-Snowden, J. (1995, April). *Towards a coherent vision of teacher development.* Paper presented at the annual meeting of the American Educational Research Association, San Francisco.

Bruner, J. (1985). Narrative and paradigmatic modes of thought. In E. Eisner (Ed.), *Learning and teaching the ways of knowing* (pp. 97–117). Chicago: National Society for the Study of Education.

Bruner, J. (1986). *Actual minds, possible worlds.* Cambridge, MA: Harvard University Press.

Clarke, A.(1995). Professional development in practicum settings: Reflective practice under scrutiny. *Teaching and Teacher Education, 11,*(3), 243–261.

Coles, R. (1989). *The call of stories: Teaching and the moral imagination.* Boston: Houghton Mifflin.

Connelly, F. M., & Clandinin, D. J. (1990). Stories of experience and narrative inquiry. *Educational Researcher, 19*(5), 2–14.

Dewey, J. (1933). *How we think: A restatement of the relation of reflective thinking to the educative process.* Chicago: Henry Regnery.

Elbaz, F. (1983). *Teacher thinking: A study of practical knowledge.* London: Croom Helm.

Fenstermacher, G. (1988). The place of science and epistemology in Schön's conception of reflective practice. In P. Grimmett & G. Erickson (Eds.), *Reflection in teacher education.* New York: Teachers College Press.

Freeman, D. (1996). "To take them at their word": Language data in the study of teachers' knowledge. *Harvard Educational Review, 66*(4), 732–761.

Grimmett, P., Erickson, G., Mac Kinnon, A., & Riecken, T. (1990). Reflective practice in teacher education. In R. Clift, R. Houston, & M. Pugach (Eds.), *Encouraging reflective practice in education* (pp. 20–38). New York: Teachers College Press.

Interstate New Teacher Assessment and Support Consortium. (1995). *Next steps: Moving toward performance-based licensing in teaching.* Washington, DC: Author.

La Boskey, V. K. (1994). *Development of reflective practice.* New York: Teachers College Press.

Lyons, N. (1983). Two perspectives: On self, relationships and morality. *Harvard Educational Review, 53,* 125–145.

Lyons, N. (1990). Dilemmas of knowing: Ethical and epistemological dimensions of teachers' work and development. *Harvard Educational Review, 60,* 159–180.

Mishler, E. (1990). Validation in inquiry-guided research: The role of exemplars in narrative studies. *Harvard Educational Review, 60,* 415–442.

Mitchell, W. J. T. (Ed.). (1981). *On narrative.* Chicago: University of Chicago Press.

Noddings, N. (1986). Fidelity in teaching, teacher education, and research for teaching. *Harvard Educational Review, 56,* 496–510.

Polkinghorne, D. E. (1988). *Narrative knowing and the human sciences.* Albany: State University of New York Press.

Schön, D. (1983). *The reflective practitioner: How professionals think in action.* New York: Basic Books.

Schön, D. (1987). *Educating the reflective practitioner: Towards a new design for teaching and learning in the professions.* San Francisco: Jossey-Bass.

Schön, D. (1991). *The reflective turn: Case studies in and on educational practice.* New York: Teachers College Press.

Witherell, C., & Noddings, N. (1991). *Stories lives tell: Narrative and dialogue in education.* New York: Teachers College Press.

Yinger, R. Y. (1990). The conversation of practice. In R. Clift, R. Houston, & M. Pugach (Eds.), *Encouraging reflective practice in education,* (pp. 72–94). New York: Teachers College Press.

Zeichner, K. (1991, April). *Conceptions of reflective teaching in contemporary U.S. teacher education program reform.* Paper presented at the annual meeting of the American Educational Research Association, Chicago.

Zeichner, K., & Liston, D. (1987). Teaching student teachers to reflect. *Harvard Educational Review, 57,* 23–48.

PART III

The Tensions: Portfolios for Professional Development or for Assessment?

PORTFOLIO PARADOXES, PORTFOLIO POLARITIES

In the adaptation of portfolios by different communities of practice, tensions emerge. A central one, well-documented in this book, appears repeatedly: whether to consider portfolios primarily for professional development or for teacher evaluation.

Each chapter in this part of the book addresses this issue and responds to it, often in profoundly different ways. Faculty at the University of California at Santa Barbara cast the problem as a question: Are portfolios to be thought of as technical or transformational? These teacher educators resolve the tension by asking their students to create two portfolios: one for high stakes certification purposes and one for the student's own development. Teachers in the Everett, Massachusetts schools view the construction of portfolios solely in the service of teacher professionalism. To cast portfolios as a means of teacher assessment, they feel, would constitute a violation of the possibilities of portfolios to promote teacher development.

The possibilities for ongoing professional development initiated by a portfolio process are traced over time by Grace Grant and Tracy Huebner. These researchers follow teacher interns through their first years of teaching to examine the usefulness of a portfolio question that structured their self-directed inquiries about teaching and learning. Larry Cuban looks at the portfolio process he put in place with his university colleagues in the unique case he made for a post-tenure review of his professional development.

The tensions surrounding these issues are not easily resolved. But there have been transformations. One teacher educator came to see that portfolios could be both celebratory of personal development and used simultaneously for determining high stakes certification: The tension dissolved. But the more likely scenario for the future is that tensions will remain, resolved only by portfolio users and their judges.

CHAPTER 8

Portfolios in Teacher Education: Technical or Transformational?

Jon Snyder

Ann Lippincott

Doug Bower

UNIVERSITY OF CALIFORNIA, SANTA BARBARA

Educators of teachers have two essential ethical and legal responsibilities. One is to support the development of the teachers (pre- and in-service) with whom they work; the other, to ensure the integrity of their programs for the competency accrediting and credentialing purposes. The two responsibilities create inherent tensions.

The tension between support and accountability in teacher education is manifested in the increasing use of portfolios as an assessment tool. On the one hand, portfolios are used as developmental reflective tools to engage teachers in sustained and rigorous inquiry into their own professional growth. On the other hand, portfolios increasingly are being used to evaluate a candidate's ability to meet licensure standards. Thus, portfolio assessment is being used both to support learning and to evaluate it—as a transformational tool and as a technical tool.

This chapter addresses the tension that arises from these dual functions. As one student teacher questioned, "Is this for my growth as a student teacher or is this for the program's purposes to say to the state, 'Yeah, these guys should get a credential'?"

The context of the study is the Teacher Education Program at the University of California at Santa Barbara (UCSB), an institution with approximately 100 candidates each year for elementary, bilingual, and secondary teaching credentials. This fifth-year, postbaccalaureate program also provides the option of receiving a master's degree in conjunction with professional preparation. The program recognizes the competing needs embodied in the use of portfolios. The first is a response to external pressure for better assessments to increase the probability of responsible and responsive practice (Darling-Hammond & Snyder, 1992). Portfolios offer the promise of a more appropriate authentic performance assessment (Tierney, 1992) with an increased degree of consequential validity (Messick, 1989). Thus, the UCSB teacher education program requires a portfolio documenting the successful initial attainment of the standards of teaching codified in state credentialing requirements—the credential portfolio. Simultaneously, the UCSB Teacher Education Program uses portfolios to meet the needs of students and of the program itself. To meet this function, the program requires an "issue" portfolio, with a student-selected focus, as the culminating experience for a Master's of Education degree. This M.Ed. portfolio is a 12–24 month piece of work designed to be a developmentally appropriate tool for ongoing reflection to support professional growth and in-course feedback for programmatic decisions (Grant, 1994; Lichtenstein, Rubin & Grant, 1992).

Thus, the M.Ed. portfolio is designed to encourage reflection on individual practice, focusing on the growth process over time to support the candidate's ability to "learn from teaching." The credential portfolio, starting with externally defined standards, tends to be a collection of artifacts that portray one's work in its most glorious light (e.g., "proving" that the candidate has demonstrated competence on state-defined teacher standards). The fear among some UCSB teacher educators, however, is that "proving" one's competence may supersede the use of a portfolio as a workspace charting the growth of a teacher through honest reflections on the struggles and inevitable failures common to the learning process. We wonder if the portfolio's use as a summative evaluation overrides its use as a strategy and process to make visible one's own practice for the purpose of reflection and inquiry. Can both external and internal needs be met simultaneously, and, if not, what is lost? Have we set up, in the words of a cooperating teacher, "a glorious expectation that none of them can live out"?

METHODOLOGY

The data to analyze this question have been collected over 2 years. We followed two cohorts of student teachers through their professional preparation year and, with a sample of 18 candidates, into their first year of teaching. Data have been collected from interviews with preservice teachers, from first-year teachers who graduated with the first cohort group, from Teacher Education Program faculty, and from school site personnel involved in the design and instruction of preservice teachers. Additionally, portfolios and their contents have been analyzed.

Initial analysis organized data into the naturally occurring categories of "credential portfolios" and "issue/M.Ed. portfolios." Those categories then were further analyzed using constant comparative and discrepancy analysis techniques until the information was distilled into the findings presented. This level of analysis resulted in the abandonment of the original categories and the construction of new ones. Unanticipated outcomes emerged and were scrutinized—primarily by seeking verification from multiple sources and developmental levels of teachers.

Perhaps the most insightful analysis was more "practice" oriented in that over the course of the 2 years we were in the midst of an ongoing construction of the use of portfolios in the teacher education program. In effect, this kind of analysis could be called the "ready, fire, aim" technique. We would: (1) come up with a plan; (2) begin to implement it; (3) reflect on what was happening (usually in small-group discussions among college and school-based teacher educators); (4) make in-course adjustments grounded in our data-based reflections; and (5) begin the process anew.

CONTEXT

Understanding our findings requires a general overview of the process we followed. We began with solely a credential portfolio. In the first year of program-wide use of portfolios, we used the 10 outcome standards outlined by the California Commission on Teacher Credentialing (CTC), the state credentialing agency, as our criteria. We listed these 10 standards on a grid down the left side of a page. Across the top of the grid we identified the three sources of evidence (test/test-like event, observations, performance/work sample) that we *required* students to use to document their meeting of the state-defined standards. This resulted in the credential portfolio matrix presented in Figure 8.1.

Students were to collect artifacts, primarily from their professional

State Competency	test or test like event	observation	performance/ work sample
Student Rapport Classroom Environment			
Curricular and Instructional Planning Skills			
Diverse and Appropriate Teaching			
Student Motivation, Involvement, and Conduct			
Presentation Skills			
Student Diagnosis, Achievement and Evaluation			
Cognitive Outcomes of Teaching			
Affective Outcomes of Teaching			
Capacity to Teach Crossculturally			
Professional Obligations			

FIGURE 8.1. Credential Portfolio Matrix.

preparation year, documenting their satisfactory proficiency in the state standards. They had the opportunity to share their emerging portfolio contents weekly in supervisory seminar groups from September through June; in December, at the end of their limited student teaching placement, in a three-way conference with their cooperating teacher and college-based supervisor; in late January at the inception of their full-time student teaching placement in a three-way conference with their cooperating teacher and college-based supervisor; and finally in a summative evaluative format in June in a three-way conference where all three parties "signed off" on a form verifying that they agreed that the collection of artifacts provided compelling evidence that the student had met all state outcome standards. Thus, the initial purpose of our portfolio work was accountability—a better mousetrap with which to capture the knowledge, skills, and dispositions possessed by our students in order to ensure the state (and ourselves) that our students were capable of working as teachers in a responsible and responsive manner.

Embedded in the matrix are three essential conceptual assumptions. First is the notion of *multiple sources of evidence*. Test and test-like events are defined as tasks assigned by others to be completed within a set time (e.g., papers for a class, a standardized achievement test, a curriculum unit developed as an assignment in a methods and procedures class, etc.). Observations are defined as the record of what other people noted when they watched the student in action (e.g., notes from a supervisor's observations, comments from a cooperating teacher, a principal's evaluation, a colleague's notes from peer coaching observations, etc.). Performance/work samples are defined as direct evidence of a student teacher's work (e.g., videotapes of the student teacher's classroom, lesson plans/reflections actually used, student work resulting from a lesson, notes from parents, student teacher communications with families or with other school personnel, etc.). This way of thinking about multiple sources of evidence distinguishes the approach we used with the approach used from the National Board for Professional Teaching Standards (NBPTS) and others (e.g., state of Connecticut), which define what must go into a portfolio. By our definitions, because everything that enters an NBPTS portfolio is assigned by another to be completed within a set frame of time, student teachers would "fill in" only one column of our matrix. In this regard, successful NBPTS portfolios would not have met our credential portfolio requirements. While the NBPTS portfolio and our initial attempts both were primarily accountability driven, they differ in underlying notions of reliability and validity. Both models result in the making of decisions about "competence," but the NBPTS model requires candidate comparison across common tasks, an aggregative approach. The initial UCSB model, more like the academic evaluation of a dissertation, required that candidates collect, select, and reflect upon *different* tasks, an integrative approach. (See Moss, 1994, for a thorough and elucidating exposition of the distinction between the two.)

The second assumption is that accurate information for assessment purposes requires that data be collected *over time*. Teacher educators have the luxury of working with their students intimately over an extended period of time. This provides them both with "change" data as well as extensive contextual—psychological and social—knowledge. Even in our "accountability"-driven portfolios, rather than viewing this wealth of knowledge as variables to be controlled for comparative consistency, we viewed it as an advantage to assess teachers with the same caliber of context-specific information that teaching itself requires (Darling-Hammond, et al., 1993; Snyder, Chittenden, & Ellington, 1993). In our first implementation of portfolios, we countered reliability issues by having a minimum of five (two cooperating teachers, two college-based teacher educators, and the candidate) perspectives evaluating the work.

The third conceptual assumption was that, given the profound social welfare implications of preparing future teachers effectively, it was appropriate to use *externally defined categories* (e.g., state standards) as the criteria of good teaching. Because we felt it fair to our students to let them know in advance the criteria by which they would be evaluated, within the first week of the program, we provided them with the state's written explanation of the standards and engaged students in an activity to help them construct their own understandings of those standards.

Over the course of 3 years of using portfolios, the first two assumptions, with minor revisions, have proven to be powerfully useful. The third assumption, however, met with early concerns. One major concern was that externally defined categories were limiting our students' ability to construct their own sophisticated knowledge, skills, and dispositions of teaching. For example, some students' portfolios exhibited a mechanistic understanding of teaching which was inconsistent with the program's goals and often with the kind of holistic learner- and learning-centered teaching and learning the students were exhibiting in their field experiences and college assignments. The philosophical argument emerging from such disconcerting empirical data was that if we provided opportunities for thoughtful practice and practical reflection, our students would generate equally appropriate, generally consistent, higher caliber, and more personally valuable "standards" of their own.

The second major concern regarding externally defined standards was a disgruntled subtext that our work as teacher educators was being defined from afar. If the learning of K–12 students is enhanced by curriculum, teaching, and assessment designed by those with the most knowledge of the students and their contexts (Holmes Group, 1986), why does that not hold true for teacher educators?

One instructor, sensing the value of the first two assumptions but concerned with the third, created an assignment for her class that she labeled an "issue portfolio." The issue portfolio kept the "multiple sources collected over time" components but eliminated the external standards and the mechanistic tendencies of the credential portfolio grid. Students chose their own issue, related to bilingual education, the course in which the assignment was made, and documented their growth in knowledge and practice about their issue. Because the bilingual course is a year-long sequence of three courses and because most of the artifacts used had already been collected for the credential portfolio, the notion of multiple sources of evidence collected over time was

built into the structure without the "checklist" potential of the externally imposed credential portfolio grid. While the issue portfolios were
not of universally exceptional quality, enough of them were, to suggest
there might be something to the idea. They provided justification and
motivation to pursue portfolios growing out of the student teachers' own
issues and passions.

Lengthy and occasionally heated conversations among program faculty, coupled with the development of a combined masters/credential
program of study, led us to require *both* the credential portfolio and the
M.Ed. portfolio. The credential portfolio remained essentially as outlined above, with the major difference being a "strong permission" from
program faculty to organize the portfolio starting with "life" rather than
with the 10 standards. Students were asked to choose a teaching episode
and trace it from the initial idea and its source, into the classroom dance,
through to the assessment of student work and professional reflection.
Students documented the episode by selecting artifacts from the three
sources of evidence. They then located examples of the 10 standards
and how they were exhibited in the students' teaching as well as how
they interrelated with each other.

In addition to the credential portfolio, student teachers are required
to develop an M.Ed. portfolio as the culmination of the masters program of study. The M.Ed. portfolio is basically an "issue portfolio" developed over the course of at least 11 months. Early in their professional
preparation year (August), students take an ethnography course to begin
developing their ability to "collect data" in natural settings. By December, most students have identified an inchoate passion about some element of teaching and learning. In January students are released from all
school and college responsibilities for a week to "pursue their passion."
They identify their passion, explain how they will spend their week to
further their understanding of their passion, and determine how they
will share their learnings from the week. From January through March,
through a series of workshops and field-based experiences, students refine and focus their passion—moving between abstract questioning and
reflecting upon the concrete artifacts they have been collecting in their
field experiences and in their coursework. By March, students form self-
selected support groups and are assigned a facilitator. These support
groups meet regularly with the purpose of informing and being informed by each other of their thinking/practice regarding *their* issue and
the evidence they have selected to document their growth over time. In
the summer (June/July) following their full-time student teaching experience, students complete their M.Ed. portfolio.

Successful completion of the M.Ed. portfolio consists of two checkpoints. First, the group facilitator and every member of the support group must approve the document. Once the document has been approved by the group, the students schedule a *public conversation* where they receive feedback on the issues raised in their portfolio from five critical friends. Candidates select their critical friends so that the following five perspectives are present: (1) a school-based educator who knows the candidate well (i.e., the cooperating teacher); (2) a school-based educator who does not know the candidate well (i.e., a principal, a teacher they respect); (3) a university-based educator who knows the candidate well (i.e., the supervisor); (4) a university-based educator who does not know the candidate well (i.e., a content expert or researcher in the issue); and (5) a colleague (i.e., another candidate, a community-based educator with whom the candidate has worked).

Several of these public conversations occur simultaneously in a large room, somewhat like a poster session at AERA or a "Portfolio Fair." The conversation is not a "defense" of the work, but rather a focused 2-hour conversation about teaching and learning among professional educators. To enhance the conversation, critical friends arrive prior to the session and review the entire document without the candidate present. A set of criteria and questions (presented in Figure 8.2) are used by students to help shape their M.Ed. portfolio, as well as by the support group and the critical friends to assess the portfolio. The questions cover such issues as:

- What is the big idea? How deep is the theme?
- How does the candidate's thinking about the theme affect/support the way he or she teaches?
- How does the theme affect the teaching and learning of the candidate? Of his or her students?
- How have the questions about the big idea/theme changed?
- How has this work shaped plans for future growth?

The questions serve as both potential stimuli and entry points to the public conversation—not as a checklist.

By expecting candidates to complete two different portfolios from the same collection of artifacts, the program uses portfolios for both technical (accountability) and transformational (educative) purposes. The following section analyzes what did, and did not, in this context, make a difference in the abilities of neophyte teachers to construct portfolios and to learn from teaching.

I. Composition

What is the big idea? The framing issue?
How is the portfolio organized so that its major themes are understood?
What makes the portfolio coherent?
What was your process (before, through, and beyond) of working with the big idea?
What teaching /learning incident(s) led you to the big idea? (For example, include any lesson plan, journal, student work, text, etc., that led you to this theme.)
Are the common threads of the portfolio clear?

II. Power of the Big Idea/Theme

How deep is the idea?
What is its significance to the social world?
How is this idea connected to the field?
What other educators have similar concerns/ideas? (Through educational literature? Other teachers with whom you have spoken?)
What is its significance to teaching and learning?
How does your thinking about this big idea/theme affect/support the way you go about teaching?
How does the idea reach into the student experience?
Where is the area of greatest growth?

III. Growth Over Time

How have the questions about the big idea/theme changed?
How has the way you think about these questions changed?
What incidents and experiences may have contributed to this change?
What lessons were learned from "limited successes"?
What problems were growth providers? How?
What evidence is there of changed techniques? Attitudes?

IV. Implications for Future Growth

What interesting questions are raised?
How has this work shaped plans for future growth?
How will this work affect the teaching and learning of the candidate? Of his or her students?
How will the candidate go about finding answers to essential questions?

FIGURE 8.2. Criteria and Guiding Questions for M.Ed. portfolios.

FINDINGS

The value of the portfolio process, as evidenced by the successful meeting of the criteria and by student feedback (in formal program review documents, focus group interviews, and tape recordings of three-way credential portfolio meetings and M.Ed. support group sessions), proved to be related to reflection possibilities constructed over time more than to the function or the audience of the portfolios.

Reflection

One of the themes of the UCSB Teacher Education Program is reflection. From the onset, we have maintained that one of the primary functions of the portfolios was to enhance sustained hard personal looks at oneself and one's practice. We wanted the portfolios to both improve and document our students' belief in the importance of looking critically at themselves, the skills that enable that process to happen, and the wisdom to change what one can to improve one's professional knowledge, skills, and dispositions. Our concern was that the kind of reflection we sought was not a given of the human condition (Bolin, 1988). Were our portfolio processes providing students the kind of learning opportunities required?

Our students did not share this concern—which is perhaps one indication that we provided opportunities to learn and to enrich their abilities to reflect. One student commented, "I can't imagine that a teacher can't, in some way, shape, or form, say how they have progressed and what they have learned. Isn't reflection saying, 'I have learned this'?" Another indicator of the students' capacity to take up the portfolios as opportunities to reflect is exemplified in a student's comment made during the final "defense" of her credential portfolio in a June meeting with her supervisor and cooperating teacher.

> I think my philosophy has been pretty much a constant. . . . I like to look back and remember what my philosophy was like. . . . I still believe all those things. . . . They all still sound really good . . . but my ways of going about achieving those things . . . are different. I have different methods and procedures. . . . I learned those skills that I didn't have before. . . . I feel like a lot of this year I've been learning how to undo what I've learned before—like my impression of what a teacher was. I thought a teacher was a lecturer. That was how I was taught—rows and a person who hands you a book and you read it and you spit back what you read. . . .

I knew that I had never been involved in teaching the way I wanted it to be, the way it should be. . . . So I'm unlearning the ways that I make sense of what I know.

Growth over Time

The kind of reflection exemplified above was made possible because the process for both portfolios required documenting thought and practice as they co-evolved over time. In order to make their own growth visible to themselves, students needed to collect, select, and reflect upon concrete evidence of how they were thinking and what they were doing at various points throughout, at least, their professional preparation year. This meant making the portfolios a safe place to "show the bombs".

> I kept the bombs in my issue portfolio. . . . I had to look at what I did . . . good and bad. . . . I felt like that was what I was supposed to do. So I tried to find the ones that were bombs and the ones that were good to compare and contrast. It was almost like rather than saying, "Show your competencies," it was "Show your growth in this area." . . . The purpose of this is not to show perfection in any of these things, it is to show your change in practice and thinking over time.

When students were allowed the luxury of failure, they could explicitly articulate their own growth. In this way they became more able to build on their strengths, gained a greater control over their own development, increased their motivation to keep failing (because anything worth doing, is worth doing wrong until you learn to do it right), and enhanced their potential for continual learning.

> One of the big things . . . I felt afterwards was, "Wow!" Because when I went in the program I really had very little experience and I didn't know anything, really, about teaching. And then when I finished and looked and saw what I'd done, I had a real sense of competence.
>
> It is really hard for me to say, "This is a great lesson." It is easier for me to look at the things I am working on . . . to look at the first times I tried it and then later on. When I did that, I felt real . . . satisfaction seeing how it had improved each time. It was the lessons that didn't work so well that I really learned from.
>
> I came in saying, "I'm going to be a teacher." It took me a long time to say, "I am a teacher."

Personal or Public Entry Point?

Our programmatic portfolio discussions never called into question the value of reflection or the time required for the changes to occur in order to provide students with opportunities to reflect upon the growth in their thinking and practice. (It takes time to establish something upon which to reflect!) Our debates centered around the initial locus of control for collecting and selecting the artifacts that would become the grist for that reflection. Essentially, advocates of the credential portfolio argued for an external entry point into reflection because: (1) it was unfair to make high stakes assessment decisions (e.g., credential decisions) without informing students of the criteria; (2) the state standards were not merely hoops to jump through, they were reflections of the combined wisdom of tradition, practice, and research; and (3) the credentialing/accreditation process embodied in those standards was an essential element of democratic institutions such as public schools and universities. As one student noted, "You don't want to just throw out the 10 competencies. I mean, I don't feel comfortable with completely throwing them out and hoping that somehow you created a competent teacher."

Advocates of the M.Ed. portfolio essentially argued for an internal entry point for reflection because beginning with the external: (1) would limit the creativity of students; (2) would inhibit student ownership of their own work; (3) was inconsistent with the constructivist philosophy espoused by the program; and (4) devalued and limited the opportunities for teacher educators to use their context-specific knowledge and expertise. Another student summarized this position when she remarked:

> The [credential portfolio] never seemed real to me because . . . it was just something external coming down on me. I was looking around for the perfect little lesson, the perfect little unit to stick in. . . . Teaching is an ongoing process and you're always trying to improve by reflecting. So when I was doing the [credential portfolio], I couldn't stand it because I don't feel like I've perfected anything at all.

When our students arrived, we lost argumentation time in lieu of the day-to-day work of teacher education. As the year progressed, empirical data started coming in and we, like our students, had the opportunity to observe artifacts of our practice and reflect upon what they meant about our own growth in thinking about teaching and learning.

As one student capsulized for us, the entry point was less a factor than the opportunities to reflect over time: "The whole notion of it being over time is what is useful because it makes visible those different benchmarks in your own learning. . . . If it came from the 10 competencies or if it came from you . . . doesn't make that big of a difference. That may just be preference." Both an internal and an external entry point enhance learning from teaching as long as supported reflection over time is available—neither enhances one's goals if supported reflection over time is not present.

For some students, the external entry point was of value.

> See, if you're talking about establishing a continuing rapport [a state standard], you can't just show a letter that shows you've established rapport. You have to show an *anthology* of letters that is the continuing rapport—with the teachers, parents, students, and whoever you're talking with.
>
> I like the grid. I am a grid person. . . . I'm very proud of the credential portfolio. I own it. I was collecting it all year and we got to discuss it lots of times. . . . And the fact that I typed up each competency and really reflected on it made me really realize what I learned all year, what it was that I focused on, and what I got out of the program. It was like, "Wow, I am competent in these areas and this is what I learned. This is why I *can be* an educator." I guess that's what I got out of having all those different competencies. I saw a bunch of different areas that I grew in and I reflected on because I had this list of things. I like having the criterion that I have to meet so I know some guidelines, have some guidance. . . .
>
> I think sometimes those sorts of competencies make you look at things that you might not think of. Like maybe I wouldn't think about professional growth. . . . But it would make me look at that and then look at my own teaching and say, "What's going on?" I mean, what are those guidelines for? I understand what they mean now. When I first tried those last year, they didn't make much sense to me, and now they do.

For other students, the internal entry point was of value—and, in fact, they usually began with the internal, even for the externally defined credential portfolio.

> I think if I chose one area, and it came from within, I bet I could then look at the list and I still would meet all those competencies naturally.

I just took all my lessons and fit them into the categories. I
didn't guide what I did by those categories, but I tried to see how,
reflect upon how, they fit. It gave me a way to reflect. In other
words, I could take this lesson and really read through it, reflect
on it, and I could see it really fit into this competency and why.
And then reflect on why I chose it. I learned something from that.
But I didn't change anything I did to fit into those competencies. I
took whatever I wanted and reflected on where it went afterward.
I picked a lesson . . . and then took it to the grid—not from the
grid to the lesson.

In short, although the audiences and functions of the two portfolios
differed, students linked the two. For instance, in the following excerpt
from a portfolio conference, it is not until the very end that it becomes
clear that the student is "defending" a credential portfolio (in December) rather than conversing about an M.Ed. portfolio. In this comment,
she is explaining why she asked her students to complete a report card
on her performance as a teacher.

I was curious about what they thought about my teaching and [I
wanted] to show them that I was willing to take a risk and let
them grade me. . . . The day before I asked my students to evaluate me, my cooperating teacher had asked them to evaluate themselves. I rarely ask the students to do something that I haven't
done or to do something I'm afraid of or uncomfortable or unwilling to do. I was very pleased and impressed with the way parent–
student conferences were going . . . but there was still something
missing from this process. My rationale behind asking students to
complete a report on [me] was to show students that just as they
were willing to allow others to give them grades, I was willing to
be graded. I knew that it was difficult for students to be receiving
grades, but I also wanted to let them have the experience of grading someone and to realize this is difficult also. I was looking forward to their input on my teaching. To complete the evaluative
process, I recorded my self-evaluation prior to reading their report
cards. Like the self-evaluations and the report cards of students
that my cooperating teacher constructed, my self-evaluation and
students' report cards of me showed similar strengths and goals.
That students were able to be honest and express their beliefs
about my teaching illustrates their trust. . . . Students observed
me taking a risk and consequently they were prepared to take
risks. These report cards show me that there is mutual respect be-

tween the student and myself and they illustrate Student Rapport [a state competency] in our classroom environment.

One of the only differences between the two types of portfolios was in the nature of the artifacts selected to document the students' growth over time. The M.Ed. portfolios, starting with a personal passion, often included educational literature (e.g., university-based "traditional" research, school-based action research, and conceptual articles) as evidence documenting growth. In 3 years of credential portfolios, starting with state standards, not one has included educational literature as evidence. Starting with the personal/subjective led into a larger public dialogue with the world beyond one's own classroom practice more often than did starting with the public/objective.

In the simplest terms, both portfolio processes involved collecting artifacts from multiple sources over time, selecting artifacts for particular purposes and audiences, and using those artifacts as tools for reflection (making one's own growth explicit, moving between levels of abstraction). Our initial hypothesis, or at least our bone of contention, was that the different purposes and audiences for the portfolios would not affect collection (there would still be the same "pile of stuff" saved), but selection and reflection would differ greatly between the two. In fact, neither collection nor reflection differed in any substantive manner, and the selection differences (e.g., proving oneself wonderful versus documenting growth over time) seem to be narrowing as students and faculty become more familiar with the use of portfolios.

Anticipated Outcomes: Connecting with Teaching

Although we wanted to believe that students would learn from how we structured the program and would take up comparable practices in their work with their students, prior to the research presented here, it was an ephemeral belief. Until we systematically and rigorously studied performance samples of our students, we could not know what our students were learning from how we structured the program and how we taught our courses—let alone the processes of that learning. In short, both portfolio processes helped teachers connect their self-assessment with their assessment practices with students.

> I thought it was interesting that the things I put in my portfolio, I put in not only because they make me feel good, but because they are an example of a program I would like to create in my future classroom. (student teacher)

> I think it would be more beneficial if you collected stuff, reflected on it, then made a goal. Then a few months later, saw if you met that goal, and reflected on it. . . . I've done this. . . . The students are collecting a portfolio and I . . . have them go through their work and say, "OK, this is the language arts one. Take out your best writing piece, take out your worst writing piece." . . . Then they write about why they are the best and the worst and what their goal is in 4 months for their writing. "What would you like to see yourself do?" So it is used as a goal setter for them and at the end of the year they can see if they have progressed in a way they wanted to progress. (first-year teacher)

In fact, some of *our* students' work with *their* students dealt with the same issues as we were dealing with as teacher educators and helped inform our thinking and practice. As one of our graduates pondered, "I was just doing [portfolios] for the kids, but should I really be focusing on the state? Or if I focus on the kids, will it naturally work for the state and how? You know, are they really two different portfolios?"

Unanticipated Outcomes: Program Improvement

Another benefit to the program of portfolios is their use as a feedback mechanism for program improvement. For instance, certain classes traditionally receive low student evaluations and we have a sense that they are not "working." Yet, many students used knowledge, skills, and dispositions gained from those courses in their portfolios. Conversely, some classes we think of as successful did not show up in portfolios at all. In program breast-beating sessions, we share our concerns about what our students are not getting. Once again, there were occasions when content we thought they were not "getting" would end up in the portfolios. In these cases, the portfolios made our program more visible to us as well as illuminated the developmental nature of teaching. That is, perhaps our students "did not get" something in December, but by June, with additional experiences, they exhibited a high level of achievement.

Finally, both portfolio processes included cooperating teachers and other school-based educators in their development and ultimate structure. We did this from a sense of the cooperating teachers' value to us and to our students. An unanticipated outcome is that their "helping us" to develop and carry out portfolio assessment also served educative functions for them. As a result of their portfolio work with us and with our students, they gained a greater understanding of our program, its philosophy, and how it works. This increased understanding enhanced the cohesion between college and school-based experiences for our student teachers, which in turn enriched our students' experiences in both settings. In addition, teachers took up the "content" of both portfolios to make their own practices visible to themselves. In fact, many (if not a majority) of cooperating teachers are now constructing their own portfolios. Some schools with which we work are taking on teacher portfolios as a school-wide effort.

CONCLUSION

The tension between assessment for support and assessment for high stakes decision making will never disappear. Still, that tension is constructively dealt with daily (and has been for generations) by supervisors of student teachers throughout the nation. Supervisors of student teachers both support their students and deliver high stakes accountability evaluations (e.g., thumbs up or thumbs down on successful completion of student teaching). Given the developmental and context-specific nature of the teaching/learning process as well as the need for over-time/in-depth observations for responsible evaluative evidence, it may be that the accountability function cannot be separated from the support function. If the information with which to make a major decision can best be gained through the context-specific relationships and conversations inherent in an over-time support role, how can one defend a high stakes decision without access to such information? In other words, while a support provider does not have to be an evaluator, an evaluator may have to be a support provider. As has always been the case in effective teacher education programs, accurate evaluation may not be separable from support.

Our study indicates that efforts to combine the dual purposes of support and accountability in a *single* portfolio do not always result in a constructive tension. It appears that an essential element to use the tension constructively is the belief that a key ingredient in the process of learning to teach is the maintenance of a large collection of process artifacts that represent work over time. This collection of artifacts then is used to make one's practice visible and as a basis for reflection in order to understand and improve one's teaching. From the collection, different artifacts can be selected, organized, and presented in different portfolios for different functions and different audiences. In this way, but not without peril, teaching, learning, assessment, and evaluation can support each other. When collections of the artifacts of teaching and learning from multiple sources of evidence collected over time are used for both functions, they give teacher educators better tools to support the growth of students, better information to make the responsible decisions about credentialing that students and families deserve, improve the assessment practices of teachers, and provide rich data for improvement of teacher education programs.

POSTSCRIPT

In the 2 years since this chapter was written, the UCSB teacher education programs have edited the two portfolio processes as well as embarked on programmatic improvement efforts based on the portfolio work of our students.

We have made two major changes in the credential portfolio. The first is the use of the new California Standards for the Teaching Profession as the foundation criteria for credentialing purposes. These National Board compatible standards have undergone a rigorous validity study that assessed their content, construct, and consequence validity. We, and our students, have found them to be more grounded in teacher development than the previous competencies and, thus, more useful in accessing practice in such a way as to support both growth and evaluation.

The second major change in the credential portfolio is the addition of a "growth over time" criterion. As a result of making this an explicit criterion, teacher candidates no longer attempt to dazzle with perfection but rather, as our research indicated was useful, "keep the bombs." In addition, our students are more likely to "start with practice" rather than the standards to exemplify their growth over time. Most students analyze several teaching episodes from early in their professional preparation year and from late in the year—then reflect on the differences between the two sets of teaching episodes as a way to enrich their understanding of teaching as well as to enhance their emerging sense of their current state of professional development. In this way, reflective opportunities have become embedded in the credential portfolio structure and process.

We have made three major changes in the M.Ed. portfolio. The first was to strongly urge students to continue work on the M.Ed. portfolio for another academic year and complete the process the summer following their first year of full-time teaching. Initially, some students postponed completion of the M.Ed. portfolio, electing to give themselves more time in the belief that additional experience and reflection would enrich their portfolio, their teaching, and the learning of their students.

Especially at the elementary level, these beliefs proved true in the caliber of their work. Thus, we not only urge students to postpone completing the master's degree for 1 year, but have restructured the program in such a way that employment possibilities are greater if they "wait a year." During the first year of full-time teaching, the program holds a series of Saturday workshops to support the growth of these students. In addition, the program is linked with California's Beginning Teacher Support and Assessment Project (BTSA) so that graduates participating in that induction support program receive additional support directly related to completing the M.Ed. portfolio. Despite the logistical problems and the unpaid time and labor demands of this model, it remains the preferred choice of the program faculty and the BTSA support providers who work with these first-year teachers.

A second change in the M.Ed. portfolio is a switch in the "perspectives" required at the public conversation. We replaced the "colleague" member of the conversation with someone who brings to the table the primary perspective of a parent. The colleague perspective was more than adequately shared in the support group, and the systematic inclusion of the parent perspective in a professional conversation served two functions: (1) a symbolic representation of the significance of the family in the education of children; and (2) conceptual and practical growth based on the perspective of an "outsider" with a keen interest in the caliber of teaching and learning.

Third, we accentuated the role of "theory" in the M.Ed. portfolio process. While we still want the work grounded in their own personal practice, we also want candidates to develop theory. Our issue is where and how to incorporate "research and theory" into the M.Ed. work. We still start with *their* issue and *their* practice as we did originally. We altered, however, the role of the facilitator and the other group members. A new significant role for the support group is to send the candidate to the theorists and researchers who have studied the candidate's issue. This happens *after* the candidate's generation of a "big idea" and a set of practice-grounded frames to understand that big idea. Thus, the purpose of educational "theory" is not simply to validate the candidate's thinking but rather to extend and enrich it through placing it within historical, philosophical, and conceptual traditions.

As a program and for our own professional development, we are moving in two directions. The first is to enhance our ability to assess our students' growth and development over time—especially regarding the education of second-language learners. Based on classroom observations and document analysis, we are in the initial stages of constructing indicators of what our standards "look like" at varying phases in the process of learning to teach—from earliest field experiences, through professional preparation, and into the initial 2 years of employment as a teacher. Our second programmatic improvement stream is to develop internal communication structures and processes. Through our work with portfolios we have come to realize the extraordinary wealth of information we have about our students from multiple sources of evidence collected over multiple years. Our challenge is to invent structures and processes, and create the necessary time, to collaboratively construct knowledge from that information and then use that knowledge to support the education of our students—and theirs.

REFERENCES

Bird, T. (1990). The schoolteacher's portfolio: An essay on possibilities. In J. Millman & L. Darling-Hammond (Eds.), *The new handbook of teacher evaluation: Assessing elementary and secondary school teachers* (2nd ed., pp. 241–256). Newbury Park, CA: Sage.

Bolin, F. (1988, March–April). Helping student teachers think about teaching. *Journal of Teacher Education, 39,* (2), 48–54.

Darling-Hammond, L., & Snyder, J. (1992). Framing accountability: Creating learner-centered schools. In A. Lieberman (Ed.), *The changing contexts of teaching* (pp. 11–36). Chicago: University of Chicago Press.

Darling-Hammond, L., Snyder, J., Ancess, J., Einbender, L., Goodin, A. L., & Macdonald, M. (1993). *Creating learner-centered accountability.* New York: NCREST.

Grant, G. E. (1994, April). *Teachers' portfolio and professional knowledge: A case of multiyear teacher reflection.* Paper presented at the annual meeting of the American Educational Research Association, New Orleans.

Holmes Group. (1986). *Tomorrow's teachers: A report of the Holmes Group.* East Lansing, MI: Author.

Lichtenstein, G., Rubin, T., & Grant, G. E. (1992, April). *Teacher portfolios and professional development.* Paper presented at the annual meeting of the American Educational Research Association, San Francisco.

Messick, S. (1989). Validity. In R. L. Linn (Ed.), *Educational measurement,* 3rd edition. (pp. 13–104). New York Macmillan.

Moss, P. (1994, May). *An interpretive approach to setting and applying standards.* Paper presented at the Conference on Standard Setting, Sponsored by the National Assessment Governing Board and the National Center for Education Statistics, Washington, DC.

Snyder, J., Chittenden, E., & Ellington, P. (1993). *Assessment of children's reading: A comparison of sources of evidence.* New York: NCREST.

Tierney, D. (1992). *Teaching portfolios: 1992 update on research and practice.* Los Angeles: Far West Laboratory for Educational Research and Development.

CHAPTER 9

Experienced Teachers Construct Teaching Portfolios: A Culture of Compliance vs. a Culture of Professional Development

Lee Teitel

UNIVERSITY OF MASSACHUSETTS

Maria Ricci
Jacqueline Coogan

EVERETT (MA) PUBLIC SCHOOLS

In 1993, the authors did a simple, but still very rare, bit of collaboration: We worked together to develop teaching portfolios for our own reflection and professional growth. Our portfolios, unlike most of those described in this book, were not connected with student teachers or other preservice work, or with any inservice assessment or recertification. Ours was not a mandated effort; there were no incentives or external motivations to do it. We were all seasoned teachers, each with at least 20 years of experience and we did the portfolio simply for our own professional development.

This chapter tells the story of that collaboration and its aftermath. The first section describes why we chose to construct portfolios and what the impacts on us were at the time. We have chosen to write this section in the same collaborative style we used in portfolio development: Although there is a strong common narrative, our individual voices are interspersed, with personal comments adapted from our presentation at the January 1994 Portfolio Conference (Cambridge, Massachusetts) and from subsequent reflective writings. The second section describes the aftermath—what we did in the 2 years after we completed the portfolios and how we tried to engage other experienced teachers in portfolio development. It includes the findings of a modest action research project to follow what happens when other experienced teachers develop portfolios. The chapter concludes with our recommendations about effective use of portfolios for experienced teachers and with our thoughts and concerns about the future.

THE PORTFOLIO PROCESS

Context

The portfolio development project grew out of a larger collaboration around student teaching between Everett Public Schools (where Jackie and Maria teach) and U-Mass Boston (where Lee teaches). In 1992, Lee organized a seminar for cooperating teachers who were working with university students. The teachers shared strategies for working effectively with student teachers; they developed skills in observation and feedback; and they made suggestions for improving the student teaching experience. As a culminating project, Jackie and Maria proposed forming a partnership between the University and the Centre School in Everett.

> Maria: We felt there was inadequate communication between all of the parties involved in the training of student teachers: the supervisors, the cooperating teachers, and the student teachers. We modeled our project after one we had seen which assigned a "cluster" of student teachers in one location with one supervisor who would become a regular visitor to the host school on a weekly basis. We also designed the program to break the isolation which existed not only for the student teachers, but for the cooperating teachers as well. With much administrative support, we were able to schedule regular meetings with student teachers to share ideas and to discuss problems and possible solutions. The student teachers identified areas they wished to explore and we, in turn, attempted to accommodate them by providing tailored semi-

nars—not only with our own staff members, but with outside staff members from other schools and colleges. It was during one of those seminars that all three of us saw our first teaching portfolios, brought in by Carol Pelletier, a first-grade teacher with extensive experience with student teachers.

After seeing Carol's portfolios, we decided to have student teachers prepare similar ones as part of their requirements for the next semester. When no student teachers were assigned to the Centre School for that semester, we decided to use the "down time" for our own professional development. Maria and Jackie suggested that the cooperating teachers do teaching portfolios. The school administration supported us by purchasing materials and providing classroom coverage. Jackie, Maria, Lee, and three other teachers met seven times during the next 8 months, discussing, creating, and revising our portfolios. Most of the time was during the school day, with four afternoon releases and one full day (which we used for much of the production and assembly). We also held two sessions after school, including a pot-luck dinner at the end to share our finished products. Between sessions, each of us put in an additional 20 to 30 hours, assembling materials or writing our philosophies and reflections.

Process

When we embarked on our portfolio creation, we had seen only one set of portfolios, Carol's. We had no formal background regarding the creation or utilization of professional portfolios, so we shaped what we were doing as we went along. Lee said,

> The first thing I did when we started the seminar was to acknowledge how little I knew about how to proceed and to promise myself that I would be as much a participant as anybody else. I did not do the kind of hyperactive preparation that a college or university person usually would. I didn't go and read everything possible on portfolios. Maybe I should have, but I didn't. So I ended up learning about portfolios by doing—we experienced this by doing it together and made a lot of it up together. We had inspiration and continued guidance from Carol Pelletier, who talked to us occasionally about what we were doing—but mostly we were on our own.

We began our process by brainstorming thoughts and ideas about portfolios and we kept cycling back to what it meant for us to be teachers. We felt that our teaching philosophy should be at the core of the portfolio, but it was not easy for us to verbalize and express exactly what our philosophies were. At times, the process appeared to be a struggle, since we were not accustomed to doing deep personal reflection—either individually or in a group. Lee said:

> Putting this together with a group of elementary school teachers was both a challenge and an important lesson for me. Like many people in higher education, I find I am accustomed to—and fairly comfortable with—expressing myself in writing. For me, writing the philosophy wasn't the hardest part; it was what came afterwards—putting together the various artifacts needed for a portfolio. That was a challenge. If I had been working on this by myself, I probably would have just done a lot of reflective writing. This wouldn't have stretched me in the same way that doing the portfolio with a group of elementary teachers did. Layout, art, cutting with scissors, etc., was not my thing. I didn't do this particularly well. Visual presentation is something that I stutter and stammer my way through. Sitting in a room with people who were whipping together things and laying them out beautifully was tough. They would put a little heading on something, add some color and a few photos, and put a piece of backing paper on it and—all of a sudden—you could see a spectacular visual display. This was actually quite intimidating for me. It stretched me and encouraged me to learn from them. It was humbling. And I realize now that it is good for people in higher ed to be humbled from time to time and to appreciate how much we can learn from K–12 teachers.

Short-Term Impacts

Creating these portfolios together had a profound effect on the way each of us thinks about teaching, about ourselves as teachers, and about our colleagues.

Jackie: Getting started was exciting in that I enjoyed focusing on the many and varied activities, lessons, and teaching experiences I have had with my students. There were many I had forgotten about or had repeated in such variations that the original method almost seemed new again. In discussion with my colleagues, in particular during that first session, many memories and ideas flowed among us. It was extremely stimulating, thought-provoking, and motivating. Doing this professional portfolio, felt focused and accomplished, and became a passion. I really enjoyed doing it; the thinking, planning, focusing, processing, sharing—the accomplishing of a professional tool that was full of all of the many ideas, people, and experiences that were important to me.

Lee: I am in a different setting. I very much consider myself a teacher, but as a junior faculty member at a university, it seems that most of the reward structure is set up to focus on research and publications, with less importance given to service and teaching. During the period of time we worked on the portfolios I was simultaneously putting together the dossier for my fourth-year review—which at my university tells you if you are on the right track for tenure. The contrast between the two documents was fascinating. Since teaching had to play something of a subordinate role in the fourth-year review, I appreciated the chance to focus totally on my teaching in the portfolio work with the Everett teachers. Furthermore, the audience for the teaching portfolio was me and my collaborators; there was nothing evaluative about it and nothing that would influence my tenure at the university. I loved the opportunity to focus on just the teaching part—on "Who am I as a teacher?" and "What are the kinds of things I am trying to do as a teacher?"

A critical element in the construction of these portfolios is that we were doing them together. Although we worked individually between sessions, the bulk of our effort was shared and highly collaborative. This collaborative aspect of the portfolio process had a significant impact in its own right.

Jackie: This activity of sharing with my colleagues and friends was the most rewarding of all. So often when we teach, we feel very isolated from the adult world. The rush and demands on you and your time leave very little room to talk and explore with each other professionally in a relaxed manner. For me, this portfolio development was a wonderful and professional way of talking and sharing with my colleagues. One of the teachers in our group and I have taught together for 24 years. For 12 of those years, she taught the sixth grade with me—and although we had many opportunities to speak of our students and their needs, we had so little time to speak of ourselves and our professional needs. Doing the portfolios with a third-grade teacher, a special education teacher, a media specialist, and a first-grade teacher was important; I now understand the connections between what the first-grade teacher was doing in her language and social studies and science classes and what I am doing in the sixth grade. It was incredible to see the flow. In my portfolio and in the third-grade portfolio, you see work of one child that we have all had—an exceptional child. We never knew that we were each putting in the work of this child and it all fell in place and made the curriculum become alive for all of us.

Lee: Another collaborative aspect came out when we were sitting side by side and reading our philosophies. It was astounding to me to hear and see the similarities between and among us and to see the connections that crossed the boundaries between K–12 and higher ed. For example, you could have taken the goals of the first-grade teacher, changed a couple of words, and it would have been the same philosophy as mine. That was very powerful for both of us. It underscored what artificial boundaries often exist to separate teachers.

PORTFOLIO DEVELOPMENT: THE AFTERMATH

We completed our teaching portfolios 2 years ago, yet they continue to be very vibrant and important parts of our lives. A few months after finishing, we were invited to share our portfolios and describe our development at the first "Portfolios in Teaching and Teacher Education Conference" held at Harvard, in January 1994. Although we were initially intimidated about speaking publicly on something about which we were so unsure, the conference was tremendously affirming for each of us. What had been just us—stumbling along in the art room of an elementary school—was now part of a national movement. What had been just us—pleased with what we could share with one another, but unsure if we were doing it "right"—was now something with powerful external validation.

The positive feedback we got at the conference reinforced our desire to spread the word and to use portfolios more with our colleagues. Lee has used a portfolio as a central organizing theme for teachers enrolled in the Master in Educational Administration Program he directs; he also has begun the process of collaborating with other U-Mass faculty to develop teaching portfolios for their tenure reviews. Jackie and Maria began giving workshops on the portfolio development process to teachers in neighboring communities. In 1994–95, they took on the task of helping 25 other Everett teachers develop portfolios in a seminar series that met monthly over the entire school year.

This seminar created a natural experiment: Could our 1993 success with six teachers be repeated on a much larger scale? Several factors were different: The group was not only larger, it was more diverse, drawing a mix of high school and elementary teachers from several schools. The meetings were facilitated by teachers from inside the system, rather than by an outsider. This time teachers were offered inservice credit. Would that change the motivation? A recent change in Massachusetts state regulations required veteran teachers to apply for recertification. Would preparation for that process overshadow the professional development aspect of doing a portfolio?

Intrigued by the differences and excited by the possibilities of seeing our portfolio development "ripple out" to affect so many others, we decided to conduct a modest action research project. Lee, who had not been involved in the new workshops except to share his portfolio as a guest in an early session, came to the next-to-last session to conduct confidential interviews with about one-third of the 25 participants. In addition, we designed a short reflective survey, administered anonymously, that was completed by 15 of the teachers. The data helped to answer many of our initial questions and, at the same time, to raise some provocative new ones.

The size and diversity of the group did not seem to impinge on the abilities of the group to work well together. Most participants were pleased to have contact with people from other schools. One high school teacher described herself as "artistically challenged" and commented, as Lee had done, that most of her elementary colleagues did not seem to be so challenged. Many of the teachers did most of their work in close collaboration with one or two others from their own school, venturing out occasionally to share ideas with those from other schools.

The feedback for Jackie and Maria as facilitators was extremely positive, with all the respondents praising their professionalism, organization, approachability, enthusiasm, and caring. This suggests that, if anything, being insiders was helpful in setting up a supportive and collaborative environment.

One of the most interesting patterns of responses concerned motivation. We had wondered whether offering inservice credit and "professional development points" for recertification would be significant. We asked two related questions: "What originally was the most important motivation for taking this course?" and "As you look back on the entire experience, what was the most valuable part?"

Most responses on original motivation showed a utilitarian and extrinsically focused motivation. Six teachers referred to state recertification requirements; another six cited credits and professional development points; two commented on the convenient time and one noted the potential usefulness of a portfolio in a job search. On the other hand, only one teacher said she was motivated by a desire to reflect on her career. One saw it as a "creative" thing to do; another liked the "hands-on" approach; and two liked the 1993 portfolios they had seen.

When asked to reflect on the most valuable part of the experience, the response pattern reversed; the utilitarian and extrinsic motivations dramatically declined in importance. Only one teacher referred to organizing her portfolio for recertification; three others wrote more generally about organizing and displaying their career work. All other comments focused on the reflective and collaborative benefits of doing portfolios. Three teachers commented on the importance of writing a philosophy. Five noted the value of sifting through artifacts of their career, making comments such as:

> The most valuable and also the most frustrating part was gathering together the pieces of my teaching career and compiling them into a visual history. It's given me a better perspective on "What I've done" and "What I'd like to do."

> [The most valuable part was] deciding *what* was important to me during my teaching experiences. I had to make choices.

Another teacher noted that the experience raised her self-esteem and that the most valuable part was "learning to place an importance on the things I do and not take it for granted that it's what I'm supposed to do." For three other teachers, the workshop provided a broadening perspective—meeting new people and seeing what goes on in other classrooms and other buildings.

We asked participants about personal impacts: "What did you learn about yourself as a person?" and "What did you learn about yourself as a professional educator?" Two teachers wrote about the mechanics of assembling a portfolio: "I'm better organized than I thought." For most teachers, however, the powerful learnings focused on the opportunity to reflect on their careers as teachers.

> I learned that I'm continually changing and learning—looking for new ideas to bring to the classroom. I'm never satisfied with the status quo—always trying to do more.

Many times it demonstrated to me—not what I did, but why I did it. It helped me to analyze my teaching experiences to date.

For many teachers, it was the first time they had collected all their work and looked at it together; most were quite pleased. Three commented that they had been doing more than they realized. Overall, almost half of the respondents indicated an increased self-esteem. Not only did teachers have more to offer than they thought, but, as one teacher put it, "I have taken for granted that the things I do everyday are of real importance and not 'just my job.'"

Another set of questions focused on collaboration: "What did you learn from your colleagues?" and "In what ways, if any, was the sharing of experiences at the workshops valuable?" All of the respondents were impressed by their colleagues—their creativity, their dedication, their exciting approaches. Two noted that "teachers in general don't get enough recognition for their work."

Several teachers welcomed the opportunity to "see" other classrooms through the portfolios; two specifically mentioned the advantage of seeing across grade-level boundaries (such as high school and elementary levels). Sharing portfolios helped respondents in different ways: to crystallize a vision; to jog memory; to provide organizational formats; and, more generally, to energize and revitalize the teachers as they worked on this task.

We asked the teachers what they might do with their portfolios once they were finished so that "these wonderful portfolios won't end up in a closet." We asked also about their willingness to share their portfolios with teachers in their own building or other buildings.

Participants had few clear ideas for follow-up. More than half left the question blank, inserted a question mark, or wrote "none." Two respondents indicated they would continue to add to their portfolios; two wrote that they would share the portfolio with colleagues, parents, and educators in other systems (one already had); another suggested that follow-up on the portfolio might be more suitable for a newer teacher (who might use it for advancement).

Approximately half of the respondents indicated that they would be willing—without reservations—to share their portfolio with others. Several added restrictions: only in their own building; only after removing "personal" sections. One replied that, if asked, she would share the portfolio, but she did not want to display it. Two teachers were unwilling to share their portfolios because they viewed them as too personal or too unfinished.

RECOMMENDATIONS

Our own experiences in developing our own portfolios, combined with what we learned from our work with 25 seasoned teachers, leave us with a strong belief in the value of teaching portfolios for experienced teachers, with several recommendations for ways in which they could be developed, and with a few lingering questions. Our recommendations follow:

• Portfolios are key tools for teacher development and they should be designed to promote reflective practice. They should be tied to carefully articulated philosophies—with thoughtful consideration given to the process of sorting and selection. Portfolios should not be just glorified scrapbooks.
• Portfolios should be shared with colleagues, because colleagues are an important source of creative input and because such sharing promotes collaboration.
• Portfolios should be encouraged for cooperating teachers as well as for student teachers. Portfolios present a model of teachers as learners and as professionals who "make sense" of their work.
• Portfolio development should be a "bottom-up," voluntary process that is owned by teachers and not used for evaluation purposes. The best way to kill it would be to make it mandatory or to use it for evaluation. Key benefits are lost if the reflective culture of professional development is replaced by a "culture of compliance"—where teachers go through the motions of assembling materials according to a predated checklist.
• Portfolio development for experienced teachers should be supported by enabling conditions: for example, time, money for materials, some structure or facilitation for the development process. Modest extrinsic motivations, such as credit, may be used to encourage teachers so long as they do not take over and transform the activity into a compliance experience.

QUESTIONS

We conclude with two sets of questions concerning follow-up after portfolio development and the impact of portfolio development on teaching.

What comes next for experienced teachers who have created portfolios? Each of us and virtually all the experienced teachers we have worked with are enthusiastically recharged by the process. But what next? Will we revisit our portfolios in 5 or 10 years? What can be done to make that likely? How can we get beyond having the portfolios become a fond memory? ("Remember when we did portfolios?") How can we help tap the enthusiasm of these teachers in ways that are good for schools and for children? Furthermore, what can we do with the portfolios themselves so that they do not simply gather dust in a closet? We have some ideas, but we are unsure of the steps that need to be taken to make sure they happen.

Follow-up activities to build on the enthusiasm of teachers might include working with other teachers (as we did) on developing portfolios. If each teacher or a group of teachers returned to their school and began a portfolio workshop (even a scaled-down version), the activity would have an impact on the faculty of the schools in a small city like Everett. As Jackie wistfully put it: "Wouldn't it be wonderful for them to do seven little inservice presentations in each of the seven schools represented." Just showing their portfolios might spread the word and reduce teacher isolation. Maria added: "There are perhaps 25 teachers in each of their buildings and only three of them are in this course. If those three teachers talk to the teachers in their building and show them what it was all about, then there might be interest in the teachers on their own."

The portfolios themselves could be used as public relations tools. At open houses or PTA conferences, for example, instead of just describing a program or handing out a syllabus, teachers could use their portfolios as a wonderful visual way for parents to see and understand what is going on in the classrooms. Portfolios could be a creative part of working with student teachers. For students, a school system might use portfolios as part of reflective learning that starts in kindergarten and continues through high school. The opportunities for teachers to connect to these efforts and to share and model reflective practice would be very valuable. Portfolios could be the basis for starting substantial conversations about teaching. When we made the presentations at the Portfolio Conference, one of the best parts was the opportunity to share our work with conference participants and to very quickly get to the specific aspects of our teaching approaches. Lee added: "I keep my teaching portfolio in a prominent place in my U-Mass office, hoping one of my colleagues will ask to see it. No one has yet, and I realize I have to be more proactive in setting up times and places to share it."

These suggestions start to answer the important question about follow-up. But we are not sure what conditions will promote the use of portfolios. The initial development of a portfolio is a concrete and tangible task that results in a product. Most of our suggestions here are more amorphous; they have to do with promoting an attitude and approach that value collaboration and value teachers as professionals. These are more difficult steps and, not surprisingly, the Everett teachers we surveyed seemed much less sure of what to do next than they were about the value of what they had just done. Without clear paths and supporting structures, without school cultures that encourage collaboration, we worry that many portfolios will end up in closets. We are convinced that to "get people charged up" and then provide no outlets for that energy is a missed opportunity. As Jackie observed: "I think it's tragic to be brought out like that, to have this rebirth—only to do nothing with it."

Finally, what impact does experienced teacher portfolio development have on classroom teaching? The most important follow-up for a portfolio is one that leads to improvement in instruction—what is described as "consequential validity." Yet, we saw little evidence of that and even began to wonder if it can be an expected outcome for a portfolio development experience.

When interviewing participants in the Everett workshop, Lee asked if developing the portfolio had led to any changes in teaching approach. All but one teacher said, "No." At the same time, Jackie and Maria (who had known these teachers for most of their professional lives) saw tremendous growth in them as a result of the experience. When asked to explain the discrepancy, Maria commented that she would not expect the portfolio to have any effect on their teaching, but it had changed how teachers think about themselves. In her words: "I don't think that they are going to change what they do because they do it wonderfully—and they showed us what they do. I think that now that they have shared what they do with other people, that has made a difference in them. It won't change what they do, but I do think it will change how they feel about their role."

This leaves us with a deeper question about the ultimate impact of portfolios for improving teaching. If portfolios are the wonderfully positive, validating experiences that they have been for us and the other Everett teachers, will they lead to improvement of instruction or simply to a greater satisfaction with who we are currently as teachers? Validation of oneself as a teacher is important nourishment for members of an undervalued profession. Yet, striving for improvement in experienced teachers usually comes out of some small edge of dissatisfaction. Although some Everett teachers see themselves as continuously improving and seeking new ways to work effectively with their students, will that apply to everyone? Do we need to build into the development process some disconfirming edge to challenge us, to push ourselves more? The student teachers described elsewhere in this book who are doing portfolios receive some critical feedback from faculty members at the school and college—feedback that will help them to see where they are and where they want to go as teachers. Convinced of the importance of keeping traditional evaluation processes far away from teacher portfolios, we wonder what the analogous experience would be for experienced teachers. How can this wonderful activity of portfolio development lead us to understand and validate ourselves as teachers—and also lead us to continue to perfect our craft?

CHAPTER 10

The Portfolio Question:
The Power of Self-Directed Inquiry

Grace E. Grant

DOMINICAN COLLEGE

Tracy A. Huebner

STANFORD UNIVERSITY

A powerful means of developing autonomy and conceptual change in prospective teachers is a teacher's portfolio focused on an important, essential question. Drawn from classroom experience, or from classroom incidents that trigger recollections of prior learning, student teachers in a graduate teacher education program first framed a portfolio question and then refined and clarified its meaning. Later, they used this self-designed question to focus a 12-week inquiry into their own classroom practice. Finally, they displayed selections from these portfolio entries in a professional conference. Three years later, we interviewed these individuals about the power of that early experience to sustain their efficacy as professionals who think, talk, and know about teaching. Their stories of constructing questions and carrying out self-directed classroom inquiry illustrate the portfolio question's potency for instilling two important professional habits of mind: the view of teaching as inquiry; and the view of collaborative learning as the way to come to know teaching.

CONCEPTUAL LEARNING

Increasingly, teacher educators are coming to recognize that significant shifts in conceptual understandings about learning to teach are the result of the coordination of agency and collaboration during powerful learning experiences. The notion of agency—that is, of the mind taking more control of its own mental activity (Bruner, 1994)—is a view of mind that is proactive, problem-oriented, attentionally focused, selective, constructive, and directed toward ends. What becomes integrated into the mind is more a function of the hypotheses an individual harbors than of information present in the learning context at any given moment. Constructivist theory, beginning with Piaget (1950), poses learning as the result of observation and experiences with novel stimuli; children learn by incorporating new information into their world view, thereby constructing new knowledge and a new world view. Learning, Piaget notes, "*forms* the mind, rather than *furnishing* it." In this constructivist environment, learning experiences are empowering because they provide learners with both raw materials and a situation in which to construct knowledge. Moreover, learners have a high degree of responsibility for this process of discovery. They must resolve the inner cognitive conflicts that often become apparent through concrete experience and reflection on that experience (Brooks & Brooks, 1993). Thus, learning is a self-regulated process.

To promote self-regulated learning, a guiding principle of constructivist pedagogy is structuring learning around primary concepts. Brooks and Brooks (1993) advocate a curriculum of problems organized by "big ideas" that provide a context within which students can learn the component skills, gather information, and build knowledge. "When concepts are presented as wholes . . . students seek to make meaning by breaking the wholes into parts that *they* can see and understand. Students initiate this process to make sense of the information; they construct the process and the understanding rather than having it done *for* them" (p. 47, emphasis in original). Others promote learning through question posing and problem seeking. For Wiggins (1987), education for thoughtfulness is centered on "essential questions" that tap into core beliefs of a discipline, have no one obvious answer, require higher-order thinking in response, and generate a personalized interest in the subject. Essential questions provide a provocative or generative entry point, a manageable introduction to intriguing human problems. Cochran-Smith (1991) highlights the posing of questions, and the pursuit of problems contained within them, as a critical feature in learning the complexities of teaching. "The ability to pose questions," she writes, "to struggle with uncertainty and build evidence for reasoning . . . is an indispensable resource in the education of teachers" (pp. 280–281).

In the past decade we also have come to know a great deal more about the significance of collaborative learning, for many now believe that how we come principally to know ourselves is in interaction with each other. Beginning with the work of Vygotsky (1978), we have come to the view that thinking is a social activity, initially shared among people but gradually internalized to reappear again as an individual achievement. The conception of mind inherent in the constructivist view not only is active in nature, but also seeks out dialogue and discourse with other minds. For it is in the sharing of resources of the mix of human beings involved in teaching and learning that mind becomes both what is in the head and what is with others (Bruner, 1994). These social settings provide an audience for an individual's attitudes, opinions, and beliefs, where audiences request clarification, justification, and elaboration. Brown and Palincsar (1989) note that the persistent claim of group settings is that they force learning with understanding and are therefore likely to foster conceptual change. Learning with understanding is more likely when one is required to explain, elaborate, or defend one's position to others, as well as to oneself; striving for an explanation often makes a learner integrate and structure knowledge in new ways. Brown and Palincsar note that environments that encourage questioning, evaluating, criticizing, and generally worrying about knowledge as an object of thought—that is, taking what we know and how we come to know it as a part of the curriculum—are believed to be precisely the kind of learning environments in which knowledge is restructured.

Further, as Cochran-Smith (1991) adds, it is the posing of questions within a learning community that links theory and practice through the process of self-critical and systematic inquiry about teaching and learning. The social environment establishes important patterns of thinking, talking, and knowing about teaching. For it is a teacher's ability to frame and reframe questions in discourse—elaborating explanations that repeatedly direct teachers to return to observations of student learning, which direct them to uncover prior unanswered questions embedded in present ones—that develops the generative structures of inquiry. Learners must be able to discover new information and integrate it into their existing knowledge structures. Thus, powerful learning is active and relevant; it engages the learner intellectually and socially.

THE TEACHER'S PORTFOLIO

The dramatic pace with which teachers' portfolios have captured educators' imaginations speaks to their increased power to capture the complexities of teaching in ways that no other form can, by providing a view of teaching and learning as they develop over time across different contexts in authentic settings (Barton & Collins, 1993; Shulman, 1988; Wiggins, 1989; Wolf, 1991, 1994). In fact, it is probably because of, rather than in spite of, the ambiguity surrounding portfolio development that the teacher's portfolio has the potential to be so illuminating about practice and about the development of teacher knowledge. This work has been influenced greatly by Shulman (1992, 1994) and his colleagues (Barton & Collins, 1993; Bird, 1990; Wolf, 1991, 1994). It uses a definition of "portfolio" first stated by Shulman (1992) and later clarified by Wolf (1994).

> A portfolio is the structured documentary history of a [carefully selected] set of coached or mentored accomplishments substantiated by samples of work and fully realized only through reflective writing, deliberation, and serious conversation. (p. 111, brackets in original)

Elsewhere (Grant, 1995; Lichtenstein, Rubin, & Grant, 1992) we have argued that a teacher's portfolio should be structured, although there is considerable discussion about the nature and focus of that structuring (see, for example, Barton & Collins, 1993; Mosenthal, Daniels, & Hull, 1993; Wolf, 1991, 1994). We believe that the focus must be selective—highlighting core pedagogical knowledge or skills of an individual teacher or focusing on professional knowledge and habits. We believe that the documentary evidence must be gathered over time, must be representative of both teacher and student work, and must be captioned, so that it is understandable to others. We insist that portfolio development is a collaborative venture of coached teaching acts and that portfolio conversations (see Wolf, Whinery, & Hagerty, 1995) are essential to this process. We believe that it should include a reflective commentary, the result of deliberation and conversation with colleagues, which allows others to examine the thinking and pedagogical decisions behind the documented teaching (see also Shulman, 1994). We recognize that teacher-constructed portfolios make teaching public, including making explicit tacit knowledge, in order to increase professional autonomy, and making public the standards for good work as a source of future wise action.

CONSTRUCTING A PORTFOLIO QUESTION

While it is possible for a teacher-constructed portfolio to take a variety of shapes, we wish to argue that one successful vehicle for powerful learning in teacher education is the teacher's portfolio focused on a self-designed question. In the 1990–91 academic year, we instituted portfolio development as an integral part of the cohort-based, graduate teacher education program at Stanford University (Grant, 1990; see also Lichtenstein, Rubin, & Grant, 1992). Others at that time had used teacher's portfolios as a means of assessing experienced teachers; ours was an effort to adapt those processes to the development, rather than the assessment, of prospective teachers. Our purpose was to use the portfolio process to develop two professional habits of mind: (1) the habit of mind that views teaching as inquiry; and (2) the habit of mind that views collaborative learning as the way to come to know teaching. The construction of this portfolio entry was sustained in a seminar that accompanied a 9-month period of supervised teaching. Grace was one of the co-instructors for this seminar[1] and, as a student, Tracy wrote her own portfolio question.

Within this seminar, student teachers had a wide choice in the framing of a self-designed pedagogical question that would guide their inquiry. However, we posed five characteristics or qualities in a powerful question.

* *Practice-Based:* The question must emanate from puzzling experiences and issues arising in the student teacher's classroom practice.
* *Professionally Relevant:* It must revolve around an issue or a set of issues that sincerely and deeply concern the student teacher.
* *Significant:* It must have the power to sustain a student teacher's interest and attention throughout the 9-month period of supervised teaching.
* *Honest:* It must be a question for which a student teacher does not have a preconceived set of answers.
* *Precisely Stated:* The wording of the question must represent clear, concise thinking about pedagogical issues.

This portfolio question will be, by its very nature, selective; it can encompass only a small portion of what is to be known of classroom complexities. At the same time, it must be an "essential" question, one that focuses on core issues in teaching.

It took student teachers most of the 10-week fall quarter to formulate portfolio questions. Typically, their initial stabs at questions reflected poorly developed conceptions of their domains of inquiry. Questions were broadly phrased and lacked awareness of the subtleties and complexities of classrooms and schools. Working with student teachers as they constructed their portfolio questions required us to coach them in the process of interpreting the complicated and complex situations that characterize professional practice. For most, framing a question was a difficult and wrenching process.

This framing and refining occurred within a constellation of supporting structures: biweekly question sessions, conferences with their instructors, and peer reviews. Each of these supporting structures asked them to explain, elaborate upon, and defend their conceptions of teaching to others. For once student teachers had questions that satisfied the first four characteristics, we began a careful process of refining the question. With a refined question, student teachers wrote narrative introductions, which were shared with peers, to explain the circumstances and experiences that made the question professionally and personally salient. This process generated considerable peer dialogue about meaningful elements of classroom practice.

In the winter and early spring, student teachers documented their question with artifacts, selected from documentary evidence collected over the normal course of teaching—student work, unit and lesson plans, videotapes, logs and journals, and classroom photographs. Each selected artifact was captioned with a three-sentence explanation of what the evidence was, what it showed, and how it was related to the focused inquiry of the portfolio question. Student teachers were encouraged to draw upon readings, theories, and research, as well as classroom practice, in explaining the professional importance of their issue. They completed two drafts and a final draft of the entry rationale; each early draft was reviewed, commented on, and returned for further revision and development. These discussions merged imperatives of classroom practice with the values of research-based knowledge.

The final draft of this portfolio entry contained a commentary, reviewing the purpose, the artifacts, and what was learned about teaching in the process of constructing the entry. Finally, student teachers designed a conference to demonstrate the professional knowledge gained in constructing their portfolio entry.

The portfolio question, then, becomes the pedagogical focus, guiding teaching as well as directing the development of a teaching portfolio entry. It forms the framework against which all classroom events, or all classroom events of a particular nature, are compared to determine their adequacy in reaching these goals. Conversely, classroom data may illuminate the need to reframe the question. Finally, question making itself is an interpretive framing and reshaping of meaning found in classroom events. Slight changes in wording may reflect significant leaps in understanding. A portfolio entry focused on a self-designed question is not designed to promote comparability to particular aspects of student teachers' practical wisdom and practice or to produce high stakes judgments; it is designed to gain insight into a teacher's reflection on practice and, therefore, is particularly valuable in preservice teacher education.

In 1994, 3 years after their preservice training at Stanford, Tracy interviewed six of the 54 graduates of this class. We report on two of these individuals here. We selected Christina Hayashi[2] and Mehan Yektai specifically because they had continued to use their portfolio and portfolio question in their professional capacity as teachers and because of their common source for portfolio questions, previously introduced theory. Elsewhere (Grant & Huebner, in press) we report on the other common source of questions, personal experience. Christina Hayashi, an English teacher, had as her portfolio question, "How can I create and design English activities and assignments that will call on students to use different intelligences rather than the standard linguistic or logical skills that we typically use in the traditional classroom process?" For Mehan Yektai, a mathematics teacher, the portfolio question was, "How do I make my students good mathematical problem solvers?"

Primarily, our interviews focused on understanding the relationship between an individual's personal pedagogical inquiry and teaching practices. We were also interested in how the portfolio question continues to weave its way through a new teacher's professional repertoire and how it continues to evolve as a part of ongoing professional development. We questioned each teacher about three key concepts.

1. *The source of the portfolio question:* What was your portfolio question? How did you generate this question?

2. *The process of constructing a question:* Can you reconstruct for me your process in developing the question? How did you come to use the words you did? What were some earlier versions of this question? Why were these words more representative than others you may have used?

3. *The sustaining influence of the portfolio question:* Were there significant changes in your understanding while developing your question? Do you still have your portfolio? Have you continued to use any aspect of your portfolio in your career?

Each interview lasted 55–60 minutes, was audiotaped and transcribed (Mishler, 1986), was reviewed by each of the teachers, and later was analyzed.

Information from the transcribed interviews[3] was divided into the sequence of the three concepts constituting the interview. Following principles of Glaser and Strauss's (1967) constant comparative method, each statement was coded based on its content: impetus, process, and impact. As a result, all statements were coded as referring to the personal or professional impetus for this self-directed inquiry; to the process of question development and conceptual changes that occurred therein; and to the continuing impact of self-directed inquiry on professional activities.

All statements then were sorted as "impetus," "process," or "impact." For each individual, a summary was written of the ideas articulated for each of the three components of the question construction process. Then, looking across the statements of an individual, final summaries were written for each of the three components.

Sources for the Portfolio Question

Both Christina and Mehan constructed portfolio questions that embedded a conceptual understanding or theory they had learned earlier in their career as a student. They used this recalled theory as the basis for the design or explanation of classroom events. This recollection came to light during the first quarter of student teaching and was harnessed into a question for inquiry.

Christina Hayashi came to teacher education directly following her undergraduate preparation in English. Following her student teaching, she accepted a full-time position in that same high school English department and is now a contributing member of that faculty. Her reacquaintance with Gardner's theory of multiple intelligences triggered a memory of her high school academic experience.

> I guess my first exposure to [Gardner's theory, embedded in my portfolio question] was when I was in high school myself and we had a GATE [a program for gifted and talented students] meeting of some sort where one of the coordinators had brought up the whole concept. And that was always something that struck me. And, in fact, one of my friends from high school—who I had grown up with—was an incredibly talented artist and yet he was someone who always struggled throughout the education process. He worked really hard and was very diligent, and yet the school didn't tap into his real talent. That was something that always bothered me, because I felt he was such a genius. Then it came up again in our [English] curriculum and instruction class. We read

an article on multiple intelligences, and the instructor had ar-
ranged different activities to focus on different intelligences
throughout the quarter. So I was really interested in that idea
and trying to incorporate that into my teaching.

Mehan Yektai decided to become a secondary mathematics teacher
after working part-time for several years as a structural engineer during
her undergraduate studies and, following graduation, working another
6 months in construction and as a tutor for a home study program. For
her first 2 years of teaching, she worked in an urban middle school before transferring to a high school in another district. She currently is
teaching mathematics at that school. Her puzzlement arose from classroom events that could not be explained by her previously held conception of mathematical thinking.

It started out as a couple of lessons that I had done that puzzled
me. A couple that I thought were open-ended and fun. But the students just acted with dismay, and they didn't want to do them.
There was all this resistance, and it was just icky and bad. Then
there were a couple of lessons that I hadn't had very high hopes
for, and they went really well. In fact, students were having these
marvelous conversations. And I sat down to analyze what was
different about these lessons.

Mehan turned from Polanyi's problem-solving heuristics, which she had
used in her own mathematical study, in favor of the concept of mathematical metacognition. "They've shown that people who are good at
problem solving kind of carry on this internal conversation with themselves that has to be in words that are real to them. You just can't teach
them a set of questions to ask themselves." Mehan found this intellectual
journey helped her transform "the way that I've learned in school into
the way that I want to teach in school." Mehan's portfolio question is:
How do I make my students good mathematical problem solvers?
    Christina's and Mehan's stimulation for inquiry comes, then, from
their initial study as teachers, which tapped into recollections and prior
learning, and from questions that arose from classroom practice.

Process of Constructing a Question

Student teachers focused their inquiry into a workable, researchable
question through writing multiple drafts of increasing refinement. They
divided their question into manageable chunks so that they could work

with the information. They replaced educational jargon with more precise understandings and articulation of focus, for their understanding of the language they use is paramount to their development as professionals.

The co-instructors assisted in this revision process through "question sessions" where questions were questioned and critiqued and constructive suggestions offered. Most students began with general notions of a topic or question. When asked to recall the earliest forms of her portfolio question, Christina began, "It had to do with using multiple intelligence activities to challenge students and allow students to achieve some degree of success." Later elaboration helped her to realize that teaching to multiple intelligences included "different levels of success, from your standards of absolute excellent work to students who are still learning English. That helped shape a lot of my philosophy in my portfolio."

The shaping and reformulation process also occurred in personal writing. In her journal, Mehan struggled with the referent for key words like "class" and "students," whether to focus her inquiry on a particular course or a particular group of students; she read from her journal during our interview.

> I wasn't sure whether I should focus on specific students or if I should keep "my students generic as if they're kind of the same from year to year. I wanted to investigate some issues in my Math A class about whether they perceived our class as being different from the rest of the school or whether they perceived me as being part of the system and our class as being part of the system."

Almost all students were uncomfortable initially with the ambiguous nature of question construction but also benefited from both the challenge and the time frame. Mehan spoke for most when she pointed out that "the requirements for the portfolio question were really fuzzy [she giggled] and at times I couldn't figure out if I even had a question. Sometimes I'd think it was a question, but the people in charge wouldn't."

Nonetheless, Mehan viewed the question framing as an opportunity to develop her educational vision, as a way of keeping herself focused on what is important in learning to think mathematically.

> In my [teacher education] year, I was trying to clarify my vision of what education is about, because I really felt like it could get lost. . . . "I said at the start that I don't want to be treated as the

authority of mathematical truth. When students get an answer from a teacher, they tend to treat it as 100% absolute valid truth. When they get an answer from another student, they evaluate it. They have to make a decision about whether they want to accept it or keep looking for a better one. This explains why I wasn't using the textbook, because [students] tend to treat the textbook as absolute truth, too, and I don't think that's how learning math occurs." So, I think a big part of the reason I wanted to hold onto this idea is because I feel if we're raising the next generation to be independent thinkers, that's how we have to teach them, too.

In the end, Mehan's question embraces a progressive view of mathematics teaching, one that placed her in strong contrast with more traditional pedagogy: "I wanted to investigate the role of collaboration between students in solving a problem in developing metacognition, in developing a kind of conversation that a student would be able to have with herself when she was solving problems alone. It's the role of mathematical conversation in problem solving." It was this process of "questioning the question" that helped Mehan and her colleagues to shape and refine their questions.

Sustaining Influence

Three years after completing the portfolio project, Mehan and Christina continued to incorporate the cognitive strategies of inquiry and collaborative learning into their teaching. Their conversations reveal that the most powerful tool taken from the portfolio project was the habit of mind that views teaching as inquiry and in which talk about practice is incorporated as a regular occurrence. Although neither teacher has continued to add to and revise her original physical portfolio, both acknowledge the continuing use of the portfolio question in their everyday professional practice of planning and assessment.

Mehan reported the most dramatic sustaining use of this self-directed inquiry. Following a frustrating second year in a urban middle school where she found little support for teaching for understanding, she transferred to a more supportive high school in the same region, only to discover she was still "in trauma" while learning to be a teacher. Her crisis came in January in her third year of teaching, just after returning to school following the winter holidays.

But that Wednesday back from winter break, I just stayed at home with the flu. During the day I pulled out my [teacher education] journal and my portfolio and read through them. And I read with a kind of a funny feeling—like I remembered what it was that I wanted to do. But at the same time, I was thinking maybe this is just a chapter that's going to close—I don't know if I'm going to stay in teaching after this year. I was literally sick, but also sick of feeling like I don't know what I am doing and I keep trying and wasn't getting it right. But I thought, OK, I'll go to school tomorrow and I'll see what happens. And I just decided to back off a little bit and not force things so much, partly because I was still getting well. I decided to just sort of observe the group working together and not try to push them that much, and I have to say that was the turning point in my year. My year has been really good since that Thursday.

Following her dramatic turnaround, Mehan has been mentally documenting her progress in teaching. "I feel like I've been able to grow again, to learn new things." But when asked if she was putting these in a collection that could be called a portfolio, Mehan admitted that she was not documenting her inquiry. "I keep thinking—next year, next year. So now I'm doing some of it. I'm kind of creating a portfolio in my mind but, no, I'm not writing it down."

Like Mehan, Christina continues to revisit her portfolio question because of its centrality to her conception of teaching English. She keeps samples of student work as assessment of her instruction.

I guess I keep coming back to it [my portfolio inquiry] just because it was such a broad question because it incorporated different facets that I find very important in my teaching. One is seeing the student as a whole, not as just an English student. Trying to draw out their different skills and help them develop in different ways. I always try to see how I can take these activities and link them back into what people expect from an English class. Trying to make meaningful connections. And just coming back to the other side of it is how to challenge students and yet within a broad range of ability how to allow them to be successful. I see those as the four main things that I originally was trying to get through in my portfolio. It's always good to have that in the back of my mind just because those are critical issues that I see that shape my teaching and how I want to approach what I do in the classroom, how I interact with students. It's kind of an accountability measure in some ways, you know. I have to remember to come back to those key issues.

She has continued to add strategies for multiple intelligences, the most recent being service learning: "I guess the most recent would be just different things that have come across in community service learning that we've done. Part of it is just how in different ways students have exceeded my expectations, and areas in which I need to clarify certain things or things that I really need to watch for in future times when I work with kids."

CONCLUSION

While interviewing these two teachers 3 years after completing the portfolio project, we were struck with the clarity, the specificity, and the passion with which they described the experience and its impact on their professional lives. Each could remember the focus of her question and its exact wording, for she continues to apply the same question to new situations. Both have internalized and sustained the habits of mind fostered by this self-generated inquiry: the habit of mind that views teaching as inquiry, and the habit of mind that views collaborative learning as the way to come to know teaching. Particularly when the school culture fosters this kind of inquiry and dialogue, each has blossomed into a respected, accomplished professional in her school. Christina moved immediately into a school setting where she could continue this work. Mehan, discovering its absence in her first teaching assignment, used it as a criterion for selecting her new school, and now is continuing this work.

As a curriculum design strategy for teacher education, constructing a self-generated portfolio question helps students to transform prior conceptual understandings into professional practice. For these two individuals, the issue of the question arose when a classroom incident triggered the recall of previously learned theory—Christina remembered Gardner's multiple intelligences and Mehan studied her own problem-solving strategies and questioned Polanyi's heuristics. With coaching and revisions, both were able to transform these prior understandings into professional inquiry and to focus each question on the interconnection of teaching a particular subject matter and teaching a particular group of students. Their questions are embedded in the nexus of student and content.

But centering most discussions of student teaching on the inquiry generated from a portfolio question raises the issue of curricular priorities. Portfolio development based on this design is, in the final analysis, a student-constructed curriculum. Devoting a portion of a teacher education curriculum to core questions arising out of a particular classroom experience raises for teacher educators, as Wiggins's essential questions raise for teachers, issues of appropriate curricular coverage. The conceptual understandings about classroom practice constructed by this self-designed question appear to be personally bounded and contextualized. But as Cochran-Smith (1991) reminds us, it is "only in the apparent 'narrowness' of work in particular classrooms and in the 'boundedness' of discussions of highly contextualized instances of practice that student teachers actually have opportunities to confront the broadest themes of reform" (p. 307).

This is a "less is more" curriculum; it calls upon teacher educators to reorganize information and enhance the likelihood of powerful student learning. It places equal emphasis on making sense of classroom events and on the social interactions within which conceptual changes are possible—through clarification, elaboration, and justification. It devotes adequate time to conversation and dialogue. A curriculum based on self-designed inquiry, framed around a portfolio question, is a curriculum where the central core is establishing professional habits of mind, and where the primary focus is helping teacher education students learn to think like teachers. Within this depth, students changed their understanding of teaching from a conception that teachers predict and control learning to a view that teaching is "intellectual problem setting" (Cochran-Smith, 1991, p. 293). Prior conceptual understandings help them to interpret and transform their work as teachers.

NOTES

1. We are indebted to Gary Lichtenstein, the other co-instructor in this seminar, for his extensive contributions to the design of this portfolio entry and in coaching students' development of portfolio questions.

2. All names are pseudonyms to protect the confidentiality of these individuals and their schools.

3. For improved readability, we removed pauses and filler words from any quotations drawn from these statements.

REFERENCES

Barton, J., & Collins, A. (1993). Portfolios in teacher education. *Journal of Teacher Education, 44*(3), 200–211.

Bird, T. (1990). The schoolteacher's portfolio: An essay on possibilities. In J. Millman & L. Darling-Hammond (Eds.), *The new handbook of teacher evaluation: Assessing elementary and secondary school teachers* (2nd ed.; pp. 241–256). Newbury Park, CA: Sage.

Brooks, J. G., & Brooks, M. G. (1993). *In search of understanding: The case for constructivist classrooms.* Washington, DC: Association for Supervision and Curriculum Development.

Brown, A. L., & Palincsar, A. S. (1989). Guided, cooperative learning and individual knowledge acquisition. In L. B. Resnick (Ed.), *Knowledge, learning and instruction: Essays in honor of Robert Glaser* (pp. 19–39). Hillsdale, NJ: Lawrence Erlbaum.

Bruner, J. (1994, April). *The human and interpretively possible.* Address at the annual meeting of the American Educational Research Association, New Orleans.

Cochran-Smith, M. (1991). Learning to teach against the grain. *Harvard Educational Review, 61*(3), 279–310.

Glaser, B. G., & Strauss, A. L. (1967). *The discovery of grounded theory: Strategies for qualitative research.* New York: Aldine.

Grant, G. E. (1990). *A STEP teacher's portfolio.* Unpublished manuscript, Stanford University, School of Education.

Grant, G. E. (1995). Interpreting text as pedagogy and pedagogy as text. *Teachers and Teaching, 1*(1), 87–100.

Grant, G. E., & Huebner, T. A. (in press). The portfolio question: Synthesizing the personal and the professional. *Teacher Education Quarterly.*

Lichtenstein, G., Rubin, T., & Grant, G. E. (1992, April). *Teacher portfolios and professional development.* Paper presented at the annual meeting of the American Educational Research Association, San Francisco.

Mishler, E. G. (1986). *Research interviewing: Context and narrative.* Cambridge, MA: Harvard University Press.

Mosenthal, J., Daniels, P., & Hull, S. (1993, April). *From the bottom up: The perspective of preservice undergraduates on constructing teacher portfolios.* Paper presented at the annual meeting of the American Educational Research Association, Atlanta.

Piaget, J. (1959). *The language and thought of the child.* London: Routledge & Kegan Paul.

Shulman, L. S. (1988). A union of insufficiencies: Strategies for teacher assessment in a period of educational reform. *Educational Leadership, 46*(3), 36–41.

Shulman, L. S. (1992, April). *Portfolios in teacher education: A component of reflective teacher education.* Paper presented at the annual meeting of the American Educational Research Association, San Francisco.

Shulman, L. S. (1994, January). *Portfolios in historical perspective: Why portfolios?* Paper presented at Portfolios in Teacher Education Working Conference, Cambridge, MA.

Vygotsky, L. S. (1978). *Mind in society: The development of higher psychological processes* (M. Cole, V. John-Steiner, S. Scribner, & E. Souberman, Eds.). Cambridge, MA: Harvard University Press.

Wiggins, G. (1987). Creating a thought-provoking curriculum: Lessons from whodunits and others. *American Educator, 11*(4), 10–17.

Wiggins, G. (1989). The futility of trying to teach everything of importance. *Educational Leadership, 46*(3), 44–59.

Wolf, K. (1991). The schoolteacher's portfolio: Issues in design, implementation, and evaluation. *Phi Delta Kappan, 73(2),* 129–136.

Wolf, K. (1994). Teaching portfolios: Capturing the complexity of teaching. In L. Ingvarson & R. Chadbourne (Eds.), *Teacher appraisal: New directions* (pp. 108–132). Victoria: Australian Council for Educational Research.

Wolf, K., Whinery, B., & Hagerty, P. (1995). Teaching portfolios and portfolio conversations for teacher educators and teachers. *Action in Teacher Education, 17*(1), 30–39.

CHAPTER 11

A Post-Tenure Review Portfolio: A Collaborative Venture

Larry Cuban

STANFORD UNIVERSITY

All I ever wanted from my colleagues was a tough and fair post-tenure review. I got that *and* a portfolio, something I had barely heard of previously. Therein lies a story.

Between November 1990 and May 1991 a committee of three colleagues appointed by Dean Mike Smith met with me five times, read at least 35 pages of memos and an additional 100 pages of articles and book excerpts that I had prepared and gathered, watched a videotape of one class that I had taught, and discussed at length with me particular facets of my teaching and research agendas. In January 1992, both the committee and I reported to our faculty what we had done and there was an hour-long discussion of my post-tenure review.

RATIONALE

No such process is authorized in Stanford University's Faculty Handbook, the document that includes the policies guiding faculty rights and responsibilities. So why did I want such a review, what did I want to be reviewed, how was it done, and of what worth was it to me? I will answer these questions in turn but I want to make clear that what I produced has been called a "portfolio" but it was not my intention to create one.

Having done so, I am glad that I did and will know better what to put into one next time. I say this because the portfolio is not central to my experience; what it did was permit me to examine, in depth, with colleagues I trusted, selected activities that I had been doing for 5 years as a tenured professor. On to the questions.

Why Did I Want a Post-Tenure Review?

I had already been a teacher and administrator in urban public schools for a quarter-century before coming to Stanford in 1981 as an associate professor. In 1986, after failed attempts to return to being a superintendent, I decided to seek tenure and a promotion. In the process of the tenure review, I requested from the dean a review in 5 years. He spoke with the provost and found out that no condition—such as a future review—could be attached to acquiring tenure and if I wanted to have such a review, I would need to negotiate that with whomever was dean then.

So it was that in 1990 I approached Dean Mike Smith and requested such a review. My reasons were familiar ones. Most of my career had been spent moving from post to post, so new challenges kept me dancing intellectually as fast as I could. Being a professor for almost a decade was the longest time in my adult life that I had spent in one position. Moreover, I had discovered that faculty colleagues of national and international repute were anxious to protect a precious autonomy that they had cultivated for themselves. In other words, being a member of such a distinguished group did not automatically or easily translate into sterling exchanges of ideas over lunch, coffee, or at the mailboxes in the main office. Isolation was the norm. So I needed re-potting.

But why approach the dean? I could have just as well asked a few trusted friends on the faculty to help me. My reasons for making it an official request are laid out in a memo that I wrote to the dean on October 31, 1990.

> I have come to believe that the rhetoric that we are a community of scholars in a professional school. I owe my community the full and best performance I am capable of in discharging the roles of teaching, research, and service that are expected of me. . . . When I do well in these areas it reflects well on me and the institution that I serve. The flip side of my institutional obligation . . . is the responsibility of my colleagues to help me improve in the performance of my central roles, especially when I seek their assistance. . . . I want, simply put, a collegial dialogue about my work.

To be tenured, in my judgment, does not relieve the institution of
its obligation to me.

Or, I easily could have added, my responsibility to myself to examine
what I do. Dean Smith appointed Mike Atkin, John Baugh (who had
just joined the faculty as a tenured professor), and Lee Shulman.

What About My Work Did I Want to Have Reviewed?

Two areas in particular interested me: my teaching and my current and
future research agenda. I was less interested in the arena of service since
I had been heavily active in working with Bay Area practitioners and
with AERA, and had served as associate dean of the school. It was the
intersection between teaching and research that fascinated me and that
was what I wanted the committee to examine with me.

For my teaching, I figured that the committee would examine
my syllabi since they are maps that would give the committee members
ways of inquiring into both my pedagogy and how I organized content
conceptually. I expected the committee to examine evaluations of my
teaching and, especially, consider the pedagogical dilemmas that I have
wrestled with continually over the years both in high school and graduate teaching.

For my research agenda, I wanted the committee to appraise my
past publications, less for their content and more for their direction, and
reflect on my proposed project of examining how professors have taught,
which had grown out of earlier research on a history of how teachers
taught. I also wanted their thoughts on the dilemmas that I faced as a
researcher committed to impartial scholarship while actively trying to
improve teaching and administrative practice.

How Was the Review Conducted?

The dean assigned one of his staff to collect my materials (evaluations
of previous classes; articles and books that I had written in the previous
5 years), distribute them to committee members, and set dates for
meetings.

The staff person that the dean assigned kept notes and from those
summaries, the flow of the hour-and-a-half meetings became clear.
They were highly interactive and we worked as equals; there was no
sense that heavy consequences loomed for me or for the committee in
completing their deliberations. This was not a tenure or promotion committee meeting, by any means. On the contrary, I sensed a strong feeling

that these discussions about my work were sincere probes into not only my teaching and research but opportunities for each member to consider for himself the points we lobbed back and forth about the details of my teaching and research. It was a chance to talk about things that we had never spoken about except, on occasion, to trusted friends. These discussions became, I believe, proxies for other members' self-examination as well as mine; at least two of them expressed this to me privately.

At the meetings themselves, I usually set the agenda; members also raised items as we met. For example, at the first meeting where we met with the dean, a number of obvious questions arose: How can we do this without it becoming too burdensome on anyone? Should there be a written report? Presented to what audience? The dean wanted the faculty to be aware of what went on and why. He suggested that this could be on the agenda at one of the retreats held annually by faculty. Consensus was reached that the committee would write up a report for me only and that an oral report be given to the entire faculty.

At another meeting on January 31, 1991, we discussed what I had already submitted and members asked for the following additional information from me:

- examples of student work, both exemplary and problematic;
- comments on my present and future use of case study methods;
- comments on the first time that I taught a social studies methods course and future plans with it; on how it helps or impedes in the areas of research and teaching;
- comments on institutional obligations to the professor; on this institution and my relationship with it; on how it helps or impedes my research and teaching.

Then each committee member promised to review portions of my teaching from student evaluations, videotape, and so on. (Of the above items I completed only the last two.)

This discussion of agenda points and negotiation of another set of tasks became customary for subsequent meetings. These memos and other written tasks became the de facto portfolio.

The portfolio included memos on how I analyzed my teaching and research agendas; a videotape of an hour-and-a-half class with a nine-page, single-spaced typed analysis of my teaching and student responses; an exploration of a new course I had created; a memo on the mutual obligations of a professor to a school of education and the faculty to each other; and a final memo on the process of review itself and its overall worth to me.

THE CONTENTS OF THE PORTFOLIO: TEACHING AND RESEARCH

To give readers a flavor of items in the portfolio, let me offer excerpts. I begin with the course "History of School Reform" co-taught with David Tyack. This portfolio item contained the syllabus; a videotape of one class that I taught; a close analysis of the videotape, which I wrote with materials from the class itself (questions I handed out to students, a tally of students participating, etc.); and the readings that the class discussed.

Teaching the "History of School Reform" Class

This was a graduate class of 32 students, 18 of whom were in a doctoral program, 10 were masters students, and 4 were undergraduates. As far as backgrounds, there was a mix of former urban high school teachers, administrators, community activists, medical school researchers, psychology majors with no experience in public schools, and students who had taught in other countries. Only a handful had taken history courses as undergraduates. The issue of teaching a course on the history of school reform to a class of largely nonhistory majors with a diverse range of backgrounds (and different futures) created tensions for us each time we had taught the course in the past. I quote from the analysis of the class.

> We have developed a sequence of activities for the twice-weekly, hour-and-a-half classes. Typically, there are one or two readings as-signed for each session. Each of us takes responsibility for prepar-ing a short list of questions that are distributed prior to the class in which we examine the readings. (After assignment is given, stu-dent questions answered, and announcements are made) . . . we move to a whole-class discussion of the readings guided by the questions we asked. Often those questions (given out the previous session) are placed on the chalkboard. The discussion usually lasts 40–60 minutes and is followed by a small-group activity with speci-fied tasks for each group to complete within 30–45 minutes. The final portion of the class is set aside for each group to report, ques-tions from students about unresolved issues within their groups, and, if time, an effort to pull the many threads together (this oc-curred infrequently; often, unfinished summaries required a few

minutes at the beginning of the next class). Within this typical sequence of activities, it was a rare event when either David or I
completed the [initial] questions that we had asked of the students.

The class that I had videotaped and analyzed was one in which we had
just finished the Progressive movement of school reform and had started
into the civil rights movement of the 1960s. The readings for this class
were drawn from Diane Ravitch and David Tyack. I had prepared three
questions and asked two students to take opposite sides on one question
about whether the school reforms of the Progressive years were less successful in improving schools than the reforms of the civil rights movement. I had intended this to be a variation of the usual small-group activity that followed whole-class discussion. What were my objectives for
this class?

Usually, the questions I prepare for the readings contain what concepts I would like students to understand. In this case, I was after
three. First, while both of these social movements contained many
school reforms . . . the civil rights movement challenged certain
Progressive reforms (e.g., IQ tests) and expanded others. The notion of reforms of one generation extending and challenging reforms of an earlier one was an idea that I wanted students to consider.

Second, there are at least two "ways of seeing" the school reforms
of the 1960s. One is that the reforms derived from a social movement joining diverse groups in a collective effort to bend schools
in improving them (Tyack); the other perspective (Ravitch) is that
what occurred in the 1960s resulted from varied coalitions of interest groups each seeking different agendas using political tactics in
the school arena to achieve their ends. The concept of "ways of
seeing," employing different perspectives to view events, is a major
goal of the course and we keep coming back to it in different sessions. . . .

Third, I wanted the class to re-examine a slippery concept central
to any understanding of school reform; the varied meanings of
"success" as in "it was a successful reform." We had dealt with
this notion in an earlier set of readings and I wanted to return
since I felt what we know about school reform is often based upon

narrow, implicit notions of success that are seldom examined openly.

In addition to what I had in mind prior to teaching, I had a number of collateral objectives that I pursued during each class I taught: getting students to challenge the sources they read (i.e., the assumptions of authors, the argument in the selection, the evidence used) and their professor's ideas in carrying on the discussion; and determining the degree of understanding of concepts in individual students through their participation and my probing of their responses.

I then turned to my assessment of how well I achieved these.

Objectives After Viewing the Videotape

As with all reflections on what happened in a class . . . much remains ambiguous. . . . Often I find out whether my objectives were reached in a subsequent paper a student writes, a remark in a discussion, or in formal evaluations of the course. So, as any experienced teacher would know, determining whether objectives are met is a long-term venture and a short-term risk.

Because how many students participate in discussion and what they say offers some evidence of how close I came to reaching [my] . . . objectives, I counted in the videotape how many people participated in the discussion (22, or 76%); I divided students into high (21%), moderate (17%), and low (34%), and silent ones (24%)—a fairly typical spread for this class's participation over the quarter. I listened closely to which students said what in order to gain a sense of how much the particular student understood the concepts under discussion. But even this veneer of precision leaves a great deal open to speculation . . . whether my intended objectives were reached.

What I saw after reviewing the tape twice was that the first concept I wanted students to grasp scarcely arose during class discussion. It was missing-in-action. The bulk of the class interaction was over the content of the readings and, in particular, the distinction between a social movement and interest-group politics. . . .

As for the collateral objectives, analyzing the student frequency and quality of participation become important in assessing to what degree, if any, these objectives were being met in this class. Hence, the above numbers . . . become helpful. For those that participated in class, I noted that there were numerous times that students built upon one another's ideas, challenged David and me and each other . . . , and created student-to-student exchanges rather than the usual student–teacher–student interactions. This last item of student-to-student interactions . . . I consider important in whole-class discussions because the exchanges demonstrate a slight shift in the intellectual center of gravity from the teacher who usually directs the turn taking to students. I counted five instances of where students responded directly to other students on a point either building, challenging, or elaborating on the initial statement. Our usual small-group activities, of course, are structured attempts to focus the intellectual tasks students perform while having them take charge.

What also became obvious to me in analyzing the videotape was the familiar reappearance of value conflicts that I had faced in teaching high school. These dilemmas, were classroom situations in which I had to choose between competing values, both of which I prized, knowing full well that I had to make sacrifices in one value in order to reach a threshold of satisfaction about the lesson that I taught.

The most obvious [dilemma] was coverage of content vs. depth of understanding. With 90 minutes (we take no breaks) and the clock-tower chiming every 15 minutes outside of our classroom, I am always aware of how much time is left to cover the questions on the chalkboard and whether I am spending too much time on a particular point. . . . I constantly monitor the discussion while I listen for the chimes. Where the pinch occurs is my desire to get non-participants into the discussion, ask follow-up questions for students who have responded to my initial inquiry, and encourage extended remarks from certain students who, I feel, have much to offer the class. For all of this to occur requires time, which means that certain content is sacrificed. . . .

Another durable . . . dilemma that emerged for me in the tape was that balance that I did strike in this class . . . between being a traffic cop, [that is] having all students entering the discussions get recognized by me in order to spread the turns taken by students

. . . and encouraging students to follow-up on other students' comments without waiting to take their turn. The value of broader participation (preventing hogging of air time by a vocal few) competes with the values of spontaneity, the raising of points that I had not considered. The compromises I have struck in handling this dilemma mean that I leave some students with hands stuck in the air.

My Research Agenda

In a long memo on December 28 to members of the committee, I explored what books I had written and why I had done so since coming to Stanford in 1981. I then turned to the book I was writing with David Tyack on the history of school reform, a manuscript that had grown out of our teaching the above course since the late 1980s. Finally, I described the next writing project that I had just begun to research, which was a history of how professors had taught in universities over the last century, the connection of that story to the earlier one I had written on public school teachers, and the comparison of how both groups had taught during the same period.

This memo on my past, present, and future research agenda forced me to put into words unformed thoughts and murky impressions about why I do what I do. I quote from that memo to make this point clear.

> What ties these books of the last decade together [*How Teachers Taught; Teacher and Machines; The Classroom Use of Technology Since 1920; The Managerial Imperative; The Practice of Leadership in Schools*] is a series of themes that seem, only in retrospect, fairly clear to me but may appear muddled to others: a focus on the nature of teaching at all levels of schooling; a focus of policy and administrative efforts to alter the practice of teaching, and the nature of the setting in which policy and practice come together—the school. In all honesty, had someone asked me in 1981 [when I arrived at Stanford] what my research agenda was for the next decade I would have probably said little more than an interest in historically studying teaching as I had begun in HTT and further research of the superintendency. My experiences as a professor, associate dean, and—most compelling—as a teacher and administrator are what have shaped and reshaped my intellectual interests as they get reworked over time in my mind. What is clear to me, as I write these thoughts down, is that I tend to think of doing major

research in terms of books, not articles. I think of big chunks of writing and long-term projects of 2 or 3 years.

Yet, as I point out in this memo, I write for different audiences, that is, academics, practitioners, and the general public. I also spend a large portion of my time working with practitioners through our Stanford Educational Collaborative, and yet I had no desire to write on these partnerships or the work that I did directly with schools seeking to make changes. That bothered me so I wrote about it.

> What is puzzling to me . . . is the lack of my desire to research the meaning and worth of collaboration to teachers and administrators. I read what others have written about university–school cooperation. I am very interested in helping teachers and administrators study issues in their own settings and write up what they have learned. . . . But my strong interest doesn't translate into a passion to study systematically what is occurring in university–school cooperation. I have no book in me about collaboration. I consider it very important work and valuable to me personally but separate from my research agenda. I find that gap puzzling.

Also in this memo I explored a few of the dilemmas that I, as a professor of education, faced in trying to reach varied audiences.

> The dilemma I have is between satisfying intellectual, reflective values that I prize and the action, go-go, can-do world of the practitioner which is also a highly valued part of me. What I have patched together is a compromise of hitting different audiences in no clear pattern, more akin to when I feel like writing for one or the other. . . .

> I write for scholars because the personal side of me is pleased by the intellectual stretch that such writing forces upon me and any subsequent relevance of my findings to other researchers; moreover, I realize that scholarly exchanges about policy-relevant research may influence policymaking debates. I write for policymakers because they have an influence on setting the agenda for what gets debated and determine what policies get adopted. I write for practitioners because they implement policy. Also in reaching out to practitioners I can remain faithful to my roots as a classroom teacher and administrator and, more important, allow myself to be a translator of research findings for those who ordinarily would

not have the time or inclination to seek out the original studies. . . .

This balancing of desired values may have been good enough for the last 5 years but I do need to consider other alternative compromises since I hear a clock ticking. Can you think of other mixes of writing that I may have overlooked? Or, more to the point, in reviewing the writing I do for the different audiences, do you feel that I should focus on fewer groups because the quality of the writings may be soft, unfocused, or inferior?

These questions became agenda items for a subsequent committee meeting.

In addition to this memo on teaching and research, I wrote memos on the new course in our teacher education program that I had just developed with a high school teacher. There are other memos, but these excerpts should give readers a sense of what I did and what I sought from my colleagues.

OF WHAT WORTH WAS THIS POST-TENURE REVIEW TO ME?

I had promised the committee that I would prepare a memo for them to use in assessing what our deliberations and my work had meant to me. Let me quote at length from that May 1991 memo.

The most beneficial part of all of the memos I produced, at least for me, has been how it forced me to rethink old ideas and open up new areas that I had not considered. The act of putting the words on paper knowing that three people whom I respect will read those words pressed me to be clear in what I wanted to say, succinct (I worried about the time that it would take to read) and thoughtful so that it could help me untwist tangled ideas. If there is one over-riding benefit to such a review it is the requirement placed upon the person seeking the review to lay out for others the issues that puzzle the person, the conflicting values, unclarified questions, and the like.

Another important benefit that I came to see was the opportunity to have colleagues take a step back to examine seriously a body of work that I had accumulated over time, from where it came and where it might be leading, and to ask the seldom explored "so what" question. The only time that had occurred was when I sought tenure in 1986 and a committee of peers examined my work and got opinions from outside the university.

Yet, even at that time, all one hears from the dean and faculty is what the outcome is: yes, you got tenure and a promotion; no, you got neither. You do not find out what others consider as strengths and limitations of your work and its direction, since the letters and committee report are confidential. Once tenure is awarded, that is the last review of your work. As I said in the memo:

> If you are lucky, you have trusted friends who offer you occasional insights into your career. But you can't count on it in friendships where deep affection and . . . objectivity compete. What made this review remarkably different from the usual tenure review was the clear focus on improving rather than judging and concentrating on issues raised by me or by others as we met together.

What About Shortcomings to the Process?

> If there were any weaknesses, and that is a word that is suspect since this is the first time any of us have gone through this process, it would be around my lack of structuring the discussions during the four times that we met and the uncertainty I have about what a portfolio [focusing on a review of teaching and research] should contain. . . .

> The concept of the portfolio is most appealing to me. I am afraid, however, that I have yet to grasp its essence. I understand that it is both to document and to inquire into teaching and research. It is to be selective rather than overwhelming. The pieces that I have produced for this portfolio have the traditional items with a number of reflective pieces from me. What is still missing from the portfolio is what my students have learned or at least an attempt to get at that. What I still fail to see is a coherence to them, an underlying weave to the fabric. Perhaps that is what you are to see. And perhaps that will come in time.

What has become clear to me since writing the memo, however, is the lack of any in-depth review of my work from someone, for example, who is familiar with the history of teaching, curriculum, and school reform—subjects about which I have written. The members of the committee were experts in different areas so they felt unequipped to make substantive judgments about my work. Nor did we pursue outside letters. The thought of trying to explain a voluntary post-tenure review to someone outside of the university while asking that person to take time to write an in-depth evaluation of my work that would be made available to me was sufficiently thorny to prevent any examination from the committee.

WHAT HAPPENED AFTER THE REVIEW WAS COMPLETED?

In January 1992 we reported to the faculty at a regularly scheduled monthly meeting. A member of the committee presented a brief report, a few paragraphs from which may capture the sentiment expressed by my colleagues in the subsequent discussion.

> I learned a lot about Larry's work, his professional philosophy, and areas of his scholarship that are relevant to my own research. The virtues of this effort grew from two major factors: (1) Larry worked very hard to make his review a success; he produced memos, agendas, provided publications, and was available for discussion; and (2) the committee was composed of members who place a high priority on professional collegiality; there was a pervasive aura of tolerance and respect.

> Despite my positive experience, I have had difficulty thinking of ways to formalize this process, and to do so in a manner that would not place avoidable demands on our time. Whereas Larry was willing, indeed, eager to devote hours to the preparation of a portfolio and related meetings throughout the year, I have no such desire and doubt that many of us would approach the task with equal enthusiasm. (I recognize . . . that I could be very wrong.)

He was not wrong. At the meeting others on the committee told of their experiences with the post-tenure review. I gave my impressions also. The faculty exchanges in the hour's discussion explored the worth of such voluntary reviews, whether such reviews should be made mandatory, and the time that each one would take. I believe a fair summary of the faculty's discussion would be that there were strong reservations about any post-tenure review requirement being instituted.

Since then, nothing much has happened with post-tenure reviews in the School of Education. One member of our committee, who agreed to be on the committee with the provision that I would be on his post-tenure review, after 3 years has yet to establish such a process for himself. The reasons why colleagues may be reluctant to seek such a review vary from person to person but my hunch is that, at bottom, the fundamental reason may be close to what the colleague who reported to the faculty said in his closing paragraph.

> My observations are not definite, and will, hopefully lead to more detailed discussion regarding the virtues and limitations of post-tenure reviews. During our deliberations I observed that the gatherings were among my most enjoyable meetings, but they received low priority. I value the freedom that allows us to devote substantial blocks of time to teaching, researching, and writing. Even though I recognize the importance of committee assignments to our institutional welfare, I prefer to keep bureaucracy to a minimum.

The dilemma of professional autonomy and institutional obligations emerges from the colleague's words; it persists and no easy reconciliation is in sight for him or the rest of my peers.

PART IV

Judging and Validating Portfolio Evidence: Warranting a New Vision of Teacher Professionalism

NATIONAL, STATE, AND LOCAL PORTFOLIO INITIATIVES REDEFINE TEACHER CERTIFICATION

1997 marked the tenth anniversary of the establishment of the National Board for Professional Teaching Standards (NBPTS), a defining event for the entry of portfolios into teacher education. The National Board, demanding participation by teachers in its work, guaranteed teacher voices in developing a new professionalism called for by 1980s reformers. Although there was no formal connection between the NBPTS and the work of Lee Shulman at the Stanford Teacher Assessment Project, Shulman's research developing teacher assessment prototypes resulted in the adoption of portfolios as a principal means of evaluating experienced teachers for Board certification.

Today the NBPTS is well-established and the portfolio a centerpiece of its assessment process. Several rounds of portfolio assessments have resulted in some hundreds of Board-certified experienced teachers. The Interstate New Teachers Assessment and Support Consortium (INTASC), also established in 1987, is similarly at work piloting the use of portfolios for the evaluation and credentialing of beginning teachers. Some 32 states are working with INTASC and considering the uses of portfolios in their teacher education programs and licensing practices. In some crucial ways this work with portfolios at the national and state levels mirrors certain issues raised by all portfolio users: that is, how to guarantee the validity and reliability of portfolio evidence. How should portfolios be judged? By what evidence? Using what criteria?

This part of the book addresses these issues. It does so by examining the work of individuals creating and using portfolio assessment systems with individual teacher interns in particular teacher education programs—

see the chapter by Walter Kimball and Susie Hanley and their work with the University of Southern Maine (USM)'s Extended Teacher Education Program. It also looks at the efforts of researchers working with INTASC to rethink issues of validity and reliability of portfolios when used for large state assessment and licensing systems—see the chapter by Pamela Moss. In these experiments, portfolios are not stand-alone activities, but part of a larger system of assessment. In the USM experiment, portfolios become braided into the work of a year-long internship in learning to teach, culminating in a presentation that summarizes a year of constant feedback about teaching.

This work raises other issues as well: that is, how states might go about encouraging the uses of portfolios for teacher education and teacher credentialing. The chapter by Richard Dollase documenting the Vermont experiment provides one image: of states that mandate portfolios for teacher credentialing.

Concluding this part of the book is the thoughtful query of Gloria Ladson-Billings asking about what could be a missing entry in a portfolio: How are ethical questions at the heart of all teaching and learning acknowledged and portrayed in the portfolio?

CHAPTER 12

Anatomy of a Portfolio Assessment System: Using Multiple Sources of Evidence for Credentialing and Professional Development

Walter H. Kimball

UNIVERSITY OF SOUTHERN MAINE

Susie Hanley

GORHAM (ME) SCHOOL DEPARTMENT

The teacher intern, 35-year-old Jessie, attentive and alert, stood before the small group gathered at a table on an early May morning. She held open a large notebook, her teaching portfolio. She listened as one of her mentors presented the agenda for the meeting.

> Jessie will have 45 minutes to present her portfolio, we will then have an opportunity to question her, and, after that, Jessie will leave the room as we caucus to make a decision about recommending her for initial teacher certification. I think you all know each other. You have been her cooperating teachers in the two elementary teaching placements she has just completed here in the Gorham Public Schools or her university instructors, responsible for her coursework at the University of Southern Maine's Extended Teacher Education Program.

Then signaling Jessie to begin, the teacher said: "Do enjoy yourself!"

Jessie began her presentation with a section entitled, "Who I Am and My Vision of Teaching."

> I begin with "Who Am I?" because I bring to teaching who I am as a person. I take these things with me into a community and into a school. I become part of a community of learners.

Focusing on her teaching philosophy, her belief that "every student is a learner" and that the teacher's job is "to show students how to learn, and to give them reasons and opportunities for learning," Jessie led her listeners through the elements of her teaching platform. "Getting to know my students helps me to plan, teach, and evaluate students and their learning progress," she asserted. And, she added, "I am a learner with my students. My reflections on our classroom activities help me to construct a better learning program." Jessie's vision statement included her belief that "students learn by doing" and that a teacher "plans learning projects which teach not just information, but thinking skills and the process of investigation." Jessie went on to elaborate the idea of a class as a community of learners.

As she continued through her portfolio, features and highlights of her internship were revealed. Lessons, student experiences, and samples of student work from units she had taught appeared, along with photos of students in her two classes: one at "Circle Time," a second-grade sharing event; the other a sixth-grade science unit on "Boats" showing students making observations on why some boats tilted and sank and others stayed afloat. There were samples of airplanes sixth graders had made, journal entries, and assessments students had completed. There were bibliographies of Jessie's own readings as a new unit was undertaken. There were goals for science and math.

Toward the end of her presentation, Jessie talked about some of the portfolios her students had constructed: "No matter what kind of school I go to in the future, I will use portfolios with my students. There is nothing like them to show the progress and advance of an individual student. They do that in ways a report card just cannot."

When Jessie finished, the group of mentors and her two program coordinators began asking questions: What connections did kids make in that boat unit to the real world? Beyond Bowlby and Gardner, were there other theorists she drew upon in her teaching? How did it work out to have been responsible for a multiage, grades 2/3 inclusion class? What were her exact math goals? Were there any other things besides having students keep portfolios that she felt essential for her future classroom? The mentors especially liked how Jessie included aspects of her own learning as she discussed her students' learning.

At the end of the questioning, Jessie left the room. The mentors turned to each other. They had to decide on a recommendation: Was Jessie ready to take responsibility for a class of her own? to be certified as a teacher?

THE PORTFOLIO WITHIN A PERFORMANCE ASSESSMENT SYSTEM

The scene just described initiates the last act in a performance assessment system, one based on rigorous standards and high expectations. This system, while consistent and demanding, nonetheless encourages individuality and imaginative professional development through the flexibility afforded by the portfolio, both as a measure of excellence and a means of growth. In the work of the national bodies charged with the articulation of standards for the new teacher professionalism—the National Board for Professional Teaching Standards, the National Commission on Teaching and America's Future, and so on—portfolios have shown great promise for best capturing that elusive art we call teaching. With their actual documentation of a teacher's work, of student work, with analyses and reflections by a teacher, the rich and subtle life of a classroom can be presented and assessed.

But while there has been much applause for the rigor of standards and performance assessment systems for teacher education, there also has been an uneasiness if not sometimes outright disdain for a system that easily can be construed as mindless standardization.

This case study of Jesse's work demonstrates how the model now in use at the University of Southern Maine works. It incorporates 11 standards, or outcomes, that teacher apprentices must meet (see Figure 6.1 for ETEP standards); a year-long assessment process that monitors closely an internship in learning to teach; constant evaluation and dialogue about an intern's work; and an end-of-year portfolio presentation by the candidate as evidence of learning, and a self-assessment on the part of the intern. Capping the portfolio presentation is the discussion and determination of a recommendation for—or against—certification by the intern's mentors. Here, the portfolio is embedded within the larger assessment system.

This model is predicated on the commonly shared standards of participants and on the necessity for varied perspectives of cooperating teachers, program supervisors, and the intern to judge multiple sources of intern teaching and reflection, such as lesson plans, readings, student work, and so forth. The practitioners, both novice and experienced, believe that these procedures yield knowledge and insights that enable the intern's improvement as a teacher. It also is assumed that the continuous monitoring, interpreting, and judging of intern performance will result in fair and valid decisions for certification. In this chapter, one intern's journey through this system is described in significant detail, followed by analysis of issues of reliability, validity, and fairness in teacher assessment.

JESSIE'S JOURNEY

Jessie entered the University of Southern Maine's Extended Teacher Education Program (ETEP) as an elementary education intern in the fall of 1995. One of 15 postbaccalaureate elementary and secondary preservice interns, Jessie was to take part in a full-time internship from August to May in the Gorham Public Schools. In addition to her work in classrooms and schools, Jessie simultaneously took courses in literacy development; mathematics, science, and social studies teaching methods; and lifespan development and exceptionality. After completing her internship and the State of Maine's content requirements, and passing the Core Battery of the National Teacher's Examination, she expected to be awarded an initial 2-year provisional teaching certificate.

To achieve these goals as an intern, Jessie would teach in a sixthgrade classroom from September to December, and from January to April she would be in a multiage inclusion, combined grades 2/3 program in the Gorham School District—a school district known for its leadership in school reform. But first, in August 1995, Jessie was introduced to the district and spent time becoming familiar with the program she was about to undertake.

Jesse's two teaching experiences would anchor her year. They would be the focus of weekly conferences among interns, cooperating teachers, and program supervisors; of quarterly presentations; and of the end-of-year portfolio presentation. Observations by program mentors, reflections through a dialogue journal between intern and cooperating teacher, and cooperating teacher narratives summarizing reviews of an intern's performance would be part of the process. Instructional units and lesson plans, and analyses of student work by the intern, as well as intern observations of his or her students, would be reviewed and become part of the assessment conversations.

Jesse learned that the system is monitored and coordinated by a university faculty member and a member of the local Gorham schools—

who would serve as her site coordinators. They would meet in a weekly seminar that would serve as a forum for intern peer support and deeper investigations into critical teaching issues: interdisciplinary planning, teaching, and assessment; portfolio development; and so on. Jesse's program supervisors, cooperating teachers, and professional studies instructors would be present at the end-of-year portfolio presentation to support judgments of her year-long performance with evidence from their own perspectives.

Now we follow Jessie through this system, providing samples of feedback she received at each stage of her journey.

STAGES OF THE JOURNEY

November: Mid-Placement Review

In a first mid-placement review by her cooperating teacher, Jessie received a "needs attention" rating for her planning, instructional strategies, and classroom management—one of the program outcomes. Such a rating at this point indicates that if Jessie's progress in instructional planning continues at the same or a slower pace, she could expect problems in full-time teaching, resulting in the possibility of not being recommended for certification. The evidence used to arrive at the rating is varied, nuanced, and extremely detailed. Although Jessie plans in advance and thoroughly, more clarity is needed in connecting instructional and assessment activities to the goals of a unit or project. Similarly, evidence shows that while Jessie's group learning activities are organized, there is too much whole-group sitting time. Students need to follow through more on assignments. They tend to continue talking when someone else is speaking, including Jessie. Classroom observations by Jessie's program coordinators support these judgments. For example, an observation completed in early November shows that during a discussion, the students are slow to quiet down. The observer's suggestions are for Jessie to be clearer about consequences and moving on from a whole-group explanation.

In student assessment outcome 5, however, Jesse has been rated as "developing satisfactorily." Evidence shows that she has incorporated opportunities for student and teacher reflections in her science unit on "Forces," has established criteria for research in the "Middle Ages" unit, and has conducted regular conferences with each student regarding the books they are reading and their progress on social studies projects. In other words, Jessie is successful in embedding assessment and attention to student learning in her teaching.

These program outcomes, which provide the measure for Jesse's performance, also act as an organizer for monitoring Jessie's ongoing development. Guided by these measures, each week Jessie completes an action plan that summarizes the areas she is working on and goals she has set. To guide and support her in this, one of the site coordinators visits Jessie weekly, making an observation, discussing student work, instructional plans, a journal entry, or perhaps a next step in teaching. Jessie's action plans for this phase of her internship reveal that she is working hard on classroom management and varying instructional strategies. Her journal entries also reveal her thinking about these areas. One entry from a sixth-grade unit on "Flight" states:

> Then, most of the class came in with airplanes they made for homework. I had about 10–12 people show and fly the planes in front of the class. We critiqued each plane; did it fly well, how were lift, drag, or thrust improved by that design. They seemed to like doing this; I could tell by comments they made. The flight concept began to sink in ("it's too heavy now so it sinks, it has too much drag").
>
> When I took the paper airplanes home to look at and evaluate for an "extra" homework grade, I saw that several students had really spent time and effort on it. Some were quite creative. This told me something. My hunch that they would like doing this activity and learn something was correct. If only I had structured it a little better (more clear criteria to start; and telling them more about why)! Still, I was impressed by what they could do. Most of them took making paper airplanes beyond just playing, but just a little. I think I'm getting a better idea of this hands-on learning stuff now and so are they! I hope I can expand what I've learned to some other content areas. I'm working on planning a Middle Ages unit now that should have lots of opportunities for various types of learning.

December: First Placement Exit Conference

A formal performance review occurs at the end of the intern's teaching her sixth-grade class in December. During this exit conference with her cooperating teacher and site coordinator, Jessie presented her teaching plans, her students' work, and reflections on the units she taught. Focused on improving her classroom management, Jessie prepared a graphic summary of her plans and efforts to establish a productive learning environment. Areas needing further improvement and explicit goals for the next placement were carefully delineated. Jessie made a connection between planning, classroom management, and assessment by noting that preparation to do these things takes time and that getting students aware of expectations is a challenge. The exit conference also provided an opportunity for Jessie to practice presenting evidence of her accomplishments and her progress for review and feedback by her mentors.

Following this exit conference, the two program coordinators reviewed Jesse's progress in mastery of the ETEP outcomes. This review is a major appraisal of all the evidence of an intern's progress from the beginning to this midpoint in the program: classroom visits, journal entries, the exit conference, and the cooperating teacher's mid-placement review. The coordinators rate each outcome as either "developing satisfactorily" or "needs attention." While the exit conference is an opportunity for the interns to present evidence of their work and thinking to cooperating teacher(s) and site coordinators, the midyear review is the site coordinators' turn to talk while the interns listen and respond.

Jessie's midyear review indicated that all outcomes were developing satisfactorily. The evidence showed, for example, that Jessie prepared units and lesson plans for units in several disciplines—science, math, and social studies. She was using a template introduced by the school district. In instructional strategies (outcome 4), Jessie used technology through word processing, CD-ROM research, and videotaping presentations; utilized student groupings from individual conferencing through small group to whole class; and completed several projects and experiments while studying the Middle Ages and forces. In classroom management (outcome 5), Jessie established consequences for students and enforced consequences for completing requirements; completed peer mediation training; and began designing a system for increasing student responsibility. Jessie also did more to structure groupwork and she took a close look at her class' seating arrangement. She clearly is seeing a connection between actively engaging students and management of her classroom.

March: The Second Mid-Placement Review

Jessie's spring placement in a multiage 2/3 inclusion program focused primarily on an extended interdisciplinary study of boats, integrating social studies, math, science, and literacy. Jessie's planning continued to grow in sophistication as she prepared a unit template, specific lesson plans, and a timeline of classroom events in a planbook format. During the extended "Boats" unit, Jessie designed and executed a system of ongoing assessment, including establishing criteria for the students' projects and several opportunities for feedback to students as a basis for making improvements.

Jessie's second mid-placement review of the outcomes by her cooperating teacher showed evidence that she was pulling together planning, classroom management, instructional strategies, assessment, and the other aspects of teaching into a connected system. Her cooperating teacher indicated that Jessie was assessing prior knowledge, using those data for planning, having students demonstrate learning according to established criteria, and having students reflect on their learning and skills. Classroom management continued to be an area of emphasis. In her journal Jessie included a list of strategies that she was using: gaining everyone's attention before beginning; using cues; getting students' attention over the work noise; actively monitoring the entire classroom; and using a positive tone.

May: Second Exit Conference

Jessie's significantly improved skills in planning, classroom management, and assessment were clearly evident in her second placement exit conference. Jessie explained Boat Science Research Packets for students; journal entries and boxes constructed by students for assessment in a geometry unit; and a packet of materials containing vocabulary and sample couplets for a poetry unit. During the teaching of the "Boat" unit, Jessie had prime responsibility for the classroom; her cooperating teacher documented that the class might not have done the science component of the Boat unit without Jessie.

Jessie's journal during this phase of her internship contains much about classroom management. Her goals included setting up a literacy program from scratch, collaborating with colleagues and others, and keeping richly detailed journals. The exit conference became an opportunity for Jessie to present evidence of work and thinking, provided closure to the placement, and served as a rehearsal for the year-end portfolio presentation.

Journey's End: The Portfolio Presentation

As the opening vignette of this chapter suggests, Jessie's final portfolio offering brings together all of her mentors as members of the audience. Their caucusing is summarized in notes of confirming and disconfirming evidence. The only disconfirming evidence relates to classroom management, which Jessie herself has identified as needing more work. The panel concludes that Jessie accurately articulates what she needs to do and does it. Panel members comment on her deep reflection, equal partnership with her cooperating teachers, going "well beyond" in her teaching and work with students, and exceptional integration of subject areas. Her learning from experience and desire to improve are represented in Jessie's rather understated but typical comment, "Oh yeah, I could have done that"—and then doing it. The recommendation for certification is unanimous by panel members, who by this time know their candidate's work thoroughly. Although this part of the journey is concluded for Jessie, her path through the system offers a valuable map for future interns and the mentors who guide and assess them.

THEMES FOR PRESERVICE TEACHER ASSESSMENT: HOW RELIABLE AND FAIR ARE OUR MAPS?

Assessment based on actual performance of students and teachers has gained rapid and fairly widespread acceptance and enthusiasm in education. As it does, issues emerge around reliability and validity in judging these new measures and in considering their authenticity and fairness.

Authenticity. Grant Wiggins (1989), addressing student performance assessment, considers criteria for defining authentic assessment that are pertinent for teacher assessment as well. Wiggins recommends two criteria of authenticity: that an assessment mirror the challenges, work, and standards engaging practicing professionals; and that it actually involve the student interactively with opportunities for explanation, dialogue, and inquiry. Newmann and Wehlage (1993) propose that authentic assessment must engage students in constructing meaning and producing knowledge, in using disciplined inquiry, and in "the production of discourse, products, and performances that have value or meaning beyond success in school" (p. 8; see also Meier & Schwartz, 1995).

Authenticity also concerns teacher educators. Many share the belief that the farther removed assessment is from the real work of teachers, the weaker its power for interpreting learning and performance. This is one reason why the Stanford Teacher Assessment Project found portfolios to be a stronger teacher assessment strategy than assessment center exercises (see Chapter 2). Having a teacher present to explain exhibits of his or her teaching and work with students was more promising in

accurately representing the complexities of the teacher's practice and
thinking than fragmented, out of context exercises (Wolf, 1991).

Authentic assessment of performance of context-driven learning
such as teaching implies other things as well. If, for example, teacher
interns are to be judged on their actual teaching abilities, it makes sense
that they should be given maximum opportunity to teach and work with
students. If teaching is the primary foundation of judging, then this is
the setting in which the interns should be evaluated. Inferences from
coursework and individual lesson plans are far less dependable than
whole-class, full-time teaching. Moreover, teacher candidates ought to
be given maximum opportunity to work, learn, and perform in such
genuine circumstances. They should be evaluated, receive feedback,
and set goals for themselves under the conditions of what teachers do
and with experienced teacher guidance. Here authentic teacher learning
and performance are joined.

Fairness and Validity. The validity of an assessment process is directly related to and intertwined with its fairness. Messick (in Moss,
1992) characterizes validity as "the degree to which empirical evidence
and theoretical rationales support the adequacy and appropriateness of
inferences and actions based on test scores or other forms of assessment" (p. 13). Messick (1994) argues that the issues of consequences,
evidence, and fairness at the heart of validity need to be applied fully to
performance assessment.

Stiggins (1987) suggests that validity relates to assurances that "performance ratings reflect the examinee's true capabilities and are not a
function of the perceptions and biases of the persons evaluating the performance" (p. 35). What evidence ensures that accurate judgments are
being made, that the individual does indeed possess the skills, knowledge, and disposition inferred from a performance? Usually, independent raters judge data and individual items or entries of an assessment
and then aggregate these independent scores into a single number. But
recently, Moss (1992) has argued for an alternative to this: that is, that
the assessment of all of the data relating to an individual be reviewed by a
community of interpreters who examine it in order to develop coherent
judgments and reach agreement about their judgment (see Chapter 13).
At the moment both models are in use in the assessment of the data of
teaching portfolios: the National Board for Professional Teaching Standards uses an aggregate model, and the University of Southern Maine's
Extended Teacher Education Program uses an interpretive one—wit-
ness Jessie's case.

In considering issues of fairness and validity, the field of special education can inform this discussion. Special education has placed emphasis on due process for validating decision making and guaranteeing the rights of equal protection under the law for students with special needs and their parents. Similarly, principles of individual protection can be identified for a teacher education and assessment system.

1. *Notice of criteria and standing* by which interns examine the program outcomes from the beginning of the program to the end and participate in the midyear review evaluating their level of performance with regard to each standard;
2. *Opportunity for practice and learning* whereby interns teach extensively on a continuing basis for the entire internship year;
3. *Feedback* on an ongoing basis from a variety of university and school faculty;
4. *Multiple sources of evidence* that are considered together to provide a more comprehensive picture of the individual's work and learning;
5. *Mediated action planning* for interns to design and follow through, with program faculty, on the professional development experience of reviewing areas of need and interest and accompanying activities.

When embedded in a teacher education program, these principles can serve as guarantees, not of legal protection, but of a fair learning process.

Finally, generalizability is a critical variable in teacher assessment. How can assurances be made that assessment judgments are not limited to the specific situation laid out in the assessment, but have some promise for holding up across the varied aspects of preparing, instructing, assessing, reflecting, and communicating activities of teaching (Linn, Baker, & Dunbar, 1991)? The performance assessment system presented here offers several considerations. The assessment process does not simply run parallel to the program curriculum; it is an integral thread of the learning experiences in which the interns engage. When the assessment process is grounded in evidence directly linked to intern performance and improvement, it forces a close look at how the internship curriculum is preparing interns to focus squarely on the learning of their students. When the assessment process involves ongoing discussions, explanations, and feedback about the intern's performance, understanding, and learning of the students with whom he or she works, discourse becomes an opportunity for deeper understanding and new ways of thinking about different learning settings and different learners. When judgments emerge from a thorough and thoughtful process grounded in a multifaceted body of evidence and multiple points of view, they are more likely to be valid and lead to continuing improvement rather than just a stamp of approval or disapproval.

What are the consequences of performance assessment for those involved and for the quality of education? Applying the criteria of consequences to the assessment process—asking, "What difference does it make?"—reveals possible effects. It forces the intern and program faculty to put the learning of students as the paramount concern. Considering the question, "What is the impact of the program on the students?" forces the realization that an internship placement in no way should impede the students' learning, but, in fact, should contribute to it.

CONCLUSION

The intern assessment system of the Extended Teacher Education Program turns on its head the usual procedures in determining the readiness of an intern for full-time teaching and certification. The idea for this system came from two Gorham site coordinators who saw that the usual system of judging an intern rested solely with program coordinators and cooperating teachers. They assigned grades and determined certification. Missing was the intern. To the two coordinators, the system seemed backwards. Interns needed to have a pivotal role in the system justifying their learning, offering their own evidence and appraising and documenting their work and learning.

The intern assessment system described through Jessie's case is an attempt to make the decision for certification more closely linked to ongoing professional development. Professional development and continual improvement are for everyone: those pushing the upper reaches of excellence and those working hard on the basics of teaching. In the intern assessment system represented by Jessie's case, learning to teach, to become a competent and caring teacher, is at the center and heart of it.

REFERENCES

Barton, J., & Collins, A. (1993). Portfolios in teacher education. *Journal of Teacher Education, 44*(3), 200–211.

Colton, A. (1995, January). *Judging portfolios*. Paper presented at Portfolios in Teacher Education: A Working Conference on Using and Judging Portfolios in Teaching and Teacher Education, Cambridge, MA.

Interstate New Teacher Assessment and Support Consortium. (1995). *Next steps: Moving toward performance-based licensing in teaching*. Washington, D.C.: Author.

Linn, R. L., Baker, E. L., & Dunbar, S. B. (1991). Complex, performance-based assessment: Expectations and validation criteria. *Educational Researcher, 20*(8), 15–28.

Meier, D., & Schwartz, P. (1995). Central Park East: The hard part is making it happen. In M. W. Apple & J. A. Bean (Eds.), *Democratic schools* (pp. 35–44). Alexandria, VA: Association for Supervision and Curriculum Development.

Messick, S. (1994). The interplay of evidence and consequences in the validation of performance assessments. *Educational Researcher, 23*(2), 13–23.

Moss, P. A. (1992). Shifting conceptions of validity in educational measurement: Implications for performance assessment. *Review of Educational Research, 62*(3), 229–258.

Newmann, F. M., & Wehlage, G. G. (1993). Five standards of authentic instruction. *Educational Leadership, 50*(7), 8–12.

Stiggins, R. J. (1987). Design and development of performance assessments. *Educational Measurement, 6*(3), 33–42.

Wiggins, G. (1989). A true test: Toward more authentic and equitable assessment. *Phi Delta Kappan, 70*(9), 703–713.

Wolf, K. (1991). The schoolteacher's portfolio: Issues in design, implementation, and evaluation. *Phi Delta Kappan, 73*(2), 129–136.

CHAPTER 13

Rethinking Validity for the Assessment of Teaching

Pamela A. Moss

UNIVERSITY OF MICHIGAN

Given the rich array of practical examples provided by the other authors in this volume, I assume that readers come to this chapter with a concrete sense of the kinds of evidence that might be contained in a portfolio and the kinds of standards, principles, or criteria that might inform the selection and evaluation of that evidence. This chapter, then, focuses on how a portfolio—containing multiple entries prepared by candidates to demonstrate their learnings, capabilities, or accomplishments with respect to an articulated vision of teaching—might be evaluated to inform a consequential decision about a candidate.

More particularly, I consider the validity issues associated with an approach to portfolio evaluation in which readers engage in dialogue to integrate multiple sources of evidence about a candidate to reach a sound conclusion. As I've argued elsewhere (Moss, 1996a, 1996b), conventional theory and practice in validity research privilege an aggregative approach to portfolio evaluation where readers work independently to score separate portfolio entries. In this chapter I suggest a way to expand current theory and practice in validity research so as to support (and challenge) more integrative approaches to portfolio assessment. I consider two contexts in which integrative approaches might be used: centrally administered assessments where readers have no knowledge about the candidate beyond what is contained in the portfolio, and locally administered assessments where (some) readers have extensive knowledge of the candidate.

In rethinking validity for these integrative practices, it is important to distinguish between the crucial purposes that validity research serves and the theories and practices conventionally used to accomplish those purposes. Validity refers to the soundness of the interpretations and any consequent actions based on the evidence available in an assessment. Regardless of the approach used to evaluate a portfolio, it is crucial that the resulting interpretations and actions be supported by a rigorous and critical review when consequential decisions are made.

To develop the theoretical foundation necessary to support collaborative and contextualized assessment practices, I turn to the tradition of philosophical hermeneutics. Unlike the practices based in psychometric theory, where independent readings of isolated performances are aggregated to form a composite score, practices based in hermeneutics would encourage readers to work together to construct a coherent interpretation, continually challenging and revising initial interpretations, until they account for all the available evidence about a candidate.

Although the theory and practice of validity I propose here have a long history within interpretive social science, they are relatively new within the context of large-scale educational assessment, which has been guided by psychometric theory. Substantial empirical work is needed to explore the possibilities and limitations of more integrative approaches to portfolio evaluation. I hope readers will treat this chapter as an invitation to contribute to a much needed program of research so that we may learn from one another's work.

A RATIONALE FOR THE INTEGRATIVE APPROACH

Before proceeding, I want to circumscribe the project of this chapter in terms of the uses of assessment and aspects of validity it will address. A program of validity research begins with an understanding of the purpose(s) an assessment is intended to serve. For this chapter, I will focus on "higher stakes" uses of assessments, including those resulting in decisions about licensure, certification, or graduation. While a sound validity argument is relevant to any assessment purpose, it is crucial when decisions or actions based on the assessment have significant consequences for candidates. Further, a comprehensive program of validity research incorporates issues/evidence ranging from the means through which the guiding standards or principles are constructed through consideration of the consequences of an assessment system to the community in which it is used. In this chapter I focus on those aspects of validity research associated with the way in which conclusions are drawn from portfolio-based evidence, touching only briefly on the broader range of validity issues.

I begin the characterization of the evaluation process with the assumption that content standards or principles of successful performance have been articulated and that the kinds of entries that might constitute portfolios have been considered. This is not to imply that the vision of teaching represented in the principles or the contents of the portfolio are "written in stone" for the life of an assessment system; indeed, if the assessment system remains vital, these principles and practices will evolve in light of the concrete examples of work that the portfolios provide.

A conventional "aggregative" approach to portfolio evaluation, grounded in the psychometric tradition, might have two readers rating each entry independently on one or more of the scoring dimensions related to the standards. Readers would be blind to candidates' performances on other entries. Scores assigned by individual readers to each entry would be combined algorithmically into a composite score or profile of scores. To arrive at a "passing" decision (for licensure, certification, or graduation), the composite would be compared with a predetermined cut score or set of passing profiles. In this conventional model, after the assessment system had been fully developed, the decisions would be algorithmic once the exercise scores had been determined by individual readers.[1]

While these scoring practices represent sound and thoughtful work within the psychometric tradition, it is useful to step outside that tradition to question both the quality of information and the consequences of evaluating the portfolios in this way. A portfolio is a collection of complex performances compiled by candidates to represent different aspects of their learning and teaching. It is important to ask whether the judgment of expert readers, who have become familiar with the candidate's capabilities across multiple performances, might not result in a more valid and fair decision. For instance, to understand a teacher's decision to use a particular instructional strategy, or to respond to a student's work in a particular way, it is important to understand the larger context in which that decision was made. What is the background of these individual students? What are the resources available to the teacher? What are the teacher's instructional goals, how does she orchestrate learning opportunities to achieve these goals, and where does this particular decision fit in that sequence of activities? How does she evaluate what actually occurs and how does she use that information? All of this points to the importance of locating a particular performance in the preceding and subsequent context that surrounds it. Similarly, with performances as complex as these, it is important to ask whether allowing readers to engage in dialogue about the actual performances—possibly pointing to evidence that one reader has not noticed or challenging his or her interpretations with a second reader's counterinterpretations or with disconfirming evidence—might not result in a sounder decision that considers more comprehensively the complex evidence available.

In the more integrative approach suggested by these questions, a single pair of readers might evaluate a candidate's entire set of performances using the articulated principles or standards as a framework to guide the gathering and analysis of evidence. The goal would be to construct a coherent interpretation based on the entire set of portfolio entries, continually revising initial interpretations until they account for all the available evidence. Then the readers would engage in a dialogue to arrive at a consensus decision on the candidate's level of performance with respect to the standards or principles.

In this chapter, I consider two different circumstances in which an integrative approach might be used. In one circumstance, portfolios are evaluated outside the local context by readers who have no knowledge of the candidate beyond what is contained in the portfolio. Here, as with the aggregative approach, the candidate's participation in the evaluation is limited to the evidence provided in the portfolio entries. In the other circumstance, the portfolios are locally scored by readers who have unique and extensive knowledge of a candidate beyond what is available in the portfolio. Here, the candidate also may participate more actively in negotiating the contents and contributing to the evaluation of the portfolio through self-assessment and/or dialogue with the readers. These circumstances present somewhat different challenges for validity.

Such collaborative and contextualized assessment practices have been used for consequential decisions in a few local contexts in both higher education (e.g., Alverno College Faculty, 1994; Kimball & Hanley, 1995; Lyons & Faculty of the University of Southern Maine's Extended Teacher Education Program, 1995) and K–12 education (Darling-Hammond, Ancess, & Falk, 1995; Mabry, 1992; Meier, 1995). However, existing theory in educational measurement does not provide an adequate epistemological basis to support this promising work. What is needed is a research agenda that investigates the validity of these integrative assessment practices while maintaining rigorous standards appropriate to a high stakes assessment context.

HERMENEUTICS AS A THEORETICAL BASIS FOR
INTEGRATIVE ASSESSMENT PRACTICES

A promising theoretical direction for more contextualized and collaborative approaches to assessment can be found in the research tradition
of hermeneutics. Like psychometrics, hermeneutics characterizes a general approach to the interpretation of human products, expressions, or
actions. Like psychometrics, hermeneutics provides means of combining information across multiple pieces of evidence and of dealing with
disabling biases that readers may bring. Differences between these disciplines lie in the ways in which the information is combined and readers'
biases are addressed. Although hermeneutics is not a unitary tradition,
most hermeneutic philosophers share a holistic and integrative approach
to interpretation of human phenomena, which seeks to understand the
whole in light of its parts, repeatedly testing interpretations against the
available evidence, until each of the parts can be accounted for in a coherent interpretation of the whole (Bleicher, 1980; Ormiston & Schrift,
1990; Schmidt, 1995). This iterative process often is referred to as the
hermeneutic circle.

The approach to hermeneutics on which I draw most heavily is
based in the hermeneutic philosophy of Gadamer (1963/1987). Here
the hermeneutic circle can be characterized as representing a dual dialectic: one between the parts of the text and the whole, and one between
the text and the reader's foreknowledge, preconceptions, or "enabling"
prejudices. Gadamer argues that there is no knowledge without foreknowledge—without preconceptions or prejudices. "The task is not to
remove all such preconceptions, but to test them critically in the course
of inquiry . . . to make the all important distinction between blind prejudices and 'justified . . . [or enabling] prejudices that are productive of
knowledge'" (Bernstein, 1985, p. 128).

The process of testing preconceptions in the course of inquiry begins with the respectful assumption that the text, which may contain
apparent holes or contradictions, is coherent and can inform us of something (Gadamer, 1963/1987; Taylor, 1967/1987). The dialogue between
the text and the reader, and among readers, is guided by the intent to
understand and learn from the text. Through this process, we raise to a
conscious level those "prejudices which govern understanding" (Gadamer, 1963/1987, p. 137) and enable them to evolve. An elaboration of
philosophical hermeneutics, "depth hermeneutics" (Habermas, 1980/
1990), which is informed by critical theory, locates validity in the consensus among readers who approach one another as equals, self-
conscious of the ways that different ideologies (or biases) may constrain

their interpretations. Of course, systematically distorted communication, influenced by social, political, or economic forces of which interpreters are unaware, can result in a "false consensus." Here, critical hermeneutics (e.g., Hoy & McCarthy, 1994; Kogler, 1996) highlights the role that readers from outside the interpretive community can play—bringing an alternative perspective that illuminates the values and theories taken for granted by those within the interpretive community, so that they may be self-consciously considered.

From a hermeneutic perspective, the process through which general principles or standards are applied to particular cases is dialectical—rather than fixed principles simply being applied to particular cases, the meaning of the case and the principles are co-determined. As Gadamer suggests (1963/1987), the hermeneutic process used in making a legal judgment exemplifies the hermeneutic process as a whole. He argues that "the judge does not simply 'apply' fixed, determinate laws to particular situations. Rather the judge must interpret and appropriate precedents and law to each new, particular situation. It is by virtue of such considered judgment that the meaning of the law and the meaning of the particular case are co-determined" (p. 148).

Thus, hermeneutic philosophy points to an integrative and dialogic approach to assessment—one where readers' developing conceptions of competent performance are evaluated continually; where the meaning of the principles guiding the assessment is mediated by the contingencies of the cases to which they are applied; where interpretations are revised continually until they account for all the available evidence; and where the validity of the conclusion is warranted, in part, in the consensus among readers who are empowered to challenge one another's developing interpretations in light of the case at hand.

THE INTEGRATIVE APPROACH IN PRACTICE

The principles of hermeneutics suggest research questions to ask, habits of mind and practices to foster with portfolio readers, kinds of empirical materials to collect, issues to attend to in analyzing the empirical materials, and ways to foster critical dialogue and reflection on our practices and principles. Moreover, given the value that hermeneutics places on the role of alternative perspectives in constructing and evaluating interpretations, it points to an important, complementary role for psychometrics in a program of validity research.

The two integrative contexts described above are illustrated here. First, I describe a context in which portfolios are centrally evaluated by readers who know nothing about the candidates beyond what is contained in the portfolios. Following that, I characterize the ways in which locally evaluated portfolios raise somewhat different validity issues.

Context 1: A Centralized Assessment System

To illustrate an integrative approach to assessment, I turn to the work my colleagues and I have undertaken for the Performance Assessment Development Project (PADP) of the Interstate New Teacher Assessment and Support Consortium (INTASC).[2] Drawing on INTASC's standards for beginning teaching (see INTASC, 1992, for a description of the development and review effort), the PADP is developing a process of portfolio assessment to aid participating states both in the professional development and licensure of beginning teachers. Here, I characterize both the process of portfolio evaluation and some of the strategies we are using to investigate its validity for the purpose of licensure.

The INTASC portfolio assessment tasks ask candidates for licensure to prepare an extensive portfolio with entries that document and reflect critically on their teaching practices. Entries include descriptions of the contexts in which they work, goals for student learning with plans for achieving those goals, lesson plans or logs, videotapes of actual lessons, assessment activities with samples of evaluated student work, and critical analyses and reflections on their teaching practices.

To guide portfolio evaluation, interpretive categories are being developed based on INTASC standards and standards from the relevant professional organizations. (For instance, in mathematics, the interpretive categories include mathematical tasks, mathematical discourse, learning environment, and analysis of teaching and learning.) Individual readers first work through the portfolio alone, noting and recording evidence relevant to any of the interpretive categories wherever it occurs. Then readers work together to prepare interpretive summaries with supporting evidence for each category. To assist readers in developing their interpretive summaries, INTASC staff have prepared a set of guiding questions organized under major interpretive categories.[3] (For instance, under mathematical discourse, guiding questions might include, "What role does the teacher play in fostering discourse in the classroom?" "What roles do students play in the discourse?" What is talked and written about?" "How are 'errors' treated?") Guidelines encourage readers to consider all of the evidence in the portfolio—looking across the videotapes, the student artifacts, and the teacher's plans and reflections to develop coherent explanations of the teaching practices observed; to actively seek counterexamples that challenge developing interpretations;

and to value conflicting interpretations, reaching consensus if possible, and documenting differences where consensus cannot be reached. After completing interpretive summaries and supporting evidence records, readers debate and reach consensus on an overall level of performance. They then prepare a written justification tying the evidence they have analyzed to their decision.

The performance standards are operationalized in reader preparation through exemplars of performance at different levels. Exemplars include entire portfolios, completed evaluations, and explanations of those evaluations. Initially, the potential exemplars will be selected by the lead developers and the assessment development team in each subject area, which includes teachers and teacher educators from each of the participating states. Through a number of planned validity studies, exemplars will be critically reviewed and elaborated by a broad range of teachers, teacher educators, and other discipline-specific scholars. These exemplars, some of which will be made publicly available, will serve a particularly important purpose in addition to reader preparation. In essence, they will concretize the INTASC standards in examples from teaching practice and open them for ongoing professional dialogue and critique.

One concern that typically arises about this approach is how readers can possibly keep that much information in their minds at one time. The response is that they don't have to. Here, it is important to distinguish between an integrative approach to portfolio evaluation and what is commonly understood as holistic scoring. Holistic scoring originally was associated with the scoring of written compositions. It encourages readers to form a general impression of an essay (usually informed by a scoring guide and/or benchmarks). Typically, no explicit intermediate analysis is required in determining the holistic score. In contrast, INTASC'S integrative approach to portfolio evaluation is highly analytic. The process takes readers through a series of explicit steps involving data reduction and integration guided by questions from a detailed evaluation framework. At different stages, readers take written notes, determine and record relevant evidence, and construct interpretive summaries of the evidence in response to the guiding questions. At each stage, the steps of data reduction and integration are recorded for consideration at the next stage. By the time they are ready to reach consensus on the overall conclusion, readers have produced a written record of steps in data reduction and integration to which they can return easily.

A more problematic concern with the integrative approach is that fewer expert readers are involved in the process of reviewing a portfolio. Instead of having different readers evaluate each performance, the same readers evaluate all performances. Here, it becomes crucial to monitor and control idiosyncratic perspectives (or "disabling biases" in Gadamer's terms) that readers may bring and that are inconsistent with the INTASC principles. As part of the ongoing assessment system, there are activities that occur before, during, and after the actual portfolio evaluation to monitor and control idiosyncratic perspectives. *Before* the evaluation, there is the process of reader preparation and, eventually, certification, as with any high stakes performance assessment. Reader preparation takes readers through a series of scaffolded learning opportunities that enable them to internalize the INTASC principles and to practice applying them to a variety of previously evaluated portfolios. In the process of discussing the portfolios, their own perspectives on competent teaching can be illuminated and reflected on in light of the INTASC standards. *During* the process of evaluation, idiosyncratic perspectives are controlled in two ways. First, this occurs by having readers look, continuously, for counterevidence that challenges their developing interpretations, consider the appropriate weight that should be given to the counterevidence, and reconfirm or revise their interpretations accordingly. Second, it occurs when readers challenge, elaborate, or suggest conditions that circumscribe the interpretations proposed by their partners. Taken together, these practices can highlight and confront idiosyncratic perspectives in ways that enable them to evolve. *After* the evaluation, the written record that readers produce is available for audit. Thus, the process of readers' reasoning is accessible in a way that simply is unavailable when all that is recorded is a score.

When this system is operationalized, we anticipate there will be regular audits examining the extent to which readers' interpretive summaries appropriately support their decisions consistent with the evaluation framework. For portfolios where readers cannot reach a clear consensus about a pass/fail decision or where a decision results in the candidate's inability to obtain a license, we anticipate some additional review will be given. Candidates also will have the opportunity to appeal a decision, initiating additional review themselves. In addition, a sample of portfolios will be re-evaluated independently by a second pair of readers to monitor reader reliability in terms of decision consistency. When portfolios are evaluated centrally (and readers are selected arbitrarily from a pool of possible readers), evidence should be available about the extent to which the decision would be the same regardless of which readers initially evaluated the portfolio.

The practices described above will take place as part of the ongoing monitoring of the assessment system. In addition, to help in understanding and improving the process of reader preparation and evaluation, the following kinds of analysis are underway. The data that we have collected include the written documentation produced by readers, transcribed audiotapes of dialogues among readers, and interviews with readers both before and after the preparation process. Using these data, we are closely examining the processes in which readers engage and the extent to which reader pairs, working independently with the same portfolios, achieve consistency in their interpretations and decision.

With respect to the readers' process, we approach the data with the following issues in mind: First, epistemological issues focus on the ways in which the interpretation of teaching performance is constructed and grounded: What evidence is being cited, from which data sources (artifacts, video, reflections)? What role do counterinterpretations and counterevidence play? How are interpretations evolving over the course of the discussion? Second, "political" issues focus on the extent to which readers are empowered to remain equally and critically engaged in the dialogue: What is the nature of the contribution each reader makes to the dialogue? To what extent do readers challenge one another's interpretations? How is conflict handled? To what extent do readers withhold comments or acquiesce to an interpretation they do not hold? Third, theoretical issues focus on the explicit and implicit theories about competent teaching that readers bring. To what extent are these consistent with INTASC principles? In what ways do they evolve over the course of the preparation? To what extent do particular theories disadvantage particular (subgroups of) candidates? Fourth, practical issues focus on ways in which readers manage the process: What strategies do they use? What choices do they make about how they allocate their time, together and individually? Fifth, professional development issues focus on what readers have learned as a result of participating in the process, with respect to each of the issues raised above.

In addition, comparisons of evidence and interpretations from readers working independently with the same portfolio have proven tremendously useful for pointing to areas where reader preparation can be improved. These comparisons highlight the kinds of issues where differences in interpretation consistently arise so that they may be debated and resolved by the community of readers. (See Moss, Schutz, and Collins, 1997, and Thompson, 1997, for detailed descriptions of the practices described here.)

Context 2: A Local Assessment System

Since Chapter 12 presented an extended case study of an integrative approach to portfolio assessment for certification in a local context, in this section I will touch only briefly on the way in which the factors in the local context affect the kinds of validity evidence that might be gathered. When portfolios are constructed and evaluated within a single educational community, the ongoing relationship between the candidate and the readers both can enhance the validity of the interpretation, by enabling a deeper understanding of the experiences and perspectives of each candidate, and can detract from the validity, by allowing potentially irrelevant knowledge and commitments to be brought to bear on the conclusions about a candidate's performance.

The research agenda proposed here for a centralized assessment system may seem daunting to those in the local context who are already engaged in making consequential decisions about individuals for whom they are responsible. In deciding which aspects are crucial to undertake, readers might keep the following factors in mind. The higher the stakes associated with the decision in any given assessment episode—the greater the consequences to the candidate—the more important it is to meet rigorous standards of validity. When candidates have multiple opportunities to demonstrate their learning, capabilities, or accomplishments, the stakes for any one assessment decision are reduced. This is particularly true when support for professional development is provided between assessment episodes. Similarly, when assessors can seek additional information to help in explaining the observed performance, as is true in many local contexts, the burden placed on interpreting the portfolio evidence is reduced.

Nevertheless, it will be crucial to provide some ongoing means of evaluating the soundness of consequential decisions that are made. In the INTASC project, the ongoing means of quality control involved audits of written documentation and comparisons of conclusions from readers evaluating the same portfolios independently. While audits are both feasible and useful in the local context, it may be harder to gather and interpret evidence about reader reliability—consistency among independent readings—since readers cannot be considered "interchangeable." Rather, readers typically are selected *because* of their particular expertise and/or experience with the candidate. In this circumstance, bringing together multiple readers and fostering an environment where all readers feel comfortable justifying their own interpretations and challenging the interpretations of others, will be crucial. It also will be important to bring outside perspectives to the evaluation process, so that potential disabling biases (whether favorable or unfavorable to the candidate) of readers familiar with the candidate and context can be illuminated and self-consciously considered. Readers who do not know the candidate, or who come from outside the local assessment context, can be invited to participate in the process in a variety of ways: as members of the initial portfolio review team; as auditors of the decision, written documentation, and supporting evidence produced by the team; or as independent reviewers who consider the portfolio-based evidence with no knowledge of the outcome. Although consistency in the conclusions of inside and outside reviewers will enhance the validity of the decision, high levels of consistency may be unlikely because of the differing perspectives and knowledge that the different readers bring. Here, the role of the outsider is to illuminate taken-for-granted practices and perspectives and make them available for critical review by members of the interpretive community so that they may be self-consciously affirmed or revised. In that way, the interpretive community continues to evolve in its ability to make sound judgments.

ADDITIONAL VALIDITY ISSUES

The validity issues and evidence described above touch only on a small subset of what a comprehensive program of validity research might entail. They focus on evidence that might be collected to evaluate the processes of portfolio interpretation. It is not possible to specify, in general, what *should* be included in a comprehensive program of validity research, as each research agenda depends on the particular purpose, intended interpretation, theoretical perspectives, and context of the assessment in question. Among the many additional kinds of evidence that might be considered in a comprehensive validity research agenda—one that incorporates interrelated issues of fairness, generalizability, and impact, as well as the soundness of interpretations and decisions—are:

- the processes through which the various components of the assessment system, including the standards or vision guiding the system, were developed;
- the conceptual coherence among the articulated standards or vision of teaching and learning, the intended interpretation and purposes of assessment, the portfolio tasks, the evaluation criteria, and the performance standards;
- the relevance, representativeness, and/or criticality of the performances and criteria reflected in the assessment to the kind of work in which candidates are expected to engage outside the assessment;
- the soundness of means through which performance standards (characterizing the levels of performance associated with different decisions) are set;

- the extent to which the conclusions about the candidate would be the same if the candidate had submitted a different set of entries on a different occasion (evaluated by different readers);
- the relationship between the focal assessment and other means of evaluation, including other kinds of evidence about the candidate and other perspectives or ways of evaluating the portfolio evidence;
- the opportunities candidates have to learn the capabilities on which they are assessed and to perform on the assessment with appropriate human and material support;
- the extent to which the assessment provides an appropriate range of opportunities for candidates to display expertise and recognizes differing theories or perspectives consistent with professional consensus about sound practice;
- the extent to which the soundness of the assessment remains consistent across groups that differ with respect to factors such as gender, ethnicity, socioeconomic status, context of work, context of education, and other relevant factors;
- the meaningfulness, usefulness, and appropriateness of the ways in which the assessment results are reported to candidates and other stakeholders in the system;
- the consequences of the assessment to candidates, readers, the educational communities in which they work, and other stakeholders in the assessment process, including attention to any differential consequences across relevant subgroups of candidates; and
- how the learnings obtained from various studies are incorporated into the assessment system so that it can evolve in beneficial ways.

Of course, the relative importance of these different kinds of evidence and the value judgments associated with different results will vary from context to context. Examples of more comprehensive programs of validity research that surround specific portfolio assessments of teaching are available from INTASC and NBPTS. (For instance, see Moss, Schutz, and Collins, 1997, for a description of the ongoing validity research agenda for INTASC assessments; and Bond, 1997, Hanes and Baker, 1995, and Jaeger, 1996, for examples of the range of validity studies underway for NBPTS assessments.)

CONCLUDING COMMENTS

Perhaps the most striking contrast between integrative and aggregative approaches is that, with the aggregative approach, readers rarely, if ever, review the entire set of performances for a candidate in reaching or evaluating a consequential decision. No one is asked to carefully read all the evidence available on a candidate and say, "Yes, I think this is a highly accomplished candidate, and here's why." This is, of course, one way of maintaining the objectivity and fairness of the scoring—of ensuring that the decision is not based on premature judgments or biases of individual readers. With the integrative approach, such bias can be challenged and controlled through debate, audit, and appeal—just as it is in the law. Moreover, much information is lost when performances are abstracted in scores, and decisions then are based on algorithms for combining the scores and comparing them with a predetermined cut score. It seems essential to ask whether expert judgment by knowledgeable readers— who have become familiar with the candidate's achievements across multiple performances—may not result in a more valid and fair decision. Beyond these concerns about the soundness of the conclusions, it is also important to consider the two approaches in terms of the model of intellectual work that they present for readers and candidates, and in terms of the nature of discourse about educational reform that they are likely to promote.

I am not arguing that one approach should always be preferred over another. While it is true that this chapter builds an argument for the potential of an integrative approach against the limitations of an aggregative approach, that argument is driven, in part, by the extent to which the aggregative approach has been taken for granted as the only viable approach for high stakes assessment. However, the integrative approach should not be adopted nonproblematically either. The choice among approaches depends on the particular purpose, context, and consequences of the assessment—consequences that span epistemological, ethical, political, social, economic, and legal circumstances.

In any assessment development effort, what is needed is the willingness and the means to reflect critically on alternatives. The integrative approach suggested here provides a new perspective from which the aggregative approach can be critically reviewed. Of course, the converse is also true. When we consider alternative possibilities—alternative means of serving the same purpose—the practices we take for granted become visible and open to change. At the very least, we become more aware of the consequences of the choices we make.

Acknowledgments. The work described here was supported, in part, by grants from the Interstate New Teacher Assessment and Support Consortium (INTASC) Performance Assessment Development Project (PADP) of the Council of Chief State School Officers (CCSSO) and the

Spencer Foundation. The section on hermeneutic philosophy, developed while the author was working under a grant from the National Academy of Education/Spencer Postdoctoral Fellowship Program, also appears in Moss, Schutz, and Collins (1997). The PADP validity research agenda was collaboratively developed with INTASC staff and consultants, including Ray Pecheone, Penny Pence, Bill Thompson, Jean Miller, Linda Wurzbach, Allison Kaye, Laurie Somers, Deborah Ball, Mary Diez, Jim Gee, Anne Gere, Bob Linn, Diana Pullin, and Mike Rebell. Opinions, findings, conclusions, and recommendations expressed are those of the author and do not necessarily reflect the views of CCSSO, INTASC, the PADP, or the states participating in the project.

NOTES

1. The research agenda undertaken by the National Board for Professional Teaching Standards provides a state of the art exemplar of work on how validity of an aggregative approach to portfolio evaluation can be investigated (Bond, 1997; Hanes & Baker, 1995; Jaeger, 1996). Readers who want a general overview of validity theory and practice located within the tradition of psychometrics are referred to the *Standards for Educational and Psychological Testing* (AERA, APA, NCME, 1985), Cronbach (1988), Messick (1996), Moss (1992), and Shepard (1993).

2. INTASC, a program of the Council of Chief State School Officers (CCSSO), was established in 1987 to enhance collaboration among states in promoting reform in the education, licensing, and professional development of teachers. INTASC's mission is to provide a forum for the states to learn about and collaborate on the development of programs to enhance the preparation, licensing, and professional development of teachers. In conjunction with the assessment development project described in this chapter, INTASC is fostering systemic reform by developing polices and practices that shape teacher preparation, program review, and ongoing professional development. INTASC began its work by crafting model standards for beginning teaching. To ensure compatibility and continuity in a teacher's career development, INTASC used the framework of the National Board for Professional Teaching Standards (NBPTS) to construct its core principles. Since 1995, INTASC has been developing discipline-specific standards and performance assessments in mathematics and English language arts to be used in licensing decisions.

3. This is a process similar to the one that Delandshere and Petrosky (1994) developed in their early work in teacher portfolio assessment, although their guiding questions and interpretive summaries focus on one exercise at a time, whereas those of INTASC encompass the entire portfolio.

REFERENCES

AERA, APA, and NCME. (1985). *Standards for educational and psychological testing.* Washington, DC: Authors.

Alverno College Faculty. (1994). *Student assessment-as-learning at Alverno College.* Milwaukee, WI: Alverno College Institute.

Bernstein, R. J. (1985). *Beyond objectivism and relativism: Science, hermeneutics, and praxis.* Philadelphia: University of Pennsylvania Press.

Bleicher, J. (1980). *Contemporary hermeneutics: Hermeneutics as method, philosophy, and critique.* London: Routledge & Kegan Paul.

Bond, L. (1997, March). *Adverse impact and teacher certification.* Paper presented at the annual meeting of the American Educational Research Association, Chicago.

Cronbach, L. J. (1988). Five perspectives on validity argument. In H. Wainer (Ed.), *Test validity* (pp. 3–17). Hillsdale, NJ: Lawrence Erlbaum.

Darling-Hammond, L., Ancess, J., & Falk, B. (1995). *Authentic assessment in action: Studies of schools and students at work.* New York: Teachers College Press.

Delandshere, G., & Petrosky, A. R. (1994). Capturing teachers' knowledge: Performance assessment a) and post-structuralist epistemology, b) from a post-structuralist perceptive, c) and post-structuralism, d) none of the above. *Educational Researcher, 23*(5), 11–18.

Gadamer, H. G. (1987). The problem of historical consciousness. In P. Rabinow & W. M. Sullivan (Eds.), *Interpretive social science: A second look* (pp. 82–140). Berkeley: University of California Press. (Original work published 1963)

Habermas, J. (1990). The hermeneutic claim to universality. In G. L. Ormiston & A. D. Schrift (Eds.), *The hermeneutic tradition: From Ast to Ricoeur* (pp. 245–272). Albany: State University of New York Press. (Original work published 1980)

Hanes, J. C. Jr., & Baker, W. K. (1995). *Reports of the Technical Analysis Group to the National Board for Professional Teaching Standards: An annotated bibliography.* Unpublished manuscript, National Board for Professional Teaching Standards, Southfield, MI.

Hoy, D. C., & McCarthy, T. (1994). *Critical theory.* Oxford: Blackwell.

Interstate New Teacher Assessment and Support Consortium. (1992). *Model standards for beginning teacher licensing and development: A resource for state dialogue.* Washington, DC: Author and Council of Chief State School Officers.

Interstate New Teacher Assessment and Support Consortium. (1995). *Next steps: Moving toward performance-based licensing in teaching.* Washington, DC: Author and Council of Chief State School Officers.

Jaeger, R. M. (1996). *Conclusions on the technical measurement quality of the 1995–1996 operational version of the National Board for Professional Teaching Stan-*

dards' *Middle Childhood Generalist Assessment.* Unpublished manuscript, National Board for Professional Teaching Standards, Southfield, MI.

Kimball, W. H., & Hanley, S. (1995). *Fair and defensible judging of teacher performance and understanding for certification and teacher improvement.* Unpublished manuscript, University of Southern Maine, Gorham, ME.

Kogler, H. H. (1996). *The power of dialogue* (P. Hendrickson, Trans.). Cambridge, MA: MIT Press.

Lyons, N., & Faculty of the University of Southern Maine's Extended Teacher Education Program. (1995). *Which standards? What performance? For what vision of teaching and learning?* Unpublished manuscript, University of Southern Maine, Gorham, ME.

Mabry, L. (1992, April). *Alternative assessment in an American high school.* Paper presented at the annual meeting of the American Educational Research Association, San Francisco.

Meier, D. (1995). *The power of their ideas: Lessons for America from a small school in Harlem.* Boston: Beacon Press.

Messick, S. (1996). Validity of performance assessments. In G. W. Phillips (Ed.), *Technical issues in large scale performance assessment* (pp. 1–18). Washington, DC: U.S. Department of Education.

Moss, P. A. (1992). Shifting conceptions of validity in educational measurement: Implications for performance assessment. *Review of Educational Research, 62*(3), 229–258.

Moss, P. A. (1994). Can there be validity without reliability? *Educational Researcher, 23*(2), 5–12.

Moss, P. A. (1996a). Enlarging the dialogue in educational measurement: Voices from interpretive research traditions. *Educational Researcher, 25*(1), 20–28, 43.

Moss, P. A. (1996b). An interpretive approach to setting and applying standards. In *Proceedings of the Joint Conference on Standard Setting in Large Scale Assessment* (pp. 185–202). Washington, DC: National Assessment Governing Board and National Center for Education Statistics.

Moss, P. A., Schutz, A., & Collins, K. (1997, March). *An integrative approach to portfolio evaluation for teacher licensure: Studies of readers at work.* Paper presented at the annual meeting of the American Educational Research Association, Chicago.

National Board for Professional Teaching Standards. (1994). *Report to: The U.S. Senate Committee on Labor and Human Resources, and The U.S. House of Representatives Committee on Education and Labor.* Detroit, MI: Author.

Ormiston, G. L., & Schrift, A. D. (Eds.). (1990). *The hermeneutic tradition: From Ast to Ricoeur.* Albany: State University of New York.

Schmidt, L. K. (Ed.). (1995). *The specter of relativism: Truth, dialogue, and phronesis in philosophical hermeneutics.* Evanston, IL: Northwestern University Press.

Shepard, L. A. (1993). Evaluating test validity. *Review of Research in Education, 19*, 405–450.

Taylor, C. (1987). Interpretation and the sciences of man. In P. Rabinow & W. M. Sullivan (Eds.), *Interpretive social science: A second look* (pp. 33–81). Berkeley: University of California Press. (Original work published 1967)

Thompson, W. (1997, March). *Preparing readers to evaluate INTASC mathematics teacher portfolios.* Paper presented at the annual meeting of the American Educational Research Association, Chicago.

CHAPTER 14

When the State Mandates Portfolios: The Vermont Experience

Richard H. Dollase

BROWN UNIVERSITY

As part of a major reform in teacher preparation, the State of Vermont instituted in 1992 a new program-approval system based on the creation and assessment of prospective teachers' portfolios. There are two stories to tell about this ongoing and unfolding process or innovation and reform: One concerns the establishment of the state-mandated system of evaluation by portfolio, and how it came about and how it is playing out on the state level; the second deals with the Middlebury College portfolio design—how this new outcome-based assessment system is working at the institutional level and how it has helped restructure our teacher preparation programs and our substantive focus, particularly with regard to the student teaching practicum and our professional relationships with cooperating teachers. These two stories are, of course, interrelated and their explication gives some insight into the realities, complexities, and dynamics of the restructuring of teacher preparation at both the state and the grassroots level.

STATE-MANDATED RESTRUCTURING

In the summer of 1990, Richard Mills, Vermont Commissioner of Education, and the Vermont Higher Education Council (VHEC), composed of presidents of the colleges and universities in the state, signed an agreement under which a VHEC presidential panel was established to re-design the program-approval process for reaccrediting teacher prepara-tion programs. Unlike other state or national reform commissions, which are dominated by outsiders, the presidential panel consisted of two college presidents, James Pollack (Green Mountain College) and Peggy Williams (Lyndon State College) and four teacher educators, Charles Rathbone (University of Vermont), Marilyn Richardson (Trin-ity College), Morin Smith (Norwich University), and the author of this chapter. All the teacher educators were members of the Vermont Coun-cil of Teacher Educators (VCTE), a consortium of the 11 higher educa-tion institutions in the state that have teacher preparation programs. For 18 months the presidential panel studied and deliberated. We, of course, reviewed the research literature, talked to knowledgeable professionals, and discussed the various alternatives to the Vermont input model of program approval that was an adaptation of the National Association of State Directors of Teacher Education and Certification (NASDTEC) stan-dards and regulations.

As we proceeded, it became clear that development of a new program-approval process should be portfolio-based. Such a system makes sense in Vermont. The state is pioneering portfolio assessment in the public schools, and most of the teacher educators wished not to de-velop a program-approval process that emphasized standardized tests such as the old National Teachers Examination. Instead, we wanted to create a new system that would emphasize the uniqueness and special strengths of the state's various teacher preparation institutions and that would enable our prospective teachers to demonstrate their teaching skill in a comprehensive and creative way. We did not want to recreate another cookie cutter system that involved listing and counting discrete teaching competencies, and that did not reveal a full portrait of the be-ginning teacher at work in the classroom. Finally, our portfolio system was, of course, influenced by the national trend toward performance-based assessment and the work of Lee Shulman and others at Stanford University in portfolio assessment.

Results-Oriented Teacher Preparation Program Approval in Vermont: Evaluation by Portfolio

By March 1992, the presidential panel had a final draft of its report. A statement from a related document gives a good indication of the presi-dential panel's direction and focus.

> At this time of education reform and renewal, the new Vermont system of evaluation by portfolio is a groundbreaking initiative that builds on but does not supersede past state regulations and standards for program approval. As a results-oriented system of assessment, the substantive focus and emphasis is on the demonstration of beginning-level competence and skill of the prospective teacher in accordance with the Vermont "Standards for Professional Educators" and the general standards and subject area competencies and other regulations published in the State of Vermont "Regulations Governing the Licensing of Educators and the Preparation of Educational Professionals." (Vermont Council of Teacher Educators, 1993, p. 1)

While the initiative may be groundbreaking, it clearly is not a radical departure since it is tied to existing state and interstate regulation. Perhaps it may be characterized best as an important first step away from excessive top-down regulation. While mandated from above, it was developed collaboratively within the education community, principally by the teacher educators who will have to carry it out at their colleges and universities. The principle of collegial responsibility and accountability is one that Theodore Sizer, among others, argues should hold true for all state and federal mandates, particularly those establishing national standards for teachers or for students. As he states, "Keep decisions close to the people who are affected and who know about the craft" (personal communication, February 24, 1994). The implementation of this practice can lead to a process of both effective systemic reform and enhanced decision making of the professional teacher education community.

Further, to promote statewide dialogue and to give voice to all major constituencies, drafts of the proposal were shared continually with each of the 11 teacher preparation institutions within the state. The Commissioner also set up an oversight committee of school administrators, teachers, and state board of education members, which reviewed the presidential panel's drafts and gave feedback to us. At the end of the spring semester in 1992, the framework for the new program-approval system had been developed and accepted by all the constituencies: the Commissioner, the Vermont Standards Board for Professional Educators, the Commissioner's oversight committee, and the Vermont Council of Teacher Educators. However, because the new program-approval process was a substantive change, many practical issues of implementation remained to be worked out. To that end, the Standards Board for Professional Educators asked VCTE to set up an implementation task force to write a guide for the Results-Oriented Teacher Preparation

Program-Approval System. It took another 6 months of monthly meetings to complete the guide.

THE PORTFOLIOS

In Vermont two types of portfolios are required: the prospective teacher's portfolio that reflects the teacher preparation program theme and demonstrates the individual's competence and growth as a beginning professional educator; and the institutional portfolio—Program Assessment and Planning Report—that documents the effectiveness of the institution's teacher preparation programs in preparing competent teachers and also details plans for improvement or innovation in meeting current and evolving standards of best practice in teacher preparation. Each is briefly described below.

Prospective Teacher's Theme Portfolio

This portfolio illustrates how the teacher preparation theme—the program's unifying focus and its unique perspective on teaching or learning—has been integrated into the prospective teacher's classroom and relevant course- and fieldwork. Similar to the National Council for Accreditation of Teacher Education (NCATE) requirement, the program theme is operationalized through the "goals, objectives and expected outcomes" for each prospective teacher. Such themes as Trinity College Education Department's *Learning and Teaching: Constructing Meaningful Connections* (1993) help provide a sense of purpose and direction that is important to the college's evolving identity as a teacher preparation institution. As related in its institutional report, "this determination of who we are and what we jointly believe has been central to our development as a team focused on shared goals. These common beliefs enhance our ability to deliver quality teacher education programs" (p. 6). As such, the theme portfolio helps promote greater program coherence and collaboration among teacher education staff while it demonstrates how the theme is incorporated into the "hearts and minds" and practices of prospective teachers.

   In addition to the program theme, there are, of course, other purposes that the Vermont prospective teacher's portfolio serves:

1. it documents the beginning teacher's teaching and professional competence in meeting the Vermont standards;

2. it exhibits professional growth and reflective learning;
3. it displays the beginner's best work or the individual's progress in achieving beginning-level teaching competence;
4. finally, it provides a prospective teacher with documentation to use in obtaining a teaching position.

(Presumably, it may serve other uses as well.)

According to the program-approval guidelines, the prospective teacher's portfolio must contain:

- Lesson plans
- Unit plans
- Demonstrated evidence of one's pupils' learning
- Reflective statements by the candidate about his or her learning
- Field placement observations
- Material that demonstrates learning over time and in different learning environments (The portfolio must contain not just material related to the student teaching practicum but must encompass work and effort from the beginning of the preparation program.)
- Student teaching summative evaluations
- A nationally recognized assessment instrument (Such instruments may include new versions of the Educational Testing Service's PRAXIS Series or such classroom evaluation tools as the Learning Environment Inventory, which assesses the teacher's classroom environment in comparison to other teachers in the same field.)
- College transcript(s)
- Documentation of completion of college competencies—such as a writing requirement
- Written statements attesting to teaching and learning performance from a college supervisor, cooperating teacher, and liberal arts and science faculty.

The portfolio may include other items such as journals, photo essays, videotapes of teaching episodes, endorsements by supervisors, and other evidence of competence.

Once the portfolio has been created, the teacher preparation program staff assumes the responsibility to determine how it will be assessed and by what criteria, and to document the process of assessment in its institutional portfolio.

From a review of the literature, the general criteria for development of the Vermont prospective teacher's portfolio conform to emerging good practice in portfolio design and evaluation. These criteria clearly include the five intertwined clusters of teaching activity that Bird (1990), a leading scholar on portfolio design, believes reveal and illuminate the classroom teacher's role and practice in its multiple dimensions.

1. Teaching a class
2. Planning and preparation
3. Student and program evaluation
4. Interaction with other educators
5. Interaction with parents and members of the community (One of the Vermont standards, advocacy, addresses the need of a teacher to communicate with parents and community members.)

The Vermont prospective teacher's portfolio also meets the criterion of authenticity articulated by Newmann and Archbald (1992), as "the cultivation and documentation of meaningful, significant, and worthwhile forms of accomplishment" (pp. 71–72), by the beginning teacher. As Wolf (1991), another leading expert in portfolio development, states:

> A schoolteacher's portfolio can be defined as a container for storing and displaying evidence of a teacher's knowledge and skills. However, this definition is incomplete. A portfolio is more than a container—a portfolio also represents an attitude that assessment is dynamic, and that the richest portrayals of teacher (and student) performances are based upon multiple sources of evidence collected over time in authentic settings. (p. 129)

Institutional Portfolio

The program-approval guidelines call for the inclusion of the following items in the Program Assessment and Planning Report (PAPR), or the institutional portfolio:

- Statement of program theme(s) and operational characteristics (goals, research base, oucomes)
- A representative sampling of prospective teachers' portfolios from each program area
- Aggregated data developed from prospective teachers' portfolios (general conclusions about lesson or curriculum planning, implementation of theme, etc.)
- Aggregated data from follow-up surveys of beginning teachers
- Annual collection of surveys and/or interviews with a representative sample of graduates, principals (if possible), parents of pupils, and/or other school personnel to validate or corroborate the judgments of data analysis

• Aggregated data compiled from a survey of cooperating teachers and school administrators at school sites where prospective teachers are placed on a regular basis

• Evidence of advisement/collaboration with the Vermont Council of Teacher Educators

• Program self-evaluation

• Five-Year Planning Report (including time schedule, specific changes or restructuring planned to improve quality and effectiveness, and a description of school–college partnerships to help restructure learning environments within area schools)

• Documentation that the program(s) meets the basic state regulations in regard to field experience hours, length of student teaching semester, frequency of supervision, and so on.

While containing many of the components of the traditional institutional report, the institutional portfolio has three important, if not unique, features that make it distinctive and a promising innovation. First, it requires and encourages ongoing consultation and collaboration among teacher preparation programs in the state. Such collegial consultation may be formal or informal. In the formal arrangement, the VCTE member, acting as consultant, will review the teacher education program's institutional portfolio and make a written statement of findings, suggestions, and substantive recommendations. In an informal relationship, VCTE consultants will advise the teacher education program under review when requested and during workshops or conferences held by VCTE and the Vermont Department of Education on such topics as developing programmatic themes or evaluating the prospective teacher's portfolio.

Second, the institutional portfolio requirement that an institution of higher learning report on its school–college/university partnership with area schools also helps promote collaboration of higher education with the Vermont public schools. While not a requirement for reaccreditation, it does obligate colleges and universities to detail in what ways, if any, they are working with area schools to help improve the education of the children its prospective teachers will teach in the classroom. At a minimum, school–college/university partnerships allow for dialogue and increased understanding of each institution's general perspective. Teacher education programs may benefit particularly from such partnerships. Breaking down the institutional barriers and holding sustained and thoughtful conversations with public school colleagues about substantive problems of teaching and learning can only enhance cooperation and mutual respect. It also may lead to the reduction, if not the elimination, of the perceived theory—practice dichotomy that often inhibits effective classroom and school reform.

Finally, the multiple measures—especially the prospective teacher's portfolio and the graduates' and cooperating teachers' evaluations—allow for a more holistic assessment of program effectiveness and encourage serious self-reflection on the part of the teacher education staff. It is not simply that there are more data to collect and to weigh in preparing the institutional portfolio, but the teacher preparation staff also must make a substantive judgment about what their student teachers know and what teaching skills they can effectively demonstrate, and how their judgment as teacher educators squares with the views of beginning teachers in the field and cooperating teachers in area schools. Such self-reflection on the part of the teacher education staff is valuable and can lead to constructive self-criticism that triggers practical and important steps to program improvement and institutional renewal.

Implementation of the New Program-Approval Process

As of 1996, all teacher preparation institutions in Vermont have been reviewed under the new program-approval system. These institutions—Castleton State College, Green Mountain College, Trinity College, Goddard College, Middlebury College, and the University of Vermont (UVM)—are representative of the diversity in Vermont: All are quite different from each other in their institutional mission, the composition of their student body, and their size and institutional resources. All these higher education institutions report that the new system is both workable and preferable to the old input model of program approval. The process, of course, needs fine tuning. The one serious concern voiced by all higher education institutions was with the procedures related to the visiting team review of the teacher education programs. Because of the newness of the approach, the state visiting teams not only looked at outputs (principally the prospective teachers' portfolios) but also continued to examine the old inputs as well (the course syllabi, faculty credentials, etc.). As one can imagine, the results of the reaccreditation visits were uneven and initially somewhat confusing, particularly for the two institutions that were first reviewed in 1993, Trinity and Goddard Colleges. The following academic year Middlebury College, UVM, Castleton State College, and Green Mountain College registered fewer reservations, in part because the visiting teams were clearer in their roles and in part because at this stage of implementation of the new program-approval process, it was necessary to provide both outputs and inputs to the review teams.

However, it is envisioned by the Standards Board for Professional Educators and by VCTE that in the near future the visiting team's assessment will be based chiefly and substantively on output data related to the prospective teachers' portfolios and evaluations of the teacher preparation programs provided by graduates and cooperating teachers. We are now in a transition process between the old and the new. We need to develop both new procedures for program review and a new language to describe what is to happen during the review visit of a results-oriented teacher preparation program. We also need to communicate to the review team members and remind ourselves as well that we are embarking on a new way of evaluating professional programs that involves innovating, risk taking, and demonstrating good faith.

In general, then, the new program-approval system, while representing a compromise between the old process and the innovative and more authentic assessment by portfolio, is an important step toward genuine and continual reform that can make a difference. Its implementation in the next few years holds promise to improve teacher education in Vermont because it is a form of authentic assessment and because it collaboratively involves all the Vermont teacher preparation programs that now have a greater sense of ownership and stake in its successful implementation. Finally, it also holds the promise of significant improvement over time because it is an open system of evaluation that continually calls for self-assessment and self-reflection on the part of the teacher education faculty. If the new program-approval system is taken seriously by the preparatory institutions, there is no final closure in its implementation, only the presence of new challenges that grow out of its implementation and the practice of portfolio assessment.

THE MIDDLEBURY PORTFOLIO SYSTEM

Turning now to the Middlebury portfolio system and its development—the second tale—it is important to note that the state program-approval system allowed us a considerable degree of decision making and latitude to shape the portfolio process in accordance with our goals and our special strengths as a liberal arts college. Specifically, in developing our portfolio system of evaluation, we had to determine and make choices about our portfolio theme and who was to be involved in developing and evaluating the prospective teachers' portfolios.

Portfolio Themes

The Middlebury College Teacher Education Program theme of "reflective teaching and the creation of community in the classroom and school" is grounded in and grows out of the strength of our liberal arts curriculum. The College's aim has been to educate practitioners of the liberal arts who can bring liberal learning to bear on practical and significant real-world problems and concerns. Such liberal preparation, in particular, fosters and facilitates reflection-on-practice in beginning teachers and the effective development of their problem-solving, decision-making, and communication skills. These skills are essential to the creation of a learning community in the classroom that is intellectually challenging and enabling for a diversity of students.

Reflective Teaching. As Dewey (1915) and others (e.g., Tom, 1984) held, it is essential to view teaching as dynamic and changing, and as a moral craft in which determining and pursuing worthwhile ends and means are critical and ongoing. Thus, as Schön (1987) points out, reflective teaching means careful planning and continual "reflecting-in-practice" and "reflecting-on-practice" (p. 1) about both the intellectual and ethical dimensions of classroom teaching and learning. At its best, such teaching requires a passion for the subject matter, high expectations for all students, and multicultural sensitivity to the diversity of students' needs and family backgrounds. It also must be grounded in a view of the student as an active learner whose intellectual capacity, emotional and moral levels of development, and self-esteem and self-worth deserve to be respected and enhanced.

Community of Learners. Creating community in the classroom is an increasingly central focus of our teacher preparation programs as we engage in teaching in our classrooms and as we work in the schools with cooperating teachers and student teachers. Through dialogue in our classes and thoughtful conversation in supervisory conferences and other mentoring occasions, we attempt to foster reflective practice in a supportive liberal arts context.

Central to a community of learners are three principles articulated in *The Shopping Mall High School* (Powell, Farrar, & Cohen, 1985), "purpose, push and personalization" (p. 316). These are crucial ingredients to a successful classroom and school and to a "more committed learning community" on any level of the American educational system. We endorse Sizer's (1985) metaphor of "student as worker and teacher as coach" (p. 316). We also advocate learning environments in which cooperative learning is emphasized or at least equally balanced with competitive learning, particularly in the contexts of heterogeneous classrooms. Working along with cooperating teachers, we encourage and help equip student teachers to provide their students with intellectual stimulation, moral definition, and reward for hard work, creativity, and perseverance in collaborative and individual efforts in and outside of the classroom.

In sum, the educational perspectives and dispositions that the Middlebury College prospective teacher will exhibit and strengthen in the student teaching practicum are:

- the view of teaching as a moral craft that enables and facilitates students' intellectual growth and the development of their self-esteem
- mastery of the subject matter and a deepening conviction of its relevance and value to students and society in general
- the habits of thoughtful and critical reflection about teaching and learning in their classrooms and other learning environments
- the exhibition of effective problem-solving, decision-making, and communication skills in their classroom preparation, teaching, and evaluation
- the demonstration of high expectations and multicultural understanding, empathy, and respect for all students in their classrooms
- the promotion of a shared vision of community for the classroom and the school

Collaborative Model of Teacher Preparation

Both the teacher education program staff and area school cooperating teachers played a collaborative role in the design and construction of the Middlebury College theme portfolio. The cooperating teacher and the college supervisor also are involved in ongoing evaluation of its effectiveness. For example, the college supervisor and the cooperating teacher review the student teacher's portfolio at midterm and at the end of the semester. When the portfolio is completed, there is a one-hour oral presentation by the student teacher of his or her portfolio. At the oral, the college supervisor, cooperating teacher, and outside reviewer ask substantive questions and enter into dialogue with the student teacher about teaching and learning issues. Based on a reading of the portfolio and the oral examination, the college supervisor, cooperating teacher, and outside reviewer make a holistic judgment about the competence and teaching effectiveness of the student teacher. Such collaboration between the cooperating teacher and college supervisor is important in two regards: (1) It enhances the cooperating teacher's acceptance of the new portfolio system of evaluation and enables these educators to develop a sense of ownership and investment in its successful implementation; and (2) it helps establish a genuine school–college partnership that is good for both institutions of learning, because it promotes the professionalization and status of teaching in general.

Our portfolio design is substantive, but it is important to make clear that we have only the first generation of prospective teachers' portfolios. We need continually to fine tune our portfolio designs based on our own experiences and on evolving best practice in the field.

Problematic Issues

While the Middlebury College prospective teacher's portfolio conforms to good practice, as do those of the other Vermont colleges and universities, any mandated and structured teacher portfolio also raises some problematic issues. Here are six such perceived or real problems.

1. Ownership. Whose portfolio is it really—the prospective teacher's or the institution's? Is it something that prospective teachers are proud of and find of real meaning to them, or is it viewed as another rite of passage by the neophytes—one more hurdle to overcome in becoming licensed as a professional educator?
2. Confidentiality. Who gets to see it?
3. Authenticity. Does it provide by itself a comprehensive and accurate picture of the prospective teacher's skills and competence? In what ways can it stand alone and in what ways must it be viewed in relation to other evidence?
4. Reflection-on-Practice. Does it lead to greater reflectivity and to improvement in the quality of instruction of the prospective teacher?
5. Program Accountability. Does it or can it lead to program self-evaluation and improvement?
6. Doability. Finally, can an already overworked teacher-preparation program staff handle the increased work load?

These questions will be briefly addressed below in relation to the Middlebury College system of portfolio evaluation.

Ownership. The dual ownership of the portfolio has its advantages and disadvantages. Normally, the structured portfolio that is evaluated in progress by mentors makes the end product more comprehensive and analytic and more literate and polished. Our graduates have, of course, used their portfolios to get teaching positions; it was their portfolios that helped them get both the initial interview and the job. Cooperating teachers also reinforce the portfolio's importance in obtaining a job, and thus prospective teachers come to understand the value of the portfolio in these pragmatic terms. However, on the personal and more existential level, a number of the prospective teachers do not experience that special ownership of their portfolio that a prospective teacher who voluntarily develops one on his or her own may feel. Clearly, most of the Middlebury College student teachers do feel justifiably proud about their creation, but not all of them are enthusiastic and fully invested in their portfolio work.

Confidentiality. A mandated portfolio system, of course, means that the visiting team also will review the prospective teacher's portfolio. While most of the Middlebury prospective teachers have no problem with this oversight responsibility of a state review team, it does entail that their written permission be obtained before their portfolios can be read by people other than their college supervisors and cooperating teachers. Because the teacher preparation institution must maintain portfolios of prospective teachers for 5 years, this requirement inevitably involves increased paperwork and development of files of completed informed consent forms. Moreover, a teaching portfolio that is to be viewed by a public audience often will be written differently from one that is confidential and intended in part to help the beginner communicate his or her hopes and fears as well as personal triumphs and frustrations about learning to teach.

Authenticity. On many levels, the portfolio is an accurate and in-depth portrait of the prospective teacher's teaching competence and progress and development as a beginning teacher. This is particularly true if the evaluations of the cooperating teachers and college supervisors also are included in the portfolio. However, the portfolio cannot stand alone. It must be viewed in the light of other evidence As Lee Shulman (1988) wisely points out, "A combination of methods—portfolios, direct observation, assessment centers, and better tests—can compensate for one another's shortcomings as well as reflect the richness and complexity of teaching" (p. 36).

Reflection-on-Practice. On many levels, the Middlebury College theme portfolio of reflective teaching and the creation of community encourages sustained reflection-on-practice. We also have added additional portfolio components to help prospective teachers gain a more holistic sense of classroom teaching. For example, in addition to lesson plans, curriculum units, videotapes of classroom teaching, and teaching journals, the Middlebury portfolio has added a requirement that student teachers "present a student" and "present a class." Adopting and adapting a practice from medical training, "presenting a student" allows our student teachers to be more reflective about the learning needs, learning style, and general strengths and weaknesses of individual students. "Presenting a class" in terms of the diversity of learning styles and motivational levels, particularly in a heterogeneous classroom, allows students to begin to focus on the larger picture and to recognize patterns of behavior as well as individual differences that need to be addressed. These additional components of the portfolio help make it more comprehensive in scope and more reflective and analytic in nature. When student teachers present their class or present specific students in weekly afternoon seminars, a sustained and substantive dialogue also takes place about teaching and learning issues that can help make the portfolio a living and organic document. These presentations enable student teachers to document their increasing understanding of the dynamics and complexities of teaching in a thoughtful manner and provide the database for more effective classroom planning and decision making.

However, there is another side to this issue. In their portfolios, a few of the student teachers are not always as reflective as they should be. It is not just the difficulty these prospective teachers have in seeing the "forest for the trees" in terms of course goals—that is to be expected when learning to teach and teaching a subject matter for the first time. Rather, it often relates to their not developing an adequate rationale for the lesson or not providing adequate substantive and helpful written comments on their pupils' papers. It is somewhat of a paradox. The prospective teacher has the analytic skills for reflection, and his or her teaching is often analytic and creative, but an outside reviewer who had not observed the prospective teacher in the classroom would not necessarily know it from the portfolio material.

Perhaps the explanation for the paradox relates to professional life and to the special stresses of teaching. Most teachers—indeed most professionals—are people of action in the context of dynamic and constantly changing learning environments. On a daily basis, they have little time for reflection-on-practice, and such reflection is not really valued or sustained by the school culture. Moreover, learning to teach is very stressful, as is the task of developing a portfolio of their competence and achievement. Further, the Middlebury College portfolio format favors a prospective teacher who has good writing skills and who is expressive in thought and action. More reserved but still effective student teachers, or beginners who are more articulate orally than in writing, have a harder time with developing a portfolio that is both reflective and engaging to the reader. "Are we asking too much of the rookie?" is a thought that comes to mind. Perhaps—but it is our view that spelling out our expectations in more detail, providing exemplary models of excellent portfolios, and allowing more time during the professional semester for development of the portfolio will make a difference. Also, as Lyons (1994) suggests, greater reflection and self-evaluation may occur more naturally and more fully after the end of student teaching and at a time in the lives of prospective teachers when they are free of the daily pressures of the classroom and have achieved some distance from their student teaching experience. It is an idea that makes sense and calls for follow-up interviews with student teachers after the completion of the professional semester.

Program Accountability. The process of implementing the approval system of portfolio evaluation and preparing for and undergoing the visiting team review, does encourage honest program self-evaluation. After all, the evidence of the prospective teacher's competence and adequacy of preparation is there for the college supervisor and others to see. It cannot really be trivialized or explained away in the same way a bad student evaluation (the student doesn't like me) or an outsider's criticism (the evaluator doesn't understand the full context) can be rationalized. As a professional, the teacher educator will act to improve the preparation or engage in dialogue with others on how to address the specific issue.

More important, there is a built-in dynamic for continual change and experimentation with the new portfolio system. As one reads the portfolios and discusses them with prospective teachers, cooperating teachers, and colleagues from both the department and VCTE, the resulting dialogue encourages, if not compels, a certain tinkering with the design of the prospective teacher's portfolio. Through thoughtful engagement in conversation, it often becomes evident how the portfolio might be improved. For instance, after reviewing all of the prospective teachers' portfolios in anticipation of the state visit, we decided to make a number of modifications in the portfolio design. One in particular is worth mentioning. Prospective teachers are now required to develop portfolios of the work of the students who make up the case studies related to "presenting a student." Such an additional portfolio requirement helps give greater focus to these case studies and also provides authentic evidence of how the prospective teacher's instruction makes a difference to the learning of individual students in the classroom.

Doability. It clearly takes a great deal of time, labor, and psychic energy to create and then implement the new program-approval process. It is, of course, a more manageable endeavor in a smaller teacher preparation program such as Middlebury's where the number of prospective teachers' portfolios to evaluate is limited to about 25 annually. Yet, the University of Vermont, with over 200 prospective teachers' portfolios a year to review, also is successfully implementing the new system of portfolio evaluation. But the verdict is still out. In certain critical ways the new system of portfolio evaluation is superior to the old input model. It is a more authentic form of assessment, and it promotes and can capture many of the essentials of good teaching. However, it is not a panacea. The portfolio by itself does not substitute for systematic observation and personal mentoring. Rather, it serves to augment and place in a larger context these standard forms of beginning teacher supervision. In addition, substantial photocopying costs as well as opportunity costs are incurred. Could the prospective teacher and the college supervisor not better spend their time preparing or observing classroom lessons rather than reflecting on past practice? Sometimes, it is a tough call. Yet, it is clear that significant improvement in teaching comes about by reflection on teaching practice as much as it is promoted by greater experience in the classroom.

CONCLUSION

Will the portfolio evaluation system survive? While it will take at least 5 years to determine its long-term feasibility and durability, ultimately it will depend on the commitment of the Vermont teacher education community to continue to improve the state-mandated innovation, and on the goodwill of state agencies to support the new program-approval system.

In sum, the Vermont program-approval system is a promising innovation. It is a vehicle that allows for program self-reflection and systematic documentation of teaching competence and commitment to teaching. But it will take a goodfaith effort to realize its full potential. In Vermont, we are off to a good start and so far no major complaints have been expressed by any of the state's teacher preparation institutions or by any of the state visiting teams about the new program-approval process. Over the next few years, we need to refine and fine tune the portfolio evaluation, especially with regard to the nature and procedures of the state review visit and to the improvement of the prospective teacher's portfolio. Presently, the Standards Board for Professional Educators is conducting an evaluation of the new system to determine how well it is working and what changes are necessary to improve its overall effectiveness. Such evaluation data will be helpful in our continuing efforts to improve the new Vermont program-approval process and to anticipate future needs in teacher education that again may be addressed by grassroots initiatives.

REFERENCES

Bird, T. (1990). The schoolteacher's portfolio: An essay on possibilities. In J. Millman & L. Darling-Hammond (Eds.), *The new handbook of teacher evaluation: Assessing elementary and secondary school teachers* (2nd ed.; pp. 241–256). Newbury Park, CA: Sage.

Dewey J. (1915). *School and society.* Chicago: University of Chicago Press.

Lyons, N. (1994, January). *Puzzles, questions and emerging research issues: A discussion.* Paper presented at the Portfolios in Teacher Education: A Working Conference on Using Portfolios in Teaching and Teacher Education, Cambridge, MA.

Newmann, F, & Archbald, D. (1992). The nature of authentic academic achievement. In H. Berlak, F. Newmann, E. Adams, D. Archbald, T. Burgess, J. Raven, & T. Romberg (Eds.), *Toward a new science of educational testing and assessment* (pp. 71–83). Albany: State University of New York Press.

Powell, A., Farrar, E., & Cohen, D. (1985). *The shopping mall high school.* Boston: Houghton Mifflin.

Schön, D. (1987). *Educating the reflective practitioner: Towards a new design for teaching and learning in the professions.* San Francisco: Jossey-Bass.

Shulman L. S. (1988). A union of insufficiencies: Strategies for teacher assessment in a period of educational reform, *Educational Leadership, 46*(3), 36–41.

Sizer, T. (1985). *Horace's compromise.* Boston: Houghton Mifflin.

Tom, T. (1984). *Teaching as a moral craft.* New York: Longman.

Trinity College Education Department. (1993). *Learning and teaching: Constructing meaningful connections.* Burlington, VT: Author.

Vermont Council of Teacher Educators. (1993). *A guide for results-oriented teacher preparation program approval in Vermont: Evaluation by portfolio.* Montpelier, VT: Author.

Wolf, K. (1991). The schoolteacher's portfolio: Issues in design, implementation, and evaluation. *Phi Delta Kappan, 73*(2), 129–136.

CHAPTER 15

The Case of the Missing Portfolio Entry: The Moral and Ethical Dimensions of Teaching

Gloria Ladson-Billings

THE UNIVERSITY OF WISCONSIN–MADISON

The thinking underlying the portfolio assessment process is not unlike the tenure and promotion process that takes place at colleges and universities. In order to maintain one's position and garner the rewards of the institution, faculty members select examples of scholarship that best reflect their research interests. In addition, student evaluations of teaching and service to the university and professional community are examined. The basic premise is that the teachers under review should have the opportunity to present themselves in the best possible light, showcasing the exemplary aspects of their practice, and that the people whom they serve (i.e., the students) should have input concerning that service. In the case of college and university faculty, that input comes in the form of student evaluations. In precollegiate classrooms, that input may come in the form of examples of student work and parent and community feedback.

My own experience with portfolio assessment came as a result of my involvement with the Stanford Teacher Assessment Project (TAP) elementary literacy module. A portion of the assessment center activity involved teacher portfolios. The entries of the portfolio, as described by Athanases (1990) included:

1. A prose or graphic overview of 3 to 5 weeks of instruction.
2. Details of two to three consecutive lessons.
3. A roster of literary works and other resources selected for use.
4. Copies of handouts to students.
5. Samples of student work.
6. Photos or written records of blackboard and bulletin board work (optional).
7. Videotapes of teaching: (a) large-group lesson on literature, (b) small-group discussion of literature (4–8 participants, 10–15 minutes in length), and (c) one-to-one writing conferences with students of two different skill levels.
8. Audiotape of teaching (optional).
9. Notes by observer of teaching (administrator, mentor, resource person) (optional).

As I looked with interest and fascination at the artifacts of the varied teaching careers—the pieces of paper, the video- and audiotapes, the photographs—I began to look for examples of what I have come to regard as essential elements of good teaching—the moral and ethical dimensions.

WHY TEACHERS MUST EXHIBIT A MORAL AND ETHICAL DIMENSION

The changing demographics in the United States make imperative the need for teachers to consider diversity as an important aspect of education. California presents a graphic example of just how dramatic that demographic change is. In 1980, California had a population that was approximately 76% white (Gibbs, 1991). Fifteen years later, the white population in the state dropped to 57%. In Los Angeles County, no one ethnic or racial group constitutes a numerical majority. Unfortunately, this diversity is not accompanied by equality.

The infant mortality rate in Cleveland, Detroit, and Oakland is higher than that in Costa Rica (Edelman, 1987). African American students constitute 17% of the public school population but are 41% of the special education population (Kunjufu, 1984). African American students are two to five times more likely than white children to be suspended from school (Irvine, 1990). The high school dropout rate in inner cities is almost 50% (Chan & Momparler, 1991). Although in 23 of the nation's 25 largest school districts African American students are now a majority, African American teachers constitute only 5% of the teaching population (Power, 1988).

What do these shocking statistics have to do with prospective teachers attempting to develop teaching portfolios? I would like to suggest that unless teachers pay attention to the moral and ethical dimensions of teaching, the technical aspects of the craft are for naught. These moral and ethical dimensions include informed empathy, reflective practice, and cultural relevance.

Informed Empathy

In my years of teaching preservice teachers at Santa Clara University, I met scores of caring and well-intentioned young people (primarily women) who were prompted to pursue teaching careers for a variety of reasons. In preadmission interviews, those pursuing elementary teaching careers often referred to their love of children as the reason they wanted to teach. When pushed to consider the fact that one's love of children could lead to other occupations, such as pediatric nursing, day care worker, recreation leader, and children's librarian, many of these prospective teacher candidates were at a loss to articulate why they really wanted to be teachers. They had not considered that teaching is not merely about working with students. Teachers are involved in a professional enterprise that requires interactions with both children and adults. In the classroom, teachers need to have some sense of both what they are doing and why they are there.

At the secondary level, the prospective teacher candidates I met often expressed a desire to teach because they "just *loved* mathematics (or history, English, biology, etc.)." While it was refreshing to see students intellectually excited about a field of study, few of these students had given thought to what it would be like to attempt to teach the subject they loved to students who just might *hate* it. Like their elementary counterparts, the prospective secondary teacher candidates had given little thought to what is involved in teaching and why they were pursuing it as a career. Almost none of our prospective students had given any thought to the purposes of schooling.

As I mentioned above, these prospective teachers are often well-meaning and caring. However, as primarily white middle-class students preparing to teach in classrooms of students increasingly brown and black and from working-class and poor families, the caring they exhibit is in the form of sympathy. They feel sorry for and pity their students. It is unlikely that teachers who pity their students are prepared to see those students in societal positions that exceed their own.

What I am advocating is informed empathy. Empathy means the ability to "feel with," not "feel for," the students. Informed empathy involves getting to know as much as possible about students, their families and lives away from school, their communities, and their cultural backgrounds. If you understand that students come from households where they are expected to assume flexible roles—roles that are interchangeable with adult roles—then perhaps you can understand that the classroom seems a confusing place because the roles are so fixed.

What aspects of teacher preparation help students to develop this informed empathy? What portion of the portfolio documents this informed empathy? How can we develop informed empathy in prospective teachers?

Reflective Practice

Ken Zeichner (1986) has written extensively about the role of reflection in teaching. Zeichner distinguishes his notions of reflection from those that divorce reflection from moral and ethical issues such as diversity and social justice. Building on Zeichner's ideas about reflection, I am concerned that prospective teachers do more than think about their lessons to devise better techniques for delivering instruction.

Reflective practitioners who understand the moral and ethical dimensions of their teaching are willing to ask important questions about what they do and why they do it. They understand that knowledge is socially constructed and each of their students, regardless of school performance, comes to the classroom with knowledge. In their reflection, they ask themselves, "What can/did I do in the classroom to capitalize on the knowledge that students bring with them? How often do my agendas dominate the classroom? How often do students have the opportunity to set the agenda?"

How many student teachers have taken the time to reflect on what made school meaningful for them and tried to incorporate that in their own teaching? How many have asked students what they like and don't like about school? If new teachers blindly follow the state framework, the course syllabus, and the textbook, how can they develop reflective qualities that help them improve their teaching? What aspects of the teaching portfolio document the ability to reflect on these dimensions?

Culturally Relevant Teaching

Finally, teachers must become what I have termed culturally relevant teachers. Culturally relevant teaching describes a pedagogy that empowers students intellectually, socially, emotionally, and politically by using cultural referents to impart knowledge, skills, and attitudes (Ladson-Billings, 1992). Like critical pedagogy (Giroux & Simon, 1989), culturally relevant pedagogy

> refers to a deliberate attempt to influence how and what knowledge and identities are produced within and among particular sets of social relations. It can be understood as a practice through which people are incited to acquire a particular "moral character." As both a political and practical activity, it attempts to influence the occurrence and qualities of experiences. (p. 239)

Another point of convergence between critical and culturally relevant pedagogy is the notion that they both "strive to incorporate student experience as 'official' content" (Giroux & Simon, 1989, p. 250). The place where these pedagogical approaches differ is the emphasis placed on various subjectivities. While critical pedagogy seeks to help the *individual* critique and change the social environment, culturally relevant pedagogy urges *collective* action grounded in cultural understandings, experiences, and ways of knowing the world.

In other writings, I have outlined the dimensions of culturally relevant teaching (Ladson-Billings, 1990, 1992). What is more important for this discussion is not the specifics of these dimensions but the distinction between culturally relevant teaching and assimilationist teaching. I believe most teacher preparation programs work to develop assimilationist teachers. These teachers are not "bad" teachers. However, their conception of teaching is to find ways for their students to fit into the existing social order. They often draw direct lines between school knowledge and employability. Consequently, they say things like, "You have to stay in school (or speak standard English, or dress in this particular way) in order to get a job." These teachers never question the basic injustices of the society or challenge their students to do so. Issues of knowledge construction or production never arise in these classrooms. These teachers accept failure as inevitable for some students and maintain a fixed and hierarchical structure between teacher and students in their classrooms. Rarely are the things they teach connected to the lives of the students.

Culturally relevant teachers understand the social contexts in which they teach. They recognize social inequality and incorporate information about it in their classrooms. They believe that success is possible for all students. They understand that knowledge is created, shared, and recycled in a classroom. They understand their purpose in the classroom as helping students to critically read both the word and the world. It is not enough to understand the plot, theme, and structure of a piece of literature. For them, how a particular piece of literature got selected as "good" literature, how it relates to students' everyday lives, and how students develop their own literature are all a part of the learning process. Culturally relevant teachers see their students as *producers* of knowledge, whereas assimilationist teachers see their students as *consumers* of knowledge. These very different visions of students have ethical implications.

If we see our students as producers of knowledge, then we understand them as people who come to the classroom with knowledge. If we see them as consumers of knowledge, then we see them as receptacles of the knowledge we "give" them. If we subscribe to this consumer vision, we expect students to merely replicate what we have given them. We are participating in a form of indoctrination, and this is unethical.

How is culturally relevant teaching documented in a portfolio? How do prospective teachers understand the social purposes of schooling? How do they document these understandings? How do they meaningfully link up school knowledge and experiences with students' everyday lives?

WHAT GOOD IS A TEACHING PORTFOLIO?

It may seem that this discussion is attempting to discount the significance of the portfolio as a tool in teacher assessment. Actually, it is aimed at helping teachers rethink the use and development of teaching portfolios. We are living in times when our social, cultural, and economic differences challenge all teachers to raise serious moral and ethical questions in the classroom.

As a parent, I recall being incensed at the fact that each November the teacher would ask my son to bring a can of food to school for the needy. By the third year that this had happened, I wrote a scathing note asking why the students were not being asked to think about how it could be that in a land of abundance, schoolchildren were expected to collect cans once a year to feed the hungry. Do the students understand who the hungry (and homeless) are? Do they know what conditions exist that produce these situations? Needless to say, my child was not given the opportunity to explore these questions and discrepancies in the American dream.

In the aftermath of the Los Angeles police brutality trial (note that I did not refer to this as the "Rodney King verdict"; King was not on trial—the police officers were, but somehow this event has been constructed to make Rodney King the criminal) and the subsequent civil disorder, teachers were scurrying to help students understand what happened. In most urban classrooms, the students could better explain to the teachers what was happening.

We do need new and innovative ways to get at the complexity of teaching. Portfolio assessment offers some promising ideas. However, we should not become so enamored of this new "technology" that we are rendered powerless to critique it. We have to ask important questions about equity. Our commitment to the teaching profession must force us to keep the ethical and moral dimensions of this work at the top of any educational agenda. Young people who are going into teaching during these complex and confusing times need to be supported and mentored. They need to be commended for their idealism and reinforced for their willingness to take pedagogical risks. They bring with them the newest and most innovative techniques and strategies in instruction and assessment. We are at a particular moment in history where the stakes are incredibly high. Teachers' combination of technical skill and ethical commitment can point the way to brighter futures of opportunity, equality, and social justice. Let me urge you to keep your portfolios open for the missing entry that may mean the difference between *schooling* and *education* for the nation's children.

REFERENCES

Athanases, S. Z. (1990). *Assessing the planning and teaching of integrated language arts in the elementary grades* (Technical Report No. L3). Stanford: Stanford University, School of Education, Teacher Assessment Project.

Chan, V., & Momparler, M. (1991, May/June). George Bush's report card: What's he got against our kids? *Mother Jones, 16*(3), 44–45.

Edelman, M. W. (1987). *Families in peril: An agenda for social change.* Cambridge, MA: Harvard University Press.

Gibbs, N. (1991, November 18). Shades of difference. *Time,* pp. 66–68, 70.

Giroux, H., & Simon, R. (1989). Popular culture and critical pedagogy: Everyday life as a basis for curriculum knowledge. In H. Giroux & P. McLaren (Eds.), *Critical pedagogy, the state and cultural struggle* (pp. 236–252). Albany: State University of New York Press.

Irvine, J. (1990). *Black students and school failure.* Westport, CT: Greenwood Press.

Kunjufu, J. (1984). *Developing discipline and positive self images in black children.* Chicago: Afro-American Images.

Ladson-Billings, G. (1990). Like lightning in a bottle: Attempting to capture the pedagogical excellence of successful teachers of black students. *International Journal of Qualitative Studies in Education, 11,* 335–344.

Ladson-Billings, G. (1992, April). *Liberatory consequences of literacy: A case of culturally relevant instruction for African American students.* Paper presented at the Annual Meeting of the American Educational Research Association, San Francisco.

Power, J. (1988). Black education: How far have we come? *NEA Today, 6*(9), 14–15.

Zeichner, K. (1986). Preparing reflective teachers: An overview of instructional strategies which have been employed in pre-service teacher education. *International Journal of Educational Research, 7,* 565–575.

PART V

Epilogue

With Portfolio in Hand concludes with a brief examination of the critical question of portfolio consequences: What difference do portfolios make in the lives of teachers and their students? The chapters of this book provide at least two cautionary tales.

Lee Shulman's story of his own aborted effort to create a portfolio—told in Chapter 2—points to the obstacles a teacher faces when attempting to work in isolation from the creative context of dialogue and discussion with colleagues. The task seems never to get done. Portfolio development needs collaboration; it seems impossible without it.

The story of the teachers of the Everett Public Schools—told in Chapter 9—provides a more sobering tale. Having created a new professional development experience for themselves—developing portfolios, leading workshops to facilitate other teachers' portfolios in constructing their own—these teachers are pessimistic about the future of these efforts. Where can they take this new and clearly powerful, reflective experience? Their schools—as welcoming and supportive as they have been—offer no immediate suggestion. There is no time, no place, no structure in the everyday routines of schools to foster this reflective work. As teacher educators across the country work to make reflective practitioners of their students, are schools ready to receive and support these practices?

Some answers to these dilemmas are coming from the new professionals themselves. The following chapter looks at the long-term experiences of a small group of teachers who presented portfolios as part of the requirements for program completion and certification. While no generalizations are possible from this small sample, the experiences of these teachers do suggest several things: about how reflective practice might develop, about how portfolio development fosters the knowledge of practice, and about how these learnings may fare over time.

CHAPTER 16

Portfolios and Their Consequences: Developing as a Reflective Practitioner

Nona Lyons

UNIVERSITY OF SOUTHERN MAINE

Any new model of teacher professionalism ultimately must answer the question of consequences, of what difference it makes to its clients, to those the profession serves, as well as the profession itself. If the portfolio process is an effort to forge a new teacher professionalism—a cadre of competent practitoners, capable of interrogating their practices and fostering their own reflective learning—what, then, are its consequences? What difference does engaging in a portfolio process possibly make for students, for teachers, and for teaching as a profession?

As the authors of this book attest, portfolios are yet in their infancy. While portfolios have moved from individual classrooms and teacher education programs to state departments of education, are the primary assessment used by the National Board for Professional Teaching Standards for certification of experienced teachers, and currently are being developed by the Interstate New Teacher Assessment and Support Consortium for initial teacher licensure, there is not yet a body of systematic data documenting their uses or their long-term consequences. Some consequences—the time it takes to construct, evaluate, and judge portfolios; the affordability, equity, and feasibility of implementing portfolio processes; public acceptability and legal defensibility, as well as reliabil-

ity and validity—must all be addressed in various arenas where portfolios are being implemented. Much of this work is also in its infancy
(see Moss, 1992, 1997). While research needs to be undertaken in these
domains, there are glimpses, clear glimpses, of the promising possibilities of portfolios in the development and learning of teachers and their
students. That is the focus of this chapter. In particular, it takes up a
central issue in the development of the new professional teacher: becoming a reflective practitioner.

Of the stories teachers tell of their portfolio experiences, those presented in this book as well as those reported on by the National Board and
at teacher conferences, those about reflecton are compelling. Here I turn
to look at some of these stories, focusing on the experiences of several
teachers, especially one, Martha Martinez, introduced in Chapter 7, following her into the first years of teaching in her own classroom. Then,
drawing on a longitudinal study, I sketch an outline of developmental
elements that seem to be at work in becoming a reflective practitioner.

REFLECTING, INTERROGATING, AND CHANGING ONE'S PRACTICES

One consequence of engaging in a portfolio process, reported by teachers, both masters and novices, is the power of the opportunity for reflection. While there are differences in the meaning of the experience and
in what teachers say they learn from reflection, all report that the process
helps them to identify for themselves the critical features of their own
teaching platforms and philosophies. Some experienced teachers—see
Maria Ricci's comments in Chapter 9—do not find that reflection leads
to changes in their practice. Rather, for them, a portfolio process confirms what they are already doing as valid practice. Novice teachers, on
the other hand, report a direct connection between reflection and their
actual classroom teaching and work with students (Freidus, 1996; La
Boskey, 1994, 1996; Lyons, 1996, 1997).

One teacher intern revealed the way her portfolio learning, which
she began as an undergraduate, became a part of her teaching practices
during her internship year. Seeing that the portfolio process "made me
think about my purpose . . . made me probe deeper . . . what is the driving purpose? what is it that you want to accomplish? and what purpose
does it have? is it useful?" she found the process continued into her internship: "When I prepare a lesson plan or am asked to do something
with the children, I constantly ask myself: What do I want the kids to
get out of this? Why? Why am I doing this? So in that sense it was really

beneficial. And I try to think of that as I go through this whole process [of learning to teach]."

Similarly, the student teacher, Martha Martinez, identifies an insight into her teaching values that she carried into the first years of teaching—a direct result of her portfolio experience. The year after completing her student teaching, Martha, a Mexican-American, found a job in a junior high school in a rapidly changing ethnic community. As the only person of color on the faculty, Martha found that more and more minority students were being directed to her class. One Monday in the fall of that first year, Martha arrived early to find the school had been trashed by local high school students. On a door that led from the outside into her classroom, she found satanic symbols, a swastika, and racial epithets directed against her and her students. Shocked and angry, she went to the school authorities requesting that they be erased before her students—sixth graders—arrived. The principal agreed.

When the students arrived, Martha wondered whether she should tell them what had happened and how she felt about that. Then, she said: "I remembered the [portfolio] interviews . . . and that I am an ethical person. I decided it was important and the right thing for me to discuss this with my students."

> And I took my stand. I said it is wrong [what those students did], and if you know who did it, you can tell them for me that I thought it was wrong. . . . And maybe I made [my kids] responsible. But all through the year, kids in my class were very conscious of things like that, very conscious of race relations. When that stuff broke out in LA, they wanted to talk about it and they said: "No, that's wrong." And I said, "You are right, it is wrong." I said sometimes you can have your opinion on this or that, but sometimes you have to say something is right or wrong. And I said, "I'm telling you it's wrong . . . if you don't respect people, that's wrong." The kids, they just had a more focused opinion and they weren't afraid to say, "I think this is right or wrong." Whereas I don't think the other teachers ever came out and said this. . . . I think the teachers were trying to do business as usual. . . . I think the teachers were unsure themselves. I have a sense that some of them haven't been in situations where they had to make a decision about racism.

> But the kids, when they saw a television ad [after that incident] or something, they would come in and say, "Have you seen this ad or have you seen this or that?" How they portray certain types of

people. They seemed a lot keener about it than they were before, wanting to talk about it.

AUTHORING ONE'S OWN PROFESSIONAL AND ETHICAL DEVELOPMENT

What begins to come into focus in considering these teachers is that what they are about is nothing less than authoring their own learning and professional development. Armed with the insights of reflection, seeing the ways their own beliefs can influence their students, they shape and reshape their practices.

For example, when Martha Martinez, in the second year of her teaching, was again asked to teach a low-tracked class, she was determined "not to make those assumptions about the students that I had made about the class that failed during my student teaching. I determined to go into that class assuming that these students can succeed and that I would go down fighting to make that happen." Seeing the clear implications of her own expectations for student learning, Martha seeks to ensure that she will fit her practice to the needs of a particular class of kids, in this school community. She describes how she went about this.

> It was almost as if sometimes I had a completely different lesson planned for them than the other two classes. We had been doing the same book or the same reading or whatever, but I'd have to think of a new way to do it for that class, so that they could get a positive outcome and make them feel empowered, like they might want to come to class because they know that they can do the work.

Clearly, the teacher is in command of her developing learning. Thus, through a process of reflection on her own experience, begun with a portfolio interview, Martha Martinez scaffolds her own ethical and professional development.

MAKING PUBLIC DISCUSSION AND DEBATE ABOUT WHAT CONSTITUTES GOOD TEACHING

Perhaps the most striking consequence of a portfolio process for a new teacher professionalism is the creation of a new norm for teachers: that is, making public discussion and debate about what constitutes good teaching. Most versions of a portfolio process include some public presentation of the completed portfolio. But the process itself, usually taking place over a sustained period of time—a semester, a year—is characterized by discussion of a set of standards for effective practice, the presentation of artifacts, and conversation and discussion of their meaning to the individual with peers and mentors. This dialogue is likely to center on a teaching philosophy; how a given practice, lesson, or curriculum is or is not viewed as effective; why something failed; and, most important, how the individual made sense of something, and the lesson learned about teaching and learning. For many teachers, their most prized ways of doing things have never been shared with others, and certainly have rarely been subjected to the insights or probings of critical friends. Thus, the portfolio process opens to scrutiny and interrogation debate about what constitutes good practice and sustains the conversation over a long period of time. An emerging characteristic of a teacher as a professional is this ability to articulate, evaluate, engage in, and respond to criticism about teaching, their own practice, and student learning.

FOSTERING COLLABORATION, INTERPRETIVE COMMUNITIES

When teachers engage in a portfolio process they are likely to do so in the company of their colleagues—peers or mentors—conferencing with them about potential portfolio entries, articulating their philosophy, and subjecting their ideas to interrogation and further clarification. Most teacher education programs using a portfolio process, as well as the guidelines of INTASC and the National Board for developing a portfolio, carry the injunction that the portfolio process ought to be carried out in the company of others. The isolation so long a characteristic feature of teaching is broken and collaboration becomes a new norm of professional life.

There are two ways that the portfolio process needs collaboration: in the development of a portfolio and in its assessment and evaluation. What joins these two activities—development and assessment—is what might be called an interpretive turn, the interpretive nature of portfolio work. Interpretation characterizes portfolio making in deciding what counts as evidence of teacher growth and learning to teach. And interpretation characterizes the judging of portfolio evidence. This emphasis on interpretation is not surprising. Teaching is a supremely interpretive activity. It involves constant and sometimes highly nuanced interpretations. To the extent that portfolio practices embody highly interpretive acts, they are mirrors of teaching.

These are four important achievements of the portfolio process. All are predicated on the developing ability of teachers to reflect on their experiences, to interrogate their practices, understand their affects on students, and shape their practices to their goals for students. But a critical issue emerges: How do these changes and developments in understanding and implementing reflective practice take place? The puzzle is heightened by the fact that increasingly teacher educators and other researchers report that becoming reflective is no easy achievement for apprentices or master teachers. In this Epilogue I take up the issue of the reflection and the possible path of its development.

DEVELOPING AS A REFLECTIVE PRACTITIONER

I just didn't realize that until that whole discovery. . . . I just didn't realize that until I did the portfolio. . . . Now it's a conscious decision. . . . That is what the process is about. It helps to bring things to cognition . . . through these conversations with people, it helps bring it to that part of your brain where you can realize that you know it and that it is important to you. (teacher intern)

In taking up the issue of reflection in teacher education and the possible role of development in becoming a reflective practitioner, I will consider these issues through the lens of teacher apprentices as they put together a teaching portfolio to convince their mentors that they are indeed ready to take responsibility for a class of their own. This exploration with portfolios goes on in the context of widespread discussion about the place of reflection in teacher education and some recent puzzling findings about how effectively reflection can be taught.

Reflective practice is defined here as ways in which teachers interrogate their teaching practices, asking questions about their effectiveness and about how they might be refined to meet the needs of students. The development of reflection is considered not simply as change, but as the evolution and integration of more complex ways (or processes) of engaging in a critical examination of one's teaching practices.

Using data from a longitudinal study of ten teacher apprentices to examine the experience of becoming reflective through a portfolio process, I outline several developmental elements of reflection and an interpretive framework to uncover potential theoretical as well as practical implications of portfolios in teacher education.

The Puzzle

At a time of unprecedented interest in developing skill in reflection for both new and experienced teachers, it is disconcerting to find that reflection is not uniformly achieved (Lyons, in press; Baratz-Snowden, 1995). This contradictory feedback raises compelling questions: What makes it possible for some teachers to engage in reflective practice while others are unable to do so? What—culture, epistemology, learning style—impacts on one's ability to demonstrate reflection? What role might development play? What meaning do teachers themselves make of their experience of learning to be reflective practitioners? How does that influence their teaching and their understanding of student learning? Although teacher reflection has received considerable attention of researchers, few studies—with the exception of La Boskey (1994)—outline its development.

It is within this context of exploring and elaborating ideas about reflection and how it changes over time that I turn to research I have been conducting at the University of Southern Maine. Because these data are limited to a small number of case studies, I recognize and caution that the observations being made must be considered preliminary ones, needing verification.

THE LONGITUDINAL STUDY

The study reported here involves three cohorts of students at the University of Southern Maine's Extended Teacher Education Program (ETEP): undergraduates preparing to enter the university's internship program; teacher interns or postbaccalaureate students, taking part in a year-long intensive internship in learning to teach; and graduates of this program in their first or second years of teaching. Using data from ten case studies of students in these three settings who prepared teaching portfolios and talked about the process in open-ended interviews, I examine the meaning students give to their experiences of learning about and engaging in reflection and how that changes over time.

Instructions for constructing a portfolio usually suggest including the following: a statement of one's teaching philosophy or platform and a set of entries that are the evidence of one's competency in learning to teach. Each entry includes a description, a rationale for why it is included, and a reflection on what one learned about teaching and learning from the experience. Interns also consider the 11 ETEP program outcomes or standards as one guide to the kind of evidence they include in their portfolios, such as understanding child and adolescent development, or one's subject matter in order to reach all students—to name a few. (See Chapter 6, Figure 6.1.)

Four undergraduate students constructed and presented portfolios within the context of a "Portfolio Class," part of the admission process into the ETEP internship year program: They were interviewed during the following year. Six interns, identified by their mentors as either high reflectors or not-high reflectors, created portfolios over a five-month period of their internship year, coached by a Portfolio Team of former interns, university and school faculty. This portfolio was then presented to mentors and colleagues to cap the internship and provide closure to the year: It served as one determinant of certification for the interns. The interns were interviewed immediately after completing their portfolio presentations, and in the two years following. All of these interviews provide narrative reflections on the meaning students give to the portfolio process. I taught the undergraduate "Portfolio Class" and coached three of the interns as a member of their Portfolio Team. I conducted all the interviews. Data were analyzed both cross-sectionally and longitudinally for themes. It is these themes and elements of reflective development that I will highlight in the following paragraphs.

This analysis suggests four important hypotheses described below. In brief, this work points to a needed, expanded concept of reflection to include "making connections" about teaching and student learning that take place over time and in critical, collaborative conversations with others, and not as a solitary, individual enterprise.

OBSERVATIONS SUGGEST SOME HYPOTHESES

Data from the cohorts of these pilot studies reveal various responses on the part of the interns and undergraduates to the reflective portfolio process. But what first became apparent with the undergraduates of the Portfolio Class was that there were clear differences in the initial abilities of the students to engage in either written or oral reflections. This quickly became evident in the Portfolio Teams of teacher interns as well. Not all students could go beyond simple descriptions to engage in saying *why* they had included something in their portfolios, what it represented about their teaching, and what it was they had learned about teaching and learning from that experience. In response to the interview question—*Looking back at the portfolio experiences and presentation, what stands out for you?*—a nearly universal response from undergraduates, interns, and graduates now teaching is "engaging in reflection" or "doing reflections." In nearly the same breath most said, "It is hard." Some used the words "difficult"; some called it "daunting." Other researchers have reported similar findings (see Freidus, 1996; La Boskey, 1994, 1996).

In addition, when asked to write a statement of their teaching philosophies to be included in their portfolios, some teacher interns report being clearly dismayed by the scope of that task, some "nearly terrified" by it. Many believed that they did not have a teaching philosophy. Thus, at the start of their learning to teach, students are found with a variety of abilities and with greater or less success in engaging in reflection. But no matter how challenging, nearly all students in the end report the task of constructing a teaching portfolio as an important and significant reflective learning experience.

Four themes emerge from this pilot study that suggest hypotheses for future testing:

1. that several key elements and processes seem present from the simplest efforts at reflection but are elaborated over time;

2. that critical conversations interrogating portfolio entries and their significance provide a scaffold that fosters teacher consciousness of their knowledge of practice; such reflective interrogation can become a mechanism for continued teacher growth;

3. that the reflective process reveals, over time, significant aspects of one's teaching practice that become identified as part of one's teaching philosophy, and emerge embedded in one's teaching practices; and,

4. that the process of reflection that comes about through public, collaborative inquiry paradoxically—and sometimes painfully—involves learning about the self and about the values one holds for teaching and learning.

Each observation is discussed below.

Observation 1: That several elements and processes of reflection seem present from the simplest, initial, or even the most difficult efforts at it. One important observation of this study is that while the elements of reflective processes seem present from the start, they appear in some students in almost rudimentary, elemental form. They are, however, transformed over time. Some cross-sectional examples from the longitudinal study can clarify this process. However, this is a cross-sectional view and not necessarily a developmental one, and it is only one potential pattern.

Challenged-at-Times and Daunted Reflectors. Nadine, an undergraduate science major applying for admission into the internship teacher education program, identified the difficulties she encountered with reflection. Asked in an interview to say what stands out for her at the end of the portfolio process, she said:

> Amazed—coming up with all the reflections. That was challenging. It was difficult to think back [to the experiences represented by the entries] and just get it out. I can think of something to say, but it is harder to tell others what you are trying to say . . . having my thoughts be understandable to the reader. . . . to have it have meaning. . . . That's one thing that is hard . . . talking about it, digging deeper into myself. . . . When you are trying to reflect back on experiences, you need to say things or express things in ways that you do not always do—[it's] not an everyday process that you have to say things or write things down—that's really personal, not something you would tell just anyone. That's really difficult. . . .
> It is not something you think about everyday. It takes time to think. . . .

This undergraduate confronts the difficulties she finds in the reflecting but simultaneously identifies some of the elements of the reflective process: saying what you mean, digging deeper into yourself, and sharing the personal along with exactly what you mean. Nadine also spoke about an added element. A group of Nadine's classmates decided to meet outside of class in order to have a longer, uninterrupted period of time to share their work:

> A few of us met outside of class and looked at each other's portfolios and that helped. I really liked that I could see what they put into their portfolios. They could see what I was putting in and we helped each other [by saying]: "You know, this isn't clear to me. You need to let us know what you want us to know."

Here there appears for the first time a recognition of the importance of interrogation, the questioning by a critical friend. Several elements of reflection are revealed in Nadine's discussion: the idea of engaging in saying what you mean, clarifying why you are including something in a portfolio, revealing something about yourself and doing that through inquires made in critical conversations. These all appear in stark relief.

A second piece of evidence about the elements of reflection came from a young teacher intern named Nicole, a woman who had constructed a portfolio as an undergraduate but also created one as part of her internship year. Finding the process of reflection difficult, like Nadine, Nicole identified that selecting the entries she would include and justifying them can also be difficult:

> The selection process [is difficult] because anybody can fill up a scrapbook, so selecting things that are appropriate and relevant, I think, are important and justifying those to others—which is the difficult thing for me to do because I know what I am trying to say, but someone else may not know, so I need to articulate that.

Nicole gave an example of an artifact, a tape of an interview with a student about what the student thought about a class. If she played that cassette tape to someone else, saying, ". . . this is important because it . . . shows some learning going on there," she knew that she might "be the only one who would know what learning went on there, you know. . . . Maybe the person wasn't there to see the lesson . . . doesn't know the student, and doesn't know the progress of the student." Nicole concluded with an ideal way out of her difficulty:

> So actually an ideal thing to put in a portfolio would be a student's portfolio, to show the growth and progress of a student from day one to . . . June or whatever. . . . a portfolio inside a portfolio would be kind of a neat thing.

"But," she added, "it would be huge. Ideally it would be great to do that for each student."

Nicole knew that the portfolio has the possibility to show the development, learning, and change of her students as it could for herself. But the justification of her entries are troubling: "I don't know why it's so difficult to justify it. I couldn't tell you . . . 'why'. . . . it is something I am still trying to figure out. How can I adequately justify this, this learning going on to someone else who wasn't in the experience, who wasn't in the environment? . . . Even though I see it, I need to show someone else how to see it."

When asked if there was anything else that stood out for her in the portfolio process, Nicole identified "reflections" for the first time. She continued, linking reflection with justification:

> The reflections were a big part . . . and the reflection is part of the justification of the artifact and reflections, that's the key to the artifact. And so I think it's a craft that everybody needs to develop, to

write the reflection. . . . It's kind of show, not tell. Don't tell me, show me that something's going on, so that's in the reflection . . . the artifact itself is not as important as the reflection . . . because the reflection would show my growth, what I learned from the experience. . . .

Justification as reflection, talking to others in support of uncovering meaning, are all important pieces of the experience. But for Nicole they were still isolated pieces, not connected experiences. What Nicole did see is the significance of focusing on evidence that could convey something about her learning or that of her students.

Observation 2: That critical conversations interrogating portfolio entries and their significance provide a scaffold that fosters teacher awareness of their knowledge of practice. This reflective interrogation can become a mechanism for continued growth.

Natural Reflectors. To provide a contrast to the emerging reflective processes just discussed, I turn to two examples, one from Cara, a former undergraduate who became an intern, and another from the longitudinal study of Martha Mann, a teacher now in her second year of teaching high school English. Martha, like Cara, had been identified by her university and school mentors as a high reflector, or what I call a natural reflector.

I conducted a series of interviews with Martha over 3 years as she completed her internship and her portfolio and began full-time teaching. In this longitudinal data it is possible to see how Martha's ideas and reflections—her understandings of the reflective process and insights— were reexamined and refined over time. I turn to the first interview with Martha that took place in the spring of her internship year, when she completed her teaching portfolio. In that first interview, Martha described how the process of reflection first became apparent to her through the critical conversations of her Portfolio Team members:

I remember the most important things that I got [from the Portfolio Team] was that [Team members] could pull out these themes. I think that was the most important conversation and I think that was most of the conversation. Just looking at where things fit in and trying to find patterns or themes in all of the things that you are presenting or in all of the things you wanted to include in the portfolio. And it was hard to see it yourself, so that was key, the conversations [were] key, were critical in discovering what that was. . . . And that is what it is, the word that comes to mind—it is a process of discovery. I can remember having some-

thing I was presenting, presenting it and saying what I thought I
had to say about it, having considered what I would say, saying it,
showing my artifact and having someone say, "Tell me more about
that," about some aspect of it. And then I would go off talking
about the artifact in some different way and discover some more
meaning or an underlying meaning.

Martha gave an example: She described how, in teaching *The Scarlet
Letter,* she had her students embroider the letter *A* and draw a scene
from the novel.

Everyone was assigned a scene from the novel and they had to
draw it. And [in our Portfolio Team meeting] . . . I think I said
something that I like to use art, and then someone said, "What do
you think that says about you?" and then I remember getting to a
place where I realized that it was more than having kids do art,
I knew that there were kids whose main strength was art and I
was trying to give kids a chance to succeed in the way that they
could. . . . And I remember . . . that was a moment of revelation
for me. That I really was trying to play to the strengths of my students, to have everyone experience success in a unit. So I remember that it was through that conversation that came out. That it
went deeper. It started at a level and then we had some questions
and then it got deeper into what was at the core of my doing that.
And it wasn't right there. . . . someone was there [saying]: Look
deeper.

In the second year of her teaching, Martha elaborated on a second
discovery of her use of art: She came to realize how this practice is now
a conscious decision.

Recently, I was trying to teach reflection. We were listening to
Zora Neale Hurston's *Their Eyes Were Watching God* on tape because [the] school does not have money to buy the books. So I
own the tape. . . . We listened to it. And then I had them illustrate
it by having them record a story from their life in a reflective
voice. There again some kids who are not great writers made excellent tapes that I could play and get them some recognition, get
them some applause for what they are good at. So it is something
that I recognized through my portfolio. . . . that whole discovery
as to the reason why I was using it [art]. I just didn't realize that
until I did the portfolio: I use it to give everyone their moment of

glory and it's a conscious decision. Now it is a conscious decision to use art to give everyone a chance.

This understanding happened for Martha through the collaborative inquiry with her colleagues. That process brought to the surface her awareness and her knowledge of practice. Martha spoke about this process in a larger sense:

> That is what the process is about: It helps to come to cognition. It's almost as if we are talking about that there are things in your subconscious that you know about yourself, and through these conversations with people, it helps bring it up to cognition, it helps bring it to that part of your brain where you can realize that you know it and that it is important to you.

Thus the process of reflection—the interrogation and examination of one's practice—is facilitated through critical conversations evoking the knowledge of practice. And, as Martha's friend Sarah put it: "That you are conscious of it."

Observation 3. That the process of reflection reveals over time signifi-cant aspects—knowledge—of teaching practice that become identified as a part of one's teaching philosophy and emerge embedded in one's conscious practice. Recalling that original portfolio experience, Martha, in the second year of her teaching remembered:

> The last things we did [in putting together our portfolios] were our philosophies because we found that an impossible task when we had started working on our portfolios. We all felt we could write a trite [philosophy]—"this-is-what-a-teacher-should-be" kind of philosophy if we had to. But I don't think any one of us had an idea of what our philosophies were when we started. But we did when we finished. It had emerged through dialogue, through the observations of other members of the Team. I know when I wrote my philosophy I felt terribly comfortable that I was speaking for myself. I wasn't writing down things other people had suggested, but certainly I was writing things other people had helped me realize through the process. And I still haven't changed that philosophy.

Martha presented several tenets of her philosophy: that each voice in her classroom has an equal chance of being heard, that she not dominate the class, that she be fair and consistent, and, above all, that she is a visual and verbal person and not every student is: "I am very conscious of finding opportunities for students to show me what they know in ways that they are good at something, not having to be locked onto paper and pencil or keyboard and paper." Thus as her students read Eli Wiesel's *Night*, she searched to find another medium in which they could express their varied strengths:

> . . . . for the final assignment they had to do an oral project . . . they can write a poem or they can write a song, or they can write a letter to Eli Wiesel and ask him some questions. I give them six or seven options, and one little girl who struggles with writing and reading, I saw her face light up (when she heard the assignment). . . .

This practice, identified in the portfolio process nearly 3 years before, was deeply embedded in Martha's practice and referenced by her as a critical part of her teaching philosophy.

Observation 4: That the processes of reflection that come about through public, collaborative inquiry paradoxically involve at the center learning about self, about the values one holds for teaching and learning. One difficulty students report in identifying their teaching philosophies is the seeming threat it can present. This may be so, because it involves one's sense of self as a person and a teacher. In her first interview, Martha had talked about this, suggesting that some people are better at self-disclosure. Others, like herself, are not: "I was taught you don't write about yourself . . . when you write there is no self-disclosure. . . . It's [also] risky. It's a risk to say: here I am on this page. This is what I believe about education . . . an employer could say, 'Oh, I don't want her if that's what she believes.'" And there is something else involved:

> I know that for us, for Sarah and Anna and me, it was coming to know who we were, coming to know what our philosophies about teaching were, all of this stuff coming to the surface about—Yeah, I do connect with students in special ways, I do, you know, these various things that are important to me, all the things that we came to realize, I mean, it was a powerful experience . . . compiling the portfolio, it was very much a coming to know [process], and then an experiential journey sort of through this portfolio process . . . and the portfolio is always there . . .

	Emerging Elements	**Elaborated Elements**
What Reflection Is	Telling others	Engaging in critical collaborative conversations; interrogating practice
Purpose of Reflection	Saying why; justifying entries	Bringing to the surface knowledge about teaching and learning
How the Self is Implicated	Sharing personal experiences	Knowing the self in relation to teaching: "Coming to know who we are, our philosophy, our connection to students." "That we know that we know."

FIGURE 16.1. Changing Understanding of Reflection in the Portfolio Process: Pre-Internship to First Years of Teaching.

Discussing how she connects with that currently, Martha says how it continues her mind and in her latest discussions with her current colleagues:

> . . . but it is not the static portfolio, it's the growing portfolio. I know it's the dialogue with other teachers. I know it's the reflection that I do on my own, the reflection that I do with colleagues . . . we talk about teaching and we talk about kids . . . and we reflect together—what do you think this means, and this is what happened today, how would you have done that . . . and I think some of those habits of mind come from the portfolio process. Some of those coming to know, I know this is good practice, I know soliciting student feedback is good practice, and that is something I am going to make sure I do. I know that multiple intelligences are important to me and I am going to make sure when I plan units that I do those things.

Thus it appears that there are understandings of reflection that change over time. But the elements of reflection may be present from the earliest efforts at it. These become more elaborated over time. Figure 16.1 presents this view, indicating changing understandings of what reflection is for, why/how one engages in it, and how the self is implicated. These changes may take place over long periods of time, from undergraduate experiences to the first years of one's teaching. Collaborative conversations, in which interns or teachers continue to question their practices, emerge as the critical mechanism for reflective development.

Reflection through the portfolio process presented here suggests a redefinition: Reflection in teaching is a process that takes place over long periods of time in which connections, long strands of connections, are made between one's values, purposes, and actions toward engaging students successfully in their own meaningful learning. Such understandings are constructed through conversations with colleagues, as all interrogate their practices, asking why they are engaged in them and with what effectiveness. These critical interrogations serve to foster awareness and knowledge of practice and of oneself as a teacher.

CONCLUSION

The literature of teacher reform has identified a clear vision of successful teachers as ones who integrate complex evidence of their students' learning, engage in ongoing critical reflection about their practices, and work as members of an active learning community (Moss, 1997). The teacher portfolio makers—masters or apprentices—presented here are all engaged in these kinds of activities—not occasionally or sporadically, but systematically—through the ongoing work of creating a portfolio. One potentially significant outcome of the uses of portfolios in teacher education is the growing tendency of these teachers to engage their students in these same reflective activities using portfolios and other performance assessments. If a central aspiration of the portfolio process is to make teachers reflective of their own learning, to recognize that learning is a life-long process, then that learning is beginning to accrue to their students as well. Now, through the portfolio process, the learning of teachers and students is joined—a true teacher professionalism.

REFERENCES

Baratz-Snowden, J. (1995, April). *Towards a coherent vision of teacher development.* Paper presented at the annual meeting of the American Research Association, San Francisco.

Freidus, H. (1996, April). *Reflection in teaching: Can it be taught?* Town meeting presentation at the annual meeting of the American Educational Research Association, New York.

La Boskey, V. K. (1994). *Development of reflective practice.* New York: Teachers College Press.

La Boskey, V. K. (1996, April). *Reflection in teaching: Can it be taught?* Town meeting presentation at the annual meeting of the American Educational Research Association, New York.

Lyons, N. (1996, April). *Reflection in teaching: Can it be taught?* Town meeting presentation at the 1996 annual meeting of the American Educational Research Association, New York.

Lyons, N. (1997, March). *Reflection in teaching: Is it developmental?* Town meeting presentation at the annual meeting of the American Educational Research Association, Chicago.

Moss, P. A. (1992). Shifting conceptions of validity in educational measurement: Implications for performance assessment. *Review of Educational Research, 62*(3), 229–258.

Moss, P. A. (1997, March). *Developing coherence between assessment and reform in the licensing and professional development of teachers.* Paper presented at the annual meeting of the American Educational Research Association, Chicago.

About the Contributors

Doug Bower is a third-grade teacher at Montecito Union Elementary School in Montecito, California. With Jon Snyder and Ann Lippincott, he has been engaged in developing the portfolio process at University of California at Santa Barbara.

Jackie M. Coogan has been in education for 27 years, 24 of those years as a sixth-grade teacher. Currently she is an elementary guidance counselor at the Lafayette School in Everett, Massachusetts. With her colleague, Maria Ricci, she has done extensive work on reflective portfolios for Professional Development for Educators.

Larry Cuban is Professor of Education at Stanford University. He is a former high school teacher and superintendent and has written extensively about the history of teaching, school reform, and technology.

Carol Lynn Davis, Associate Professor of Human Development at the College of Education and Human Development of the University of Southern Maine (USM), teaches graduates and undergraduates about human development at USM. With Ellen Honan of the Yarmouth Public Schools, she has been engaged in research involving the use of teams to support teacher interns who are developing a teaching portfolio.

Richard Dollase is Director of the Office of Curriculum Affairs of Brown University Medical School and was the former director of the Middlebury College Teacher Education Program. He taught at Wheaton College in Norton, Massachusetts and has been visiting professor at Louisiana State University. He is coauthor of a four-volume African-American studies curriculum, *Black in White America*. His book, *Voices of Beginning Teachers: Visions and Realities* was published by Teachers College Press in 1992.

Helen Freidus is a member of the graduate faculty of Bank Street College of Education in New York City. She is codirector of an OERI funded study of the implementation of First Steps, a holistic, developmentally organized literacy program in the Springfield Public Schools, Massachusetts. Her professional interests center around issues of literacy, assessment, and the political and social dimensions of teaching and learning.

Grace Grant is Associate Professor of Education and Chair of the Secondary Teacher Program at Dominican College of San Rafael, California. Her scholarly interests include literacy, teacher education, reflective practice, and assessment including teacher portfolios.

Susie Hanley is an elementary educator and K–12 teacher leader in the Gorham, Maine School Department. She currently works with preservice elementary and secondary interns, university and school faculty, and K–12 students in a year-long, site-based, postbaccalaureate internship. Her interests focus on teaching practices that support high quality student work, such as exemplars and ongoing assessment.

Ellen Honan is the K–4 Language Arts Coordinator for the Yarmouth, Maine Public Schools and where she has been teaching for some 17 years. She has been a leader in school reform in the school district, serving as the Literacy Learning Area Leader and, with Carol Lynn Davis, is a site coordinator of the University of Southern Maine's Extended Teacher Education Program. She is engaged in research examining the use of teams to support teacher interns as they develop teaching portfolios.

Tracy A. Huebner is a doctoral candidate in Language, Literacy, and Culture at Stanford University's School of Education. Her research traces the development of reflective practice in preservice teacher education through the implementation of teacher portfolios.

Walter H. Kimball is Associate Professor in the Teacher Education Department at the University of Southern Maine. He works with preservice elementary and secondary interns, students, school and university faculty, and administrators in the Gorham Public Schools, Maine in a year long, site-based, postbaccalaureate internship. His current scholarship focuses on performance assessment of teaching for professional improvement and the decision for initial certification.

Gloria Ladson-Billings is Associate Professor in the Curriculum and Instruction Department of the University of Wisconsin, Madison. She is author of the critically acclaimed book, *The Dreamkeepers: Successful Teachers of African American Children,* as well as numerous journal articles and book chapters. Her scholarly activities include multicultural education, critical race theory and teacher education.

Ann Lippincott is Coordinator of Bilingual Teacher Education at University of California, Santa Barbara. Her focus in teacher education addresses the special needs of students for whom English is a second language. Her research interests center around novice teachers and how they mentor each other within the context of developing professional portfolios. She is currently completing her Ph.D. in Educational Psychology with an emphasis on Language, Culture, and Literacy.

Nona Lyons is Visiting Associate Professor in Education at Dartmouth College and Associate Professor of Human Development at the University of Southern Maine. Her current research includes the study of the development of reflection through a portfolio process; an examination of the school experiences of adolescent girls; and a project looking at the ethical and intellectual dimensions of teachers' work and development for which she received a Spencer Fellowship. In 1996–97 she was a Visiting Research Scholar at the Wellesley College Center for Research on Women. Lyons is coauthor of *Making Connections: The Relational World of Adolescent Girls at Emma Willard School,* published by Harvard University Press in 1990.

Pam Moss is Associate Professor at the University of Michigan. Her speciality is educational measurement and evaluation. Currently she is engaged with INTASC, the Interstate New Teachers Assessment and Support Consortium, developing new methods to interpret portfolio evidence.

Maria Ricci has been an elementary school teacher for 20 years in the Everett Public Schools, Massachusetts where she is currently a media specialist and has been Chair for Professional Development since 1992. She was coordinator of Partners in Education Together (PET), a student teacher training project in affiliation with the University of Massachusetts, Boston and has conducted workshops and courses on "Preparing a Reflective Portfolio" for teachers in the greater Boston area.

Steve Seidel is Principal Investigator and Director of the Shakespeare & Company Research Study, and of Massachusetts Schools Network, a collaborative effort between Project Zero, the Massachusetts Department of Education, and 11 Massachusetts elementary schools. He began working with Project Zero at Harvard Graduate School of Education after 17 years of teaching theatre and language arts in high schools. His experiences as a professional actor and stage director have influenced and informed his current interest in the process of developing collaborative interpretations of various kinds of texts, especially children's writing and art work.

Lee Shulman is president of the Carnegie Foundation for the Advancement of Teaching and Professor of Education at Stanford University. Shulman directed the Stanford Teacher Assessment Project (TAP), which developed the portfolio as a prototype teacher assessment that became the centerpiece of the work of the National Board for Professional Teaching Standards.

Jon Snyder is Director of Teacher Education at the University of California at Santa Barbara. With Ann Lippincott and Doug Bower, he has been conducting research in the development and use of the portfolio process. He is currently working with the National Commission on Teaching and America's Future.

Lee Teitel is Associate Professor and Director of the educational administration program at the University of Massachusetts, Boston. He works closely with teachers and teacher-leaders in partnerships with schools and has used teaching portfolios to reflect on his own teaching, and to document his teaching for promotion and tenure review.

Index